RUSSIA AFTER YELTSIN

Russia After Yeltsin

Edited by

VLADIMIR TIKHOMIROV
Contemporary Europe Research Centre
University of Melbourne, Australia

Ashgate

Aldershot • Burlington USA • Singapore • Sydney

Published by
Ashgate Publishing Limited
Gower House
Croft Road
Aldershot
Hants GU11 3HR
England

Ashgate Publishing Company
131 Main Street
Burlington, VT 05401-5600 USA

Ashgate Website: http://www.ashgate.com

British Library Cataloguing in Publication Data
Russia after Yeltsin
　　1.Russia (Federation) - Politics and government - 1991 -
　　2.Russia (Federation) - Economic conditions - 1991 -
　　I.Tikhomirov, Vladimir
　　330.9'47'09051

Library of Congress Control Number: 2001087930

ISBN 0 7546 1731 9 ✓

Printed and bound in Great Britain by Antony Rowe Ltd.,
Chippenham, Wiltshire.

Contents

List of Figures

List of Tables

About the Contributors

Stephen Fortescue is an Associate Professor of Politics at the University of New South Wales. His principal interests cover Russian politics and economics, in particular industrial management and modernisation. His current research is concentrated on the Russian mining and metals industry. He is the author of many articles and three books: *Policy-Making for Russian Industry* (1997), *Science Policy in the Soviet Union* (1990) and *The Communist Party and Soviet Science* (1986).

Graeme Gill is a Professor of Government and Public Administration, and Head of the School of Economics and Political Science at the University of Sydney. He is the author of *Peasants and Government in the Russian Revolution* (1979), *The Origins of the Stalinist Political System* (1990), *20th Century Russia: the Search for Power and Authority* (1994), *The Collapse of a Single-Party System: the Disintegration of the CPSU* (1994), *Power in the Party* (with R.Pitty, 1997), *The Dynamics of Democratization: Elites, Civil Society, and the Transition Process* (2000), and *Russia's Stillborn Democracy?* (with R.Markwick, 2000).

Leslie Holmes is a Professor of Political Science at the University of Melbourne. He specialises in transitions (esp. democratisation processes) and corruption in post-communist states. Prof. Holmes is the author of numerous articles and a number of books, including *The Policy Process in Communist States: Industrial Administration and Politics* (1981), *Politics in the Communist World* (1986), *The End of Communist Power: Anti-Corruption Campaigns and Legitimation Crisis* (1993), and *Post-Communism* (1997).

Geoffrey Jukes is an Associate at the Centre for Arab and Islamic Studies (the Middle East and Central Asia) of the Australian National University and an Associate at the Contemporary Europe Research Centre at the University of Melbourne. He has published widely on Soviet and Russian military developments and foreign policy. His books include *Kursk: The Clash of Armour* (1969), *The Development of Soviet Strategic Thinking since 1945* (1972), *The Indian Ocean in Soviet Naval Policy* (1972), *The Soviet Union in Asia* (1973), *Hitler's Stalingrad Decisions* (1985), *Russia's*

Military and the Northern Territories Issue (1993) and *The Middle East: Prospects for Settlement and Stability?* (co-edited, 1995).

Gennadi Kazakevitch is a Senior Lecturer in Economics at Monash University. His main areas of research interest are economic reforms in former communist countries, regional economic development and policy and applied regional models. His latest publications include articles on 'Regions in Changing Economic Environment' (1999), 'Is the Transition already over in the Former Soviet Bloc Countries? An Attempt of Taxonomy of Post Communist Economies' (1998), 'Privatisation of Natural Monopolies' (1998), 'Natural Monopolies: Comparing Russian and Australian Experience' (1996) and 'Macroeconomic Issues of Privatisation in Russia and Eastern Europe' (1995).

David W. Lovell is an Associate Professor in Politics at the Australian Defence Force Academy. During the early 1990s, he edited the *Political Theory Newsletter*, and was managing editor of the *Australian Journal of Political Science*. In 1992, he was the Australian Parliamentary Political Science Fellow, and since 1993 he has been a member of the Executive Committee of the International Society for the Study of European Ideas, and is an editorial adviser on its journal, *The European Legacy*. His books include *From Marx to Lenin* (1984), *Marx's Proletariat* (1988), *The Theory of Politics* (co-authored, 1991), *The Transition from Socialism* (co-edited, 1992), *Marxism and Australian Socialism* (1997), and *The Australian Political System* (co-authored, 1998).

Alexey Muraviev is a Deputy Director of the International Relations Program at Curtin University of Technology. His major research interests include the Russian military power, Russia's defence and foreign policy, defence and strategic studies. He has published a number of articles and co-authored a book on *Russia's Armed Forces in Asia* (with Greg Austin, 2000).

Anthony Phillips is an Associate of the Contemporary Europe Research Centre at the University of Melbourne. His main interest is in the evolving political economy of the post-Soviet Russia. His recent publications include, 'Changing Characterisations of the Roots of Russia's Problems: A Look at the "Virtual Economy" Thesis', *Russian and Euro-Asian Bulletin*, vol. 8, no. 2, March 1999, and 'The Political Economy of Russia: Transition or Condition?' in Mike Bowker (ed.), *Russia After the Cold War* (2000).

Peter Shearman teaches International Relations and Russian Politics at the University of Melbourne. His books include *The Soviet Union and Cuba* (1987), *The Superpowers, Central America and the Middle East* (co-edited with Phil Williams, 1988) and *Russian Foreign Policy Since 1990* (edited, 1995).

Vladimir Tikhomirov is a Deputy Director of the Contemporary Europe Research Centre at the University of Melbourne. He is also Chief Editor of the *Russian and Euro-Asian Bulletin*. His two main areas of interest are economic developments of post-Soviet Russia and transition in South Africa. He published widely and his books include *The Party of Apartheid* (1987), *Church and the Political Struggle in South Africa* (1990), *Development of Political Thought in South Africa* (1992), *States in Transition: Russia and South Africa* (1992), *In Search of Identity: Five Years Since the Fall of the Soviet Union* (edited, 1996), *Anatomy of the 1998 Russian Crisis* (edited, 1999) and *The Political Economy of Post-Soviet Russia* (2000).

Yuri Tsyganov is an Associate of the Contemporary Europe Research Centre at the University of Melbourne. His main areas of research include Russian political economy and Northeast Asian regional developments. His recent articles include 'Russia and China: What is in the Pipeline?' (1999) and 'Political Background of the Economic Crisis in Russia' (1999). He is the author of *Russia and Northeast Asia: Economic and Security Interdependence* (edited, 1997) and *Taiwan in Regional Security Structures of East Asia* (1998).

Preface

This book is a selection of papers presented at a conference that was held at the University of Melbourne in April 2000. The conference was organised by the Research Unit for Russian and Euro-Asian Studies of the Contemporary Europe Research Centre and attracted academics engaged in research of post-Soviet Russia from all over Australia. The general feeling of all participants was that the conference was a success. It provoked very lively and interesting debates about the future of Russia and the legacy of Yeltsinism. It is my hope that this book will follow up on these debates, as well as managing to provide an accurate and up-to-date snapshot of the reality of Russia after Yeltsin.

The primary motivation for publication of this volume was to summarise results of the decade of reforms (or, rather, reform attempts) in Yeltsin's Russia, as well as to try to outline some possible main features of future Russian policies at the start of the new millennium. The book consists of eleven chapters that cover all major areas of Russia's development: its politics, economy, social and military development, and its foreign policy.

This study would not have been possible without the enthusiasm and professionalism of all contributors. I am deeply indebted to them for their support, which has enabled us to produce a print-ready copy of the book just six months after the conference. A special word of appreciation must go to Tony Phillips, who made an invaluable contribution in editing of papers written by non-English speakers, and to Gabi Mocatta for her efficient, patient and attentive work in helping me to review the amended texts. I would also like to acknowledge the support of various kinds given to me by the Contemporary Europe Research Centre at the University of Melbourne.

Notwithstanding all this support, the responsibility for any remaining mistakes, as well as for the overall editorial work, rests with me. Needless to say, each contributor takes responsibility for the contents of his chapter.

Vladimir Tikhomirov, February 2001

List of Abbreviations

ABM	Anti-ballistic missile
ACV	Armoured combat vehicles
AF	Air Forces
AF/AD	Air Force/Air Defence army
ALCM	Airborne cruise missiles
APC	Armoured personnel carriers
BBC	British Broadcasting Corporation
BW	Biological weapons
CASE	Command-and-staff exercises of the army
CCR	Forces of constant combat readiness
CFE	Conventional Forces in Europe Treaty
CG	Guided-missile cruiser
CGN	Nuclear-powered guided missile cruiser
CIA	US Central Intelligence Agency
CIS	Commonwealth of Independent States
CMEA	Council for Mutual Economic Assistance
CW	Chemical weapons
EBRD	European Bank for Reconstruction and Development
EGRPO	Unified State Register of Enterprises and Organisations
ESOGC	Eastern-Siberian Oil and Gas Company
EU	European Union
FAPSI	Federal State Communications and Information Agency
FIG	Financial-industrial group
FSB	Federal Security Service
GF	Ground Forces
GRU	Main Intelligence Directorate of the Russian Armed Forces
ICBM	Intercontinental ballistic missile
IFV	Infantry fighting vehicle
IMF	International Monetary Fund
JGFF	Joint Group of Federal Forces in Chechnya
KGB	Committee of State Security of the USSR
KPRF	Communist Party of the Russian Federation
LRA	Long-Range Aviation
MBT	Main battle tank
MD	Military District

MoD	Russian Ministry of Defence
MSD	Missile-Space Defence
MSF	Military-Space Forces
MTA	Military-Transport Aviation
NATO	North Atlantic Treaty Organisation
NMD	National Missile Defence System
OECD	Organisation for Economic Co-operation and Development
OSCE	Organisation for Security and Co-operation in Europe
OVR	Fatherland-All Russia
R&D	Research and development
ROH	Russia Is Our Home movement
SAM	Surface-to-air missile
SLBM	Submarine-launched ballistic missile
SMF	Strategic Missile Forces
SPS	Union of Rightist Forces
SSBN	Nuclear-powered ballistic missile submarine
SVR	Russian Foreign Intelligence Service
UCCR	Units of constant combat readiness
UES	Unified Energy Systems Joint Stock Company
VPK	Military-industrial complex of Russia
WTO	World Trade Organisation

1 Introduction

LESLIE HOLMES

Russia's first ever freely elected President, Boris Yeltsin, surprised the world one more time on the last day of the twentieth century. Just as everyone was preparing for the New Year of all New Years, Yeltsin suddenly announced his resignation. His term of office had not yet expired; his mandate was until June 2000. In his resignation speech, Yeltsin maintained that a new century required new vigour and hence a new leader.[1] But these words could hardly be taken at face value. Since Yeltsin had rarely shown himself to be a man who would put the interests of others, even his own people, before his personal ones in the late-1990s – when his amazing capacity to keep going despite very poor health served as a metaphor for the state of Russia – the timing of his departure had to be more than a generous gesture to his people. Hence his announcement initially appeared enigmatic. But within a few hours of his departure, at least part of the riddle was solved; the prime minister, and now acting president, Vladimir Putin, issued a decree (*ukaz*) granting Yeltsin immunity from prosecution. A corruption scandal had been developing around Yeltsin and his two daughters in the months preceding the resignation, and the decree appeared to guarantee that this would not result in any future problems for the outgoing president.[2]

But the corruption scandal was not the only reason for the President's decision to retire early. The larger context was that Yeltsin was anxious to do everything possible to ensure that his chosen successor, Putin, would be favoured by the Russian electorate. One of the most positive aspects of the Yeltsin tenure was that the days were gone – at least for the present – when a Russian or Soviet leader could arbitrarily decide on their successor without reference to the people.[3] Yeltsin had made clear his faith in Putin as the future president from the moment he appointed him as prime minister in July 1999, but also accepted that this would have to be put to the Russian electorate. Fortunately for Yeltsin, Putin rapidly acquired mass popularity, primarily because of what was perceived by most Russians to be his effective handling of the Chechen issue. They believed that here, at last, was the strong – and fit! - leader the country needed.

A clear indication of Prime Minister Putin's rapidly growing popularity was given by the Russian electorate on 19 December 1999 when, in elections to the lower house of the legislature (the Duma), the party to which Putin had given his support – Unity (also known as

Medved) – came a very close second to the Communists as the most popular political party; in the party list vote, Unity secured 23.3% of the vote, compared with the Communists' 24.3%. The significance of this achievement becomes more obvious when two points are borne in mind. One is that, in marked contrast to the Communists, the party was almost brand new; it had been established only in September 1999, and still had almost no regional infrastructure. The other is that the party had little in the way of a programme; its identity focused primarily on its support for Putin. Within a couple of days of the election, Unity's position was further strengthened, when a key component of a third bloc – a group of regional governors within Fatherland–All Russia (OVR) – pledged their support for Putin, and thus appeared willing to cooperate with Unity. Unity's success was almost certainly a major factor in the timing of Yeltsin's resignation; whatever other criticisms can be levelled against him, there is near universal agreement among analysts that the former president was a brilliant politician and survivor – and his political intuition told him to strike while the iron was hot.

According to Russia's current (December 1993) constitution, elections for a new president must be held within three months of an outgoing president dying, resigning or being declared incapable of performing his or her duties (through ill health, etc.). Once again, it was testimony to the moves taken in the direction of constitutionalism under Yeltsin that presidential elections did take place on time, being held in March 2000. Although the electoral rules permitted a run-off of the top two candidates from the first round if no-one were to achieve an absolute majority, Putin won in the first round, with some 53% of the vote – easily beating his closest rival, communist party leader Gennadi Zyuganov (who secured just over 29% of the vote) in an election that witnessed a turnout of nearly 70%. Putin was formally inaugurated as President on 7th May 2000.

This book focuses on the Yeltsin legacy, and the challenges that face both President Putin and Russia more generally. The challenges are formidable, and individual chapters consider various aspects of the political scene, the economy, relations between the polity and economy (notably the huge problem of corruption and the boundaries between the state and the private sector), the military, and Russia's place in - and relations with - the rest of the world. In this brief introduction, I shall consider in very general terms some of the major dilemmas facing this vast country at the start of the third millennium. In line with one of my own principal interests in recent years, there will be some consideration of the issue of legitimacy.

As noted above, one of Putin's very first actions as president – granting Yeltsin immunity from prosecution – was symbolically of concern. Corruption had by the end of the 1990s become one of the most serious problems in Russia, and many expected the new leader to work hard to reduce it to much lower levels (it is unrealistic to assume that corruption can ever be totally eradicated, either in Russia or in any other country; for an interesting argument outlining the restrictions on Putin's capacity to combat corruption see Shelley, 2000). This is why the decree on immunity was on one level disturbing. However, it is important not to overlook two points.

The first is that, in the grand scheme of things, the corruption scandal – as it related to Yeltsin himself – was small-scale. The allegations were that a Swiss building company (Mabetex) that had secured the rights to renovate the Kremlin had been paying off the credit card bills of Yeltsin and his two daughters for more than three years. The sum involved was less than US$90,000 for all three recipients. If the allegations are true, there is no question that it was wrong of Yeltsin to accept such indirect payments: yet the scale is trivial in comparison with what many other Russian politicians and officials had been accused of accepting or demanding in recent years.

Even if it is maintained that this was an important matter of principle (and a president *should* set a good example), so that the sum involved is not of major relevance, the granting of immunity should not necessarily be taken to indicate that Putin was 'soft' on corruption. There are historical precedents in which a new, incoming leadership has engaged in one final act along the lines of that which they have criticised in their predecessors, as a form of closure. Prime examples of this are the show trial and execution of Beria after Stalin's death, and the show trial and imprisonment of the Gang of Four after Mao's death; it could be argued that the new leaderships sought to bring rapid and effective closure to periods of terror by engaging in one final act that, in both cases, had terroristic elements. According to this argument, then, we should not make too much of Putin's pardon. Rather, it should be interpreted as an example of an incoming leader wanting to be as little burdened by messy issues from the past as possible, so that he can concentrate on the present and future.[4]

But what are we to make of the first few months of Putin's presidency? Is Russia now on the right path (whatever that might be) – or indeed any discernible path? Or are the structural constraints on the Russian president so great that even an apparently strong and determined leader like Putin cannot realistically hope to overcome the obstacles?

When Putin first came to power, many observers pointed to the ambiguities of his past career to highlight how difficult it was to predict how he was likely to act in the future. On the one hand, he had spent a long period working for the infamous Soviet security agency, the KGB, and had been head of its successor, the FSB. On the other hand, he had also been Deputy Mayor to the generally progressive and liberal Anatoly Sobchak in St.Petersburg in the early-1990s. The enigma continued even after Putin became acting president. While he showed he was prepared to be tough on the Chechen separatists, it was far from clear what else he stood for. Even by the time he was elected, neither Russians nor external observers had much idea of how he was going to solve arguably Russia's biggest problem, the appalling state of the economy. Had Russia just elected a second 'virtual president', albeit one with a proclivity to clamp down on those who stood in the way of his political ambition? Or was this simply a cautious and reasonable man, sensibly waiting until he had a firmer grasp of the problems before proposing solutions?

In this climate of uncertainty, there was no shortage of commentators, particularly in the Western mass media, who warned of the dangers of Putin becoming a new dictator, perhaps akin to his Belarusian counterpart, Alyaksandr Lukashenka. Russia, when part of the USSR, had already experienced a leader coming to power who seemed reasonable enough at the outset, but who became increasingly dictatorial; in his analysis of Stalin's rise to power, Isaac Deutscher referred to the common perception of Stalin as 'the Man of the Golden Mean'. By some criteria, Putin already appeared to be at least as tough as Stalin was at the start – and he had something Stalin did not have, legitimacy based on a constitutional description of his powers and a mandate from the electorate. After all, surely most Russians were, by the beginning of the new century, *demanding* strong leadership?

Against this was the argument that a leader can only become a dictator if s/he has a strong state at his or her disposal; at the very least, a potential dictator needs to have a tight grip on the security forces, notably the military and the secret police. But according to many evaluations, neither of these was in a very healthy or unified state at the time Putin came to office. Although Putin had talked tough on the Chechnya issue, the fact is that the Russian army had not been performing nearly as well as Moscow would have liked it to have done in 1999. Throughout the 1990s, there were numerous cases of the military not being paid for months on end, being unable to meet their utility bills, and of officers seeking to survive by engaging in corrupt sales of military equipment, including even nuclear materials! The Russian military thus hardly looked like the kind of state agency through which to implement and enforce a dictatorship. Putin's close links with the FSB were of more concern.

Despite this ambiguous legacy and start, Putin had by the middle of 2000 begun to give a clearer idea of what he stood for, and how he intended to work to overcome Russia's problems. Details will be provided in the chapters that form the core of this collection; I shall be highly selective here.

In the political sphere, Putin soon set about addressing three of the biggest issues in Russian politics in recent times – the relationships between Moscow and the regions; those between the Kremlin and the so-called oligarchs (the wealthiest and most powerful businesspeople, the majority of whom had made their fortunes as a result of the questionable privatisation processes of the early- and mid-1990s); and the state of the military. Each of these deserves some attention.

Even following the break-up of the USSR, Russia remains by far the largest country, territory-wise, on earth, being more than twice the size of the USA minus Alaska (approximately one and three quarters times larger if Alaska is included). In the Soviet era, control of such a vast area was secured through a large, highly centralised and very hierarchical party-state machinery based in Moscow. But in the 1990s, as Moscow simultaneously advocated more democratic political processes and yet was so concerned with politics at the top that it lost some of its interest in provincial Russia, a number of local political elites in the regions began to assert themselves. Although the constitution had allowed all 89 regions and republics (hereafter, for the sake of simplicity, I shall refer just to regions) a voice in Moscow, via the upper house of the legislature - the Federation Council - several regional governors clearly believed they could largely 'go it alone'. Those who headed regions that were naturally wealthy felt particularly able to assert themselves. Putin has made it clear that he is not prepared to tolerate this decentralisation, and had within months of becoming President taken two major steps to counter it. The first was to establish seven 'super-regions', and to appoint the heads of these himself (governors are chosen by their local electorate). The second was to alter both the composition and the role of the Federation Council. Hitherto, governors and speakers of local parliaments had automatically had seats on the Federation Council (though this was not specified in the Constitution); with effect from early 2001, one of the representatives on this Council from each region is to be nominated by the governor and approved by the legislature, while the other is to be elected by the legislature from a list presented either by the speaker or at least one third of the deputies (on the potential significance of this, and an interesting argument questioning the political wisdom of centralisation in Russia, see Tompson, 2000). These two moves have substantially reduced the powers of the regional governors vis-à-vis Moscow. This said, in introducing the proposed changes Putin argued that the governors' role in their regions would be increased if they did not have to spend so much time in Moscow while the interests of the regions would be better served in Moscow if the representatives on the Federation Council were full-time professionals.

Putin also soon made it clear that he was to be much stricter with the oligarchs than Yeltsin had been. The relationship is a complex one, and is considered in more detail in Yuri Tsyganov's chapter. Suffice it to say here that by mid-2000, and following a number of raids by the tax police on companies such as AvtoVAZ and Media Most, most of the oligarchs were on the back foot, seeking an amnesty on questionable privatisation deals in the past, in return for which they promised to pay their taxes in full and on time. One of the oligarchs who was particularly close to Yeltsin, and a member of the so-called 'Family' of inner advisers and close friends of the former president, had not capitulated at the time of writing, and had even given up his seat in the Duma so as to be better able to challenge Putin. But this man, Boris Berezovsky, was the exception.[5] It is important to note, however, that Berezovsky soon approached regional governors who were unhappy about their recently downgraded status, with a view to collaborating on bringing the new president to heel; Putin had not had it all his own way.

It is also worth noting at this juncture that Putin has substantially downgraded the role of the 'Family' generally, while early signs are that the punishment of officials found guilty of corruption is becoming much harsher under Putin than it ever was in Yeltsin's time. Regarding the former, both Yeltsin's daughter Tatyana Dyachenko and the head of the Kremlin's Administrative Office (Pavel Borodin) were dismissed from their privileged 'inner sanctuary' positions in January 2000. As for the latter, the punishment meted out to former Rear Admiral Vladimir Morev in April 2000 for corruption – an eight-year prison sentence for attempting to sell radar equipment for some US$3000 - was a markedly tougher sentence than was typical for this type of crime in the Yeltsin era.

Putin has certainly given various indications, both before becoming president and subsequently, that he intends to bolster the role of the military and improve its standing. For instance, he announced in January 2000 that defence expenditure would be doubled by the end of the year.

Moreover, the seven 'super-regions' mentioned earlier not only broadly correspond to Russia's major military districts, but five of the seven people named by Putin in May to head these were from either the military or the security services.

It has been argued that a leader can only become a dictator if s/he can rely on the coercive organs of the state for support. A precondition of this is that the state can afford to maintain such organs properly; promising to increase expenditure on the military and police forces and then failing to do so is quite likely to lose a leader their support. Thus, in order to create a strong state, it is usually necessary to have a well-functioning economy.[6] By the middle of 2000, Putin had at last begun to provide a clearer idea on his economic policies, and how he intended to put Russia back on its feet. In formulating these policies, he had been making extensive use of the liberal 'St. Petersburg' economists. This strongly suggested that whereas the new president was anxious to re-centralise political power, he was also committed, like his predecessor, to a more decentralised and marketised economy. One of the key aspects of this policy was seen as a commitment to breaking monopolies – so that his 'get tough' approach to the oligarchs, many of whom control absolute or near monopolies (e.g. utility and related companies, including Gazprom, Lukoil, and United Energy Systems), was consistent with his overall economic approach.

However, Putin's approach to the monopolies and oligopolies may be more complex than is often portrayed. Early signs are that his primary aim may be to bring them under control and working in a responsible manner, rather than necessarily to break them up. It is interesting to note in this context that the first large-scale privatisation since the mid-1990s occurred in September 2000, when Tyumen Oil purchased an 85% stake in Onako Oil. On one level, this was suggestive that Putin is indeed committed to further marketisation and privatisation. But on another level, it could be argued to be surprising that an already large company was allowed to be the purchaser. Perhaps the symbolism of the sale really was contradictory. However, it can also be interpreted as indicative of Putin's parallel aims of making the economy more efficient and less corrupt, while at the same time being realistic about the optimal ways of achieving this. As long as they are operating in a proper (regulated) manner, the new Russian president may not be opposed to oligopolies, at least, in areas of the economy in which investment and infrastructure costs are high; after all, even in the West, there is a diminishing number of ever-larger motor car companies, and airliner manufacturing is almost a duopoly. Given this, the most significant fact about the sale was that *The Economist*'s sister journal for Central and

Eastern Europe reported that it '... was seen as fair and transparent, unlike previous privatisations'.[7] This focus on propriety and transparency is unquestionably needed in contemporary Russia – and a good example has now been set.

Putin's foreign and defence policies might also appear at first sight to be either full of ambiguities, or else of serious concern to the West. In January 2000, a new national security blueprint was released, which reduced Russia's self-imposed constraints on the use of nuclear weapons. Then in April, Putin ratified a new military doctrine, which confirmed that Russia was prepared to resort to the use of nuclear weapons rather sooner than it would have been under its previous (1993) policy. Some, including a number of Russian commentators (readers without Russian should look at the *CDP-SP*), have adopted an essentially benign interpretation of these developments, seeing them primarily as reflective of the impoverished state of conventional weapons and military manpower in Russia. But it would be naive to be sanguine about such developments in a country that still has a vast nuclear arsenal – and in which, as mentioned above, the president promised to double defence expenditure in 2000. Even if defence expenditure does not increase as much and as quickly as Putin promised in January 2000 – and he made a commitment to additional funding following the August 2000 *Kursk* submarine affair (see below) - the general thrust of his approach is unambiguous. Russia had become increasingly dissatisfied with its relationship with the West in recent years, and particularly since 1999, in connection with issues such as NATO's eastward expansion, Serbia/Kosovo, and Chechnya. These three issues severely strained what was already a somewhat fragile relationship, and Putin was rattling his sabre.

However, while it would be ingenuous to downplay the recent developments in defence and military policy, it would also be a distortion of the overall picture to focus solely on these tensions in international relations.[8] Russia is pleased to be accepted as the de facto new member of G7 (making it G8). Moreover, while the personal relations between Putin and both President Clinton and Prime Minister Blair have been mixed, the new Russian president does appear to get on well with Chancellor Schröder, with whom he speaks in German (a legacy of the days when he worked for the KGB in East Germany). It is notoriously difficult to know how much to make of the personal chemistry between leaders. On the other hand, it is also ill-advised to make too much of formal statements and documents, i.e. to accept them unquestioningly at face value.

Ultimately, perhaps the biggest disappointment of the Russian people in Yeltsin was that he forced through a constitution that created a strong presidency – but then, and particularly in the late-1990s, was not a strong president. It was precisely Putin's apparent toughness that appealed to so many voters. But does this mean that those who have been predicting a new dictatorship under Putin are going to be proven correct? If so, does the fact that Putin was elected mean that there is such a concept as an elected dictator?

It has already been pointed out that Putin has been making public statements that would suggest a marked upgrading of the role of the military. The available evidence suggests that Putin may in the earliest stages have been less aware of all the details of the sinking of the *Kursk* nuclear submarine than he should have been, and that this reflected limitations on the relationship between him and the military. While this might be true – and while the whole *Kursk* affair represented one of the biggest failures (particularly of public relations) of the early Putin era – it is possible to read too much into this. It could be that the military initially underrated the seriousness of the problem, and had hoped to deal with it themselves. This would have been a misguided assumption – but, if true, it would cast the submarine affair in a somewhat different light than that in which it has been portrayed by some journalists. There is a difference between deliberately excluding someone, on the one hand, and attempting to cover up or minimise one's own mistakes, on the other. Overall, Putin's statements and actions suggest that he is serious about upgrading the role of the military. In doing so, he will be strengthening his own hand, and be that much closer to a situation in which he would have the power base actually to effect a dictatorship.

It is also true that there have been a number of complaints, particularly from within the ranks of the Russian media themselves, that Putin has been muzzling the mass media, especially with regard to Chechnya. Once again, the situation is less clear-cut than presented by many of the Western media. Most countries, including the leading democracies, have censorship rules on issues of national security; quite where a prime minister or president should legitimately draw the line is often a matter of debate. There is no question that some of the actions the Putin administration has taken against the only major independent media base, Media Most, are cause for serious concern to anyone interested in freedom of the press. But the Russian press has often been at least as irresponsible as the worst gutter press in the West. This is most unfortunate when a country's fledgling democracy is as fragile as Russia's; as a former German Chancellor argued at length in a recent book (Schmidt, 1999), democracy and the rise of civil society must be based on an understanding that rights also entail responsibilities and duties – and some of the Russian press can be seen to have been undermining the democratisation process through their cavalier attitudes towards reporting. At this point then, the jury on freedom of the press in Russia is still out. The apparently harsh treatment of the head of Media Most, Vladimir Gusinsky, in the (Northern) summer and autumn 2000 is troubling – but may have been related as much to the person as to the freedom of the press more generally. While there is no question that the freedom is not as extensive as it was in the Yeltsin era, on the other hand nor has it – yet – been limited to anything like the degree it has been in some of the other post-communist states (inc. Belarus and some of the Central Asian states). This is an area on which attention needs to be concentrated in any future assessment of the extent to which an attempt at strong leadership and bringing order to near chaos is in fact developing into a bid for dictatorship.[9]

Finally, it must also be acknowledged that Putin has on occasions – for example, during his formal inauguration – played the nationalist card, which can again be a sign for some of imminent dictatorship. Yet it is not unusual for leaders even in liberal democracies to play this card to gain popularity, especially when they cannot appeal to eudaemonic legitimation based on impressive or improving economic performance. One of the reasons former Australian prime minister Paul Keating won an election that pundits forecast his party could not win (largely because the economy was performing relatively poorly at the time) was because he suddenly introduced the issue of republicanism into the debate just weeks before the election; this was clearly an attempt at legitimation based on a form of nationalism. In Russia's case, there are good reasons for arguing that, within limits, the president needs to boost the sense of national identity among a people that has experienced a serious identity crisis in the past decade. The reason for this crisis becomes abundantly clear when it is borne in mind that, within a very short period, the Russians lost an outer empire (the countries of CMEA and the WTO); an inner empire (the fourteen other republics of the USSR); their role as the centre of a superpower; the Cold War; and their status as the home of a politico-economic system that was once claimed to be superior to capitalism and liberal democracy, and which crumbled like a pack of cards in most communist states in the period 1989-91. As Stefan Auer (2000) has argued, nationalism sometimes works well with liberalism, and is not invariably a reactionary or threatening ideology. If there were less uncertainty among

Russians about their own identity, this could help to further social consensus and cohesion, which in turn should help to consolidate the post-communist system (for an identification of five major discourses on national identity in contemporary Russia, see Tolz, 1998).

Thus, while it is important to be alert to all the warning signs of potential dictatorship, it would be unjust and inappropriate to jump to premature conclusions. Putin is a far more sophisticated leader than Lukashenka. He may well have a vision of a Russia that bears some resemblance to Singapore under Lee Kwan Yew and to other Asian 'tigers' of the 1980s and 1990s, in which there is a well-functioning economy coupled with a stable, if somewhat illiberal, political system. Unfortunately, the relevance of such a model must be questioned, not only because, when it did appear to work, it did so only in small countries with quite different structures and conditions from Russia's, but also in the light of the 1997-8 Asian crash. The Chilean model, which Putin is said to have considered, also has drawbacks (for an argument that Putin has a lot to learn from Pinochet's economic policies, but not from his political approach, see Piñera, 2000). For the most part, the countries that have by the start of the twenty first century performed best are those that have both a liberalised economy and a liberal polity.[10] But Russia's starting point is different, and it is both unrealistic and normatively questionable to expect this huge country suddenly to become like the USA or Australia, for instance. Russia has always been *sui generis* in various ways, and will continue to be so. But it is a naturally wealthy country, and has the elements to make a recovery under the right sort of leadership.

There is no inherent reason why a strong leader has to become a dictator. Russia still has a functioning parliament and constitutional court, a form of federalism, and reasonably free mass media. Human rights are not as well respected as in many Western states - especially if one is a Chechen – but are still better observed than they were in Soviet times or than they are in many other countries of the world. Russia maintains a dialogue with the West, tensions in the relationship notwithstanding. In recent years, the country has come close to being either an anarchy or a country run by organised crime and corrupt officials. However democratic one is in principle, it is unrealistic to expect Russian civil society at this point to play a major role in making the country functional once again (though for an upbeat assessment of the prospects for civil society in Russia see Marsh, 2000). There needs to be leadership. As long as Putin continues to respect the basics of constitutionalism, he may be the best Russians can hope for at this juncture. Two of the best indications that he is not oriented towards dictatorship are that Mikhail Gorbachev publicly expressed his support for Putin's revamping of the Federation Council; and that Putin himself has said the country needs a dictatorship – of law.[11] He also stated publicly in December 1999 his belief that political dictatorships are invariably fragile and temporary, while democracy is the only robust and enduring political arrangement.[12] Leaders intending to become dictators do not typically make such statements.

Earlier, reference was made to Putin's use of nationalism as a mode of legitimation. In fact, he has not made nearly as much use of this as might be expected (certainly by those who see him becoming a dictator).[13] Rather, his emphasis on law suggests a strong commitment to order and Max Weber's legal-rational legitimation. There are many democratic theorists who accept that emphasis on this impersonal mode is the essence of a modern state's legitimacy. Thus, while there is no question that Putin's call for a dictatorship of law could presage his moves towards political dictatorship, his reference does not have to mean this. But it does raise a fascinating theoretical question about legitimation.

In most analyses, states are seen to exercise power through a mixture of coercion and legitimation; the two concepts are treated as discrete. But if a majority of Russians want their president to use the power of the state to bring more order and fairness to society, is it time to add a new mode of legitimation to the existing ones – that of coercion? After all, most observers agree that Putin has a popular mandate to clamp down on the oligarchs and the disintegrative forces of regionalism, as well as to get the economy back on its feet. It is argued emphatically here that we do not need to add 'coercion' to our list of legitimation modes. Even if a leader is tough with some of his/her opposition, and invokes any combination of nationalism, teleologism, eudaemonism and legal-rationality to increase or sustain his/her regime's and/or system's legitimacy, this does not constitute dictatorship as long as certain 'rules of the game' continue to be observed. These include regular, free and contested elections; and recognition of the right of non-violent opposition, among other basic human rights. Just because a majority of citizens has indicated a preference for strong leadership does not mean that there can therefore be 'legitimate dictatorship', which is an oxymoron; unless the nature of the political arrangements are properly tested on a regular basis, there can be no way of knowing that the people are positively disposed towards recent developments and continue to be normatively supportive of the system. In short, if legitimacy is to mean anything, it must be testable in some way. While we can never measure it adequately, we can say that a total inability to test it would render the concept almost meaningless (at least in terms of real politics). This needs to be borne in mind as we watch the development of Putin's Russia – and post-Putin's Russia.

Anyone who has worked on Russia and the communist world for decades should have learnt the dangers of prediction. Not only did virtually everyone fail to predict the nature and timing of the collapse of communist power, but, far more recently, most analysts were surprised at how quickly Russia appeared to recover from the rouble and economic crisis of August-September 1998 (though see Breslauer et al., 2000, for an argument that the recovery was less impressive than is often assumed). However, while it would be unwise to make any predictions, we can at least outline the problems Russia is facing; emphasise the Russian context within which the new president is working; examine the global framework in which his country must operate; and analyse the ways in which Putin has been dealing with issues since he came to power. In doing this, we hope to problematise both Russia and its new president more than the Western mass media tend to; both the man and the country are far more complex and interesting than most of the more popular analyses would suggest.

It is perhaps appropriate to finish with another metaphor. In the present Russian context, it is to be hoped that Putin's interest and skill in Eastern martial arts will be reflected in his political style. In contrast to the brute force typical of boxing or wrestling, Eastern martial arts tend to depend more on skill, fitness and strategy. When exercised well, martial art skills are also highly effective.

Notes

1   For the full speech in English, see *Current Digest of the Post-Soviet Press* (hereafter *CDP-SP*), vol.52, no.1 [2000], pp.1-2.
2   The word 'appeared' is used here to indicate that decrees are not necessarily a guarantee of anything. In the case of this particular one, there was a move in early 2000 by some members of the Duma to rescind it; this motion was rejected at the end of March, but by a relatively small majority.
3   For a round-table discussion of the Yeltsin legacy see Breslauer et al., 2000.
4   The cynic might wish to point out that Putin himself has been accused on various occasions of corruption (which might explain what some might see as his excessive 'tolerance' of it). But these allegations have not so far been taken very seriously by most people, and in any case have usually referred to Putin's close association with *others* accused of corruption. This is not to deny that there might be a major corruption scandal involving Putin in the future, merely to argue that we should at this point keep an open mind.

5   Some have seen Berezovsky's move as a bold one, since renouncing his parliamentary seat also meant he lost his parliamentary immunity. But 'boldness' can also be interpreted as bravado. There are *some* similarities between Berezovsky's recent behaviour and Yeltsin's relationship with the Communist Party in the last years of the Soviet Union; but Yeltsin was far more in touch with the mood of the masses than Berezovsky is.

6   This is not invariably so. But it is assumed here that Russia's own traditions and level of development would not permit the kind of crude dictatorship that has existed in some African, Asian and Latin American states - so that our point holds in this case.

7   *Business Central Europe*, October 2000, online at www.bcemag.com/1000/mir/russia.html.

8   At the time of writing (October 2000), all three issues referred to at the end of the last paragraph had 'come off the boil' to some extent. For instance, Slobodan Milosevic had been replaced in Belgrade by someone expected to be more reasonable (Vojeslav Kostunica), and Chechnya had recently elected a representative to the Russian Duma for the first time in five years. But this might only be a temporary respite. Moreover, NATO could yet incorporate more former Soviet bloc members into its ranks (in addition to Czechia, Hungary and Poland). Thus, while it is tempting to be optimistic in this somewhat improved situation, knowledge of world history warns that a sense of realism must be maintained.

9   For a depressing picture of the treatment of the media in the early stages of Putin's presidency and comparisons with the Yeltsin era, see Panfilov, 2000; for reassuring words on Putin's own views on the role of the media, see the president's annual address to parliament of 8 July 2000 in *Rossiiskaya Gazeta*, 11 July, 2000, pp. 1 and 3, extracts from which were published in English in *CDP-SP*, 52:28 [2000], pp.4-7.

10   The most obvious exception to this is China. While this huge country has certainly been liberalising its economy, its polity is still close to being a dictatorship. I have argued on various occasions that the communist political system's days in China are numbered – though the trigger for its collapse (or conversion into another type of political system, as happened in Hungary) is very difficult to predict.

11   *Kommersant*, 1 February 2000 – translated in *CDP-SP*, 52:5 [2000], p.17.

12   Cited in Remington 2000; readers with Russian can access many of the president's speeches and other government statements at the Russian government website, http://www.government.gov.ru.

13   Not all dictators are nationalists, of course – Lukashenka is a prime example of one who is not. However, many dictators do play on nationalism if it suits them.

References

Auer, S. (2000), 'Nationalism in Central Europe - A Chance or a Threat for the Emerging Liberal Democratic Order?', *East European Politics and Societies*, vol.14, no.2, pp.1-33.

Breslauer, G., Brada, J., Gaddy, C., Ericson, R., Saivetz, C. and Winston, V. (2000), 'Russia at the End of Yel'tsin's Presidency', *Post-Soviet Affairs*, vol.16, no.1, pp.1-32.

Marsh, C. (2000), 'Social Capital and Democracy in Russia', *Communist and Post-Communist Studies*, vol.33, no.2, pp.183-99.

Panfilov, O. (2000), 'Glasnost under Siege: Putin and the Media - No Love Lost', *East European Constitutional Review*, vol.9, no.1-2, online at http://www.law.nyu.edu/eecr/vol9num_onehalf/feature/lovelost.html.

Piñera, J. (2000), 'A Chilean Model for Russia', *Foreign Affairs*, vol.79, no.5, pp.62-73.

Remington, T. (2000), 'Putin's Third Way; Russia and the "Strong State" Ideal', *East European Constitutional Review*, vol.9, no.1-2, online at http://www.law.nyu.edu/eecr/vol9num_onehalf/feature/strongstate.html.

Schmidt, H. (1999), *Auf der Suche nach einer öffentlichen Moral*, Gütersloh, Rheda-Wiedensbrück.

Shelley, L. (2000), 'Why a Corrupt State can't be a Strong State: Corruption in the Post-Yeltsin Era', *East European Constitutional Review*, vol.9, no.1-2, online at http://www.law.nyu.edu/eecr/vol9num_onehalf/feature/corruption.html.

Tolz, V. (1998), 'Forging the Nation: National Identity and Nation-Building in Post-Communist Russia', *Europe-Asia Studies*, vol.50, no.6, pp.993-1022.

Tompson, W. (2000), 'Putin's Power Plays', *World Today*, vol.56, no.7, pp.14-16.

2 Vladimir Putin and the Future of the Presidency

GRAEME GILL

The election of Vladimir Putin as Russia's president on 26th March 2000 was noteworthy for three reasons. It was the first time in Russia's history that there had been a peaceful change of national leader registered through the public electoral process. It marked the successful transfer of power from the charismatic regime founder to a successor, a process which in some other countries has produced instability and disunity. And it constituted the coming to power of someone who, a bare eight months earlier, had had no national political profile at all. One of the issues which his election raises, and which will be examined in this chapter, is the consequences for the institution of the presidency,[1] and thereby for the political system as a whole. The starting point for this analysis must be the Yeltsin legacy.

The Yeltsin Legacy

A significant element in that legacy is the hegemonic presidency that Yeltsin proceeded to build following his dispersal of the legislature in September-October 1993 (Gill and Markwick, 2000, chs.4 and 5). The basis for such a presidency was built in the period following Yeltsin's election as Russian president in June 1991. It was then that he set about constructing a political machine at the centre to sustain him and to help realise his political ambitions. Eschewing the popular basis of support that had been so important in gaining his election in the form of Democratic Russia, Yeltsin instead began to rely on a political machine built up initially from former associates in the Sverdlovsk region (Willerton, 1998). Although the membership of this changed, the importance of the presidential administration never wavered (Huskey, 1995). Indeed, as Yeltsin's difficulties with the legislature increased, he became even more reliant upon this apparatus than he had been in the past. This was not simply a case of the former party apparatchik feeling more at home with bureaucratic institutional structures than with the open politics of parliamentary life, although Yeltsin does not seem to have been temperamentally well attuned to this latter style of politics. Rather by relying upon administrative regulations and decrees, Yeltsin hoped to avoid the veto that he feared would follow increasingly from bringing his measures before the legislative body. In any event, Yeltsin built up a formidable politico-administrative machine staffed by people who were loyal to him. By 1994, the permanent professional staff of the presidential administration numbered 2,180, while the number of presidential staff numbered between 5,000 and 27,000 depending upon which bodies were included. Its budgetary allocation exceeded that of both houses of the new legislature elected at the end of 1993 (Huskey, 1995, p.116 and n.5). It was a major source of power for the president, effectively shadowing the government and giving him an important independent source of policy advice (Berezovsky, 1994). Yet it remained an organisation relatively impervious to public gaze and outside political control.

While the construction of an extensive presidential apparatus gave Yeltsin a political base upon which to stand, crucial in the moulding of the contours of the presidency was Yeltsin's defeat of the legislature in autumn 1993. The result of this defeat was the introduction of a new constitution which embedded a new, stronger conception of the presidency into the Russian political system. Although the new constitution accorded the legislature the power to pass (and thereby also to block) laws, including the budget, and to confirm the president's choice as prime minister, the new balance of power between president and legislature was now heavily weighted in favour of the former. The president had wide powers of appointment, had significant scope for legislative initiative, and had responsibility for ensuring that the 'bodies of state power' worked in a coordinated fashion. The president could issue decrees and could introduce a state of emergency. The president could also dissolve the State Duma, the lower house, much more easily than the legislature could impeach the president. While the constitution did not create a president who could ignore the legislature, it clearly projected him as the leading political actor in the Russian political system.

This bolstering of Yeltsin's political basis was accompanied by the projection of an image of the president which sought to generate a sense of charismatic authority.[2] The basis for this was Yeltsin's public role in the defeat of the August 1991 coup attempt, symbolised for all by the enduring image of him standing atop a tank in front of the White House. Building upon the image of him as a populist, which had gained currency since his arrival as Moscow *gorkom* first party secretary in 1985, Yeltsin and the people around him emphasised his role as the victor over the communists. A simplistic message was repeatedly projected across Russia: Yeltsin understood the people and had a special relationship with them, and it was only he who stood between them and the return of communist rule. This image was used extensively during the 1996 election campaign, which saw Yeltsin come back to win from a position of single digit approval ratings at the start of the campaign. What was important about this image was that it focused on Yeltsin the person rather than Yeltsin the office-holder. He was popular and powerful because of who he was, not because he occupied the office of president. The link between Yeltsin and people was thus shown to be an intensely personal one. He was a man of the people despite the trappings of high office. In this sense, he sought his legitimacy in the special tie he had with the people, not the office he held. What linked these together was that the special tie manifested itself through the electoral process, which placed him in the presidency. But it was the personalist tie which was crucial.

Following his victory in the 1996 presidential election, Yeltsin still tried to project the image of an activist president who possessed a special relationship with his people. However his capacity to sustain such an image was fundamentally undermined by his increasing personal decline. His entry into hospital for a heart by-pass operation in late 1996 followed by an extensive recuperation period punctured the picture of the activist fighter for the people's interests which he had done so much to cultivate during the election campaign. In addition, during the following years Yeltsin was often absent from the public gaze, in a performance which to many was reminiscent of the last years of the Brezhnev period. During this time when Yeltsin was clearly much more a part-time president than he had ever been before, while the presidential apparatus continued to function as an important instrument of central power and the informal group of cronies who surrounded Yeltsin wielded increasing influence over Russian affairs, the legitimation programme which those around the president sought to project underwent change. While not ignoring the person of the president, increasingly emphasis shifted in the direction of Weber's notion of legal rational authority. It was Yeltsin the president, possessing an electoral mandate and exercising powers embedded in the formal structures of the system, which came to have primacy. It was this institutional aspect rather than the personalist element which came to prominence in the imagery projected by the people around the president. It is a paradox that while the president showed greater personal unpredictability, the presidential legitimation programme increasingly emphasised routinized procedures and principles.

The partial removal of Yeltsin from the political scene during the late 1990s did not lead to the outbreak of political conflict, or even to significant public manoeuvring by his would-be successors. Had Yeltsin been as ill disposed during the early 1990s as he was in the late 1990s, legislative efforts to remove him would have been much stronger than they already were. But with Yeltsin's indisposition late in the decade, his political opposition did not make a serious and sustained attempt to remove him from the scene.[3] Two factors were probably instrumental in this. First, the outcome of the dispute in 1993 was still fresh in the minds of Yeltsin's critics in the legislature. His opponents had seen that Yeltsin was willing to use armed force to get his way and, given the increased constitutional power the presidency now had, the possible consequences of upsetting him did not seem worth the risk. This was particularly the case given the increasing unpredictability Yeltsin seemed to be demonstrating, reflected in his sacking of successive prime ministers in 1998-99. Second, Yeltsin's critics knew they only had to wait for 2000 for the next presidential election and that this should mark the end of Yeltsin's tenure in office. Given his age and health, and despite rumours that he might ignore the constitution and stand again or even postpone the election (Thornhill, 1999), most believed that the Yeltsin era would end with that presidential election. In these circumstances, the opposition believed its interests would be better served by letting Yeltsin serve out his presidency and then seeking to gain power through the electoral process. However this strategy was nullified by the rise of Vladimir Putin.

The Rise of Putin

To many observers in 1998 the Yeltsin presidency seemed to be becoming increasingly unstable. In March 1998 Yeltsin dismissed his long-serving Prime Minister Viktor Chernomyrdin and replaced him (over significant Duma reservations) with Sergei Kirienko. In August in the wake of the financial crisis, Kirienko was replaced by Yevgeny Primakov, a choice Yeltsin was forced to make following Duma resistance to his initial plan to reappoint Chernomyrdin. Primakov (who had wide support in the Duma) lasted until May 1999 when he was replaced by Sergei Stepashin who, in the wake of the failure of the attempt to impeach Yeltsin, was promptly confirmed by the Duma. In August 1999, Stepashin was dismissed and replaced by Putin. This succession of prime ministers was seen by some as an indication that the Yeltsin regime had entered a crisis stage, especially in the wake of the financial crisis in August 1998. The stable partnership between president and prime minister (albeit with occasional tensions) that had characterised Russian politics from 1993 until 1998 seemed to be a thing of the past and suggested that Yeltsin could not rely on the upper levels of Russian politics either to sustain his rule past the appointed constitutional time or support a Yeltsin candidate in the coming election. His need to promote unknowns like Stepashin and especially Putin seemed to confirm this view. Also important in generating this sense of crisis was the increasing sense of scandal and corruption that seemed to surround Yeltsin and his family. Not only were there rumours that his daughter, Tatyana Dyachenko, had made improper use of her position as a presidential adviser to enrich herself and her family, but for the first time a whiff of corruption attached to the president himself. This was the Mabetex scandal whereby Yeltsin was accused of taking kickbacks from developers for renovation work in the Kremlin.[4] Also Yeltsin's attempts to remove the State Prosecutor Yuri Skuratov, who was following up corruption allegations that were wending their way closer to the president, became a public issue when the Federation Council refused to go along with Yeltsin[5] and footage of the prosecutor apparently cavorting with prostitutes was used to publicly discredit him. The president seemed increasingly under threat and isolated.

In this context a number of attempts were made to consolidate opposition forces. The Communist Party of the Russian Federation, the perennial leading opposition force under Yeltsin, conducted negotiations with a range of leftist groups over this period in an attempt to bring together a united front behind a common candidate in the presidential election. However the distrust of Zyuganov and the communists and a lack of clarity about what they stood for discouraged the communists' putative partners from bringing such negotiations to any firm conclusion. Disunity had always been a major problem on the left, and this it was to remain. A more important attempt to unite opposition forces was made in the centre of the political spectrum.

The mayor of Moscow, Yuri Luzhkov, had for some years been emerging as a national level politician of considerable standing. Originally becoming mayor after Gavriil Popov left that post in 1992, Luzhkov had worked assiduously to bring new development to Moscow, something which he achieved with considerable success. During the 1990s new building and renovation projects, from Christ the Saviour Cathedral to the Manezh underground shopping mall, transformed the centre of the capital. Luzhkov used this development boom to promote his own leadership, directly associating himself with it and thereby projecting an image of himself as a political leader who could get things done (Zotov, 1998). His populist, activist image symbolised by his constant wearing of a worker's cloth cap contrasted sharply with that of the ailing president in the latter half of the decade. It did not matter that Moscow's development boom rested on shaky financial foundations. What was important was that while much of the country stagnated, the Moscow economy was booming. But Luzhkov's national aspirations had a major weakness: his support base was limited to Moscow. While it is clear that his support within the capital was robust and extensive, outside Moscow there was little solid support for the Moscow mayor. Indeed, there was considerable resentment against Luzhkov. The Moscow boom not only generated jealousy among many of those who did not live in the city, but fuelled the belief that the development of Moscow was occurring at the expense of the rest of the country. Many believed that Luzhkov was scooping off money that should have gone elsewhere in the country and directing it into Moscow's coffers. This restriction of his support base to the capital was a major limitation on his political aspirations.

In an attempt to overcome the limitations of his support base, Luzhkov began to look to the regional governors. Many of these people ran their regions autocratically, but they were always concerned about the possibility of a reassertion of control from the centre. By the late 1990s they were looking for ways to shore up their local positions and to establish a more effective means of operating at the national level than was provided by their membership of the Federation Council. They began to coalesce into groups. It was at this point that overtures were made from Luzhkov's supporters to some of these governors. The result was an emerging alliance between Luzhkov's Moscow machine-based organisation called Fatherland and the emergent organisation of regional governors called All-Russia. But what seemed to give this nascent alliance real political weight was the attachment to it of Yevgeny Primakov.[6] At the time he was sacked as prime minister, Primakov had been the most popular figure in Russian politics. He was widely credited with guiding Russia through the financial crisis of August 1998 and his steady hand seemed the perfect antidote to the uncertainties stemming from his erratic president.

Primakov seemed to bring personal popularity and a national political stature to the alliance of regional and Moscow political machines, a combination which threatened to be a potent political weapon in the legislative elections due at the end of 1999. The result was the organisation called Fatherland-All Russia (OVR).

The formation of OVR seemed to crystallise the danger to those surrounding Yeltsin. Increasingly during the 1990s, the environment around Yeltsin had been one in which excessive power was exercised by family, friends and cronies. That clique of informal advisers and associates, symbolised most clearly by Yeltsin's daughter, had come to be known as the 'Family',[7] while an overlapping group of powerful businessmen known as the 'oligarchs', many of whom had funded Yeltsin's re-election campaign in 1996,were widely assumed to be able to exercise excessive power in leading circles. The Yeltsin presidency had been a time when these groups were able to enrich themselves, principally through the advantages they gained from their proximity to the summit of power. A series of public scandals, from the loans for shares deal through to Mabetex and the Bank of New York money laundering scandal, ensured that the position of these people remained an issue of public notoriety. Aware of this, those close to Yeltsin were seeking ways to maintain their positions once the president had gone. They wanted at least security that they would not be prosecuted for their deeds or stripped of their gains; but preferably what they wanted was a guarantee of being able to continue as they had before. This group looked at the emergence of OVR with alarm. Not only did OVR appear to be a potential major political force on the national stage, but also Primakov was recognised as an opponent of their interests. His sacking had been in part attributed to his encouragement of Prosecutor-General Skuratov's mounting of a very public investigation into corruption in the Kremlin, and Primakov was said to be close to the communists whose opposition to the 'Family' and the 'oligarchs' was well known.

The response to this challenge was three-fold. First, the mounting of a vigorous press campaign to discredit OVR generally and Primakov in particular. Through its links in the media, and in particular through the agency of the oligarch Boris Berezovsky who owned wide media interests, a sustained campaign was mounted against OVR. Sustained over a long period, this campaign eroded the levels of popular support OVR enjoyed and generated disunity and division within its ranks. Just as the media had proved crucial in 1996, so again at the end of the decade it was an important factor in routing those who challenged the will of the Kremlin.

Second, the promotion of Vladimir Putin. The sacking of Stepashin and his replacement as prime minister by Putin in August 1999 was a crucial step in this process. Putin's appointment came as a surprise to many. Born in 1952, Putin graduated in law from Leningrad State University in 1975, and then joined the KGB. Following a period in the Chief Directorate in Moscow, he was sent to East Germany in the 1980s. His responsibilities there remain unclear, although according to his later mentor Anatoly Sobchak, they were to do with economic intelligence. He returned to Leningrad in 1989, officially leaving the KGB and entering university administration. However in 1990 he left this post, entering the administration of the newly-elected Leningrad mayor Sobchak. From this vantage point, Putin was within the interstices of the most vigorous democratic movement in the country in the closing years of the Soviet era and of the administration of the most open city in the early years of independent Russia. From 1992-96 Putin was deputy mayor (from 1994 first deputy mayor) and head of the St.Petersburg Foreign Relations Committee, a position which brought him into close contact with Western companies seeking to invest or do business in the city. Although there have since been claims that Putin was able to use this position for personal gain,[8] Putin's tenure in St.Petersburg seems to have been unremarkable. In 1996 he was transferred to Moscow, possibly on the suggestion of Yeltsin intimate Anatoly Chubais, and took up a series of high positions in the presidential apparatus. In 1998 Putin was made head of the Federal Security Service (FSB), the successor to the KGB, and in March 1999 Secretary of the Security Council. Presumably Putin's service in Moscow had attracted the attention of those around Yeltsin and convinced them that he was the best person to protect their interests. On 9th August Stepashin was dismissed, and a week later Putin was confirmed by the Duma as the new prime minister. Furthermore Yeltsin also publicly anointed him as his preferred successor as president.

The cold, seemingly ascetic, Putin looked to be a stark contrast with the more gregarious and down to earth Yeltsin. But he may have appeared to have the qualities which those around Yeltsin felt were necessary to secure an orderly transition of power and which would also protect their interests. Putin had secured significant advancement under Yeltsin, and could therefore be considered to be in their debt. His period working for Sobchak would have given him at least some credentials in the democratic movement and therefore may have blunted criticism from this quarter. But Putin's background in the security arena would also presumably have given him both sensitivity to the interests of that sector and recognition of the positive effects that the use of forceful measures could have. In this sense, Putin may have appeared as someone who would both recognise his obligations to his patrons and be willing to use forceful measures to protect them if necessary.

Third, the formation of a Kremlin party to contest the legislative elections in December 1999. In September 1999, with the media campaign against Primakov and OVR in full swing and the fighting in Chechnya underway (see below), the formation of a new political party entitled Unity was announced. This party, notionally headed by Minister for Emergency Situations Sergei Shoigu and two people not formerly involved in political life, former world champion wrestler Alexander Karelin and former police major general Alexander Gurov, refused to specify any clear policies. Instead it was presented as the party of Putin; its support for the prime minister was its sole political slogan. It had no local organisations and no mass membership, but it received extensive support through the media and its public profile and level of support increased dramatically. [9]

Unity was undoubtedly aided by its association with Putin. Since his appointment as prime minister, Putin's public popularity had risen enormously. A major factor in this was the renewal of the Chechen War. In August 1999, two Chechen military commanders, Basayev and Khattab, launched military action into neighbouring Dagestan in a misguided attempt to rouse their Islamic neighbours into a holy war against Russia. Russian troops were dispatched, and drove them back into Chechnya. In September there were a number of bombings in Moscow and Volgodonsk in which a large number of ordinary citizens were killed. The bombings were blamed on Chechens, although no convincing evidence was ever produced. There were rumours that this was a provocation by the security services, designed to produce a pretext for the renewal of the war. [10] Even if the bombs had been planted by agents of the security services (and no convincing evidence of this has been found either, although some circumstantial evidence has come to light), [11] the incursion into Dagestan and associated hostage-taking was the sort of action which would have forced the hand of most governments. In any event, the response from the Putin government in September was to renew the war in Chechnya, but this time in recognition of the lessons learnt from the war of 1994-96, it was a war conducted with an eye to minimising Russian casualties. Continuing successes were reported, and as the election approached, Putin's popularity rose.[12] Increasingly he was seen as the leading presidential contender and as a political figure virtually beyond criticism, even by his major political opponents.[13]

When the results of the legislative election came in, it was clear that the tactics adopted by those around Yeltsin had been successful and the attempt to mount a centrist challenge was in tatters. While the Communist Party remained the largest party with 24.3% of the vote, Unity with 23.3% clearly outstripped OVR which received only 13.1%. Although there were claims from the communists that there had been significant vote rigging,[14] such claims failed to gain support either from international observers or from other participants in the election. The sidelining of OVR was continued when, at the time of the first session of the Duma, an agreement was reached between Unity and the communists to divide up the chairmanship positions of the Duma committees.[15] Following the poor electoral showing of OVR, Primakov formally announced he would not contest the presidential poll, and then on 31st December Yeltsin announced his resignation as president and the take over of that position in an acting capacity by Putin. Putin's first action was to issue a decree giving immunity from prosecution to Yeltsin and his family.

Yeltsin's resignation[16] and Putin's appointment had two important implications for the forthcoming presidential election. First, the election date was moved forward from the middle of the year to March, thereby giving potential challengers less time than they thought they had to prepare. Second, it accorded Putin all the advantages of incumbency, and he used these well. The combined effect of these undercut the positions of Putin's potential opponents in the presidential race and drove them to publicly offer their support to him.[17] With leading politicians now publicly giving their support to Putin and with the media firmly on side, the campaign involved even less of a discussion of issues than had been the case in 1996. While his challengers tried to raise enthusiasm for their causes and to engage him in public debate of various issues, Putin eschewed a campaign of either electoral promises or engagement with issues. Instead he sought to exude the air of the president while emphasising only his commitment to strengthen Russia and to defeat the so-called 'Chechen bandits'. When the ballots were counted following the voting on 26th March, Putin had defeated his primary opponent, communist leader Gennady Zyuganov, by 52.9% of the vote to 29.2%.

The Putin Presidency

The election of Putin opened a new era in Russian politics and offered the chance of a new start, of making a break with the politics of cronyism and of a drift which had been all too characteristic of much of the Yeltsin period. But how likely is it that Putin will make a break with the politics of his predecessor? And even if he wants to, will he be able to do so? Crucial here is the strength of the presidency which Putin has inherited. A number of factors suggest that Putin will have the opportunity to be a very strong president, especially during the early phases of his first term.

1. Putin had a clear-cut election victory. In contrast to some who saw his victory as being quite narrow because he gained an outright majority of only 2.9% (McFaul, 2000), in fact his victory was overwhelming. He won on the first ballot, the only person to have achieved this since presidential polls were introduced in June 1991, and he won an overall majority with eleven candidates in the field. Furthermore he beat his nearest rival by 23.7% of the votes. This was an overwhelming victory, and gives his presidency substantial moral authority and an overwhelming popular mandate.

2. The nature of the mandate Putin has received gives him substantial room for manoeuvre. Putin ran a campaign with few promises and thereby came out of it with few firm policy commitments. This means that Putin has significant policy flexibility. But this does not mean that there are no criteria against which to judge his performance or that the people did not know what they were voting for in electing him. Putin was clearly associated with the values of strength and stability, with the commitment to restoring the strength of the Russian state and dealing with the lawlessness and corruption which had become such a feature of Russian life in many people's eyes. His association with the security services seemed to be one element of this commitment; his vigorous stand on Chechnya was another. So the sort of mandate with which Putin entered office had few practical policy commitments beside a generalised commitment to restore order and state power.

3. The sidelining of major opposition groups in Russian society. The effect of the legislative and presidential elections was effectively to marginalise the main sources of political opposition to Putin.

(a) On the left, the failure of the Communist Party of the Russian Federation to increase its vote in the Duma election from that achieved in 1995 and its inability to take the presidential election into a second round suggests the electoral stagnation of this body. In the presidential election, Zyuganov's vote was down 3.1% compared with 1996, and had he been able to win this number of votes from Putin, a second round would have been necessary. But the communists' inability to make any headway in the electoral arena, added to the agreement it reached with Unity over leading positions within the legislature, may compromise the role of vigorous critic it had in the past, particularly if Putin continues to adopt positions which are consistent with its own.

(b) Similar electoral stagnation characterises the major party group with a stable identity, Yabloko. In neither the legislative nor the presidential election was it able to break out of the electoral box of about 6% in which it has found itself consistently since 1993. Its exit from this dead end seems to be seen as lying in amalgamation with the Union of Rightist Forces (see below).

(c) In the centre-right, no stable party groupings emerged to act as a check on Putin. Unity was simply an electoral vehicle comprising a wide range of people with widely different political perspectives and views. It is probable that, should someone try to impose some unity upon this group based on policy commitments (as opposed to share of the spoils of legislative office), its internal tensions would lead to its dissolution. Although there have been attempts to revive OVR, it is likely that any long term development in this regard would have a different political profile to that of the organisation in 1999. Primakov's age means that he is not a long-term player, while Luzhkov's future outside the mayoralty (to which he was re-elected in December 1999) is unclear. If there is to be a new form of organisation emerging, it is likely to be based on the regional governors whose interests in Moscow seemed to be even more in need of protection during the early Putin presidency than they had before (see below). The other major group, the Union of Rightist Forces, was formed in November 1998, principally from Gaidar's Democratic Choice of Russia and a range of other 'democratic and reform-oriented'[18] parties. This group is likely to continue to press for economic reform and by so doing may find itself allied on many issues to Putin,[19] but its small basis of support (it gained 8.3% of votes in the legislative poll) means that it does not have a major bridgehead in the political system from which to exercise substantial power. Its recognition of this problem may be reflected in the talks leading to the announcement in June 2000 of the merger of the Union with Yabloko.[20]

4.   The broad basis of support for Putin that exists in the Duma. Unlike Yeltsin for much of his term of office, Putin should confront a legislative chamber in which a significant number of deputies will support his positions. His success in getting legislative ratification of the long-stalled START-2 Treaty in April 2000 is an indication of this.

5.   During the election campaign the media did not play a major role in criticising Putin or bringing the public debate of policy into play. It is not clear that the vigorous and investigative role played by the media in earlier years will be repeated.

These characteristics of the post-election political scene in Russia suggest that Putin has an opportunity to act vigorously and decisively and to stamp his mark on Russian public life. Has he availed himself of this opportunity?

The initial months of the Putin presidency have not seen the unrolling of a robust program of policy or reform. There have certainly been measures which are consistent with Putin's desire to rebuild the power of the Russian state. The earlier restoration of military training for youths in schools was a symbolic measure aimed not just at shoring up the military and its sense of self worth, but also re-investing into Russian society the commitment to rebuilding the powerful military that in recent years had been allowed to decay.[21] The continued pursuit of the war in Chechnya was another indication of this. But Putin has also sought to strengthen the central state in other ways. He has emphasised the need for a better tax system which will increase the collection by the centre, and in May the government approved of a package of new tax bills designed to achieve this. He has also sought to strengthen the centre by undermining the power of the regional governors. He has proposed legislation to enable the sacking of governors and the reform of the composition of the Federation Council to remove them from it. He has also divided Russia into seven administrative regions, each run by a 'plenipotentiary representative of the president' with extensive powers.[22] These new regions broadly match the military districts into which Russia is divided, and five of Putin's initial appointments to fill the post of plenipotentiary came from the ranks of the military, police or security services.[23] Putin is clearly trying to bring the Russian administrative system throughout the country under closer Muscovite control.

As well as moving against the power of the regional governors, there is some evidence that Putin has been seeking to distance himself from some of the cronies who had surrounded Yeltsin. In May, armed tax police wearing balaclavas raided the offices of Media Most, owned by the 'oligarch' Vladimir Gusinsky[24] who had been critical of Putin. While this action stimulated some public demonstrations in favour of freedom of speech, it was not clear whether this action was motivated by a desire to restrict such freedom, by a desire to strike at Gusinsky, or both. The desire to punish Gusinsky seemed a stronger motive when Gusinsky was briefly arrested in June.[25] In addition, Putin's plans for restructuring the federal system came under public attack by another of the 'oligarchs', Boris Berezovsky.[26] Furthermore in June, proceedings were begun by the Prosecutor General to overturn the 1997 privatisation of Norilsk Nickel, a move directed against another of the 'oligarchs', Vladimir Potanin.[27] At the same time as this apparent rift with at least some of the 'oligarchs' was becoming public, Putin has continued to build up his own personal machine within the Kremlin. While the membership of this machine reflects in part Putin's background in the security services and in St.Petersburg, it also includes people who had associations with Yeltsin; the re-appointment of former 'Family' member and Yeltsin's head of the Presidential Administration, Alexander Voloshin, on 28th May 2000 is the most obvious case of this. Putin is clearly aiming to bring the central administrative structure in Moscow under his personal control.

Putin has sought to bolster his strong man, can-do image at home by projecting himself as someone who can protect Russia's interests in the international arena. His first international steps involved gaining legislative ratification of the START-2 treaty, which had been stalled in the Russian legislature for years. This was followed by strong criticism of the expansion of NATO and the US proposals to modify the terms of the ABM treaty in order to enable the policy of National Missile Defence to go ahead. It also resulted in clear attempts to create close relations with the major European states; in part by appealing to their wariness about the US missile defence plans. Putin's strategy is a combination of opposition to the military strengthening of the West vis-à-vis Russia with the desire for greater integration into the world economy as the means of dealing with Russia's economic problems.[28] The difficulty is not only whether the military and the economic can be distinguished in this way, but whether either is consistent with his drive to strengthen the Russian state, especially if a major means of achieving this is through militaristic symbols and action.

Conclusion

Vladimir Putin has the opportunity to strengthen the Russian presidency considerably compared with the office he inherited from Boris Yeltsin. With weak opposition from the major political actors and substantial popular support for the general project upon which he is engaged, the strengthening of order, the opportunity for the centralisation of power and control seems to exist. And Putin seems to have both the will and the energy to act upon this. But it is by no means clear that he will be able to achieve his ends, at least not without even greater militarisation than has thus far been evident. His personal popularity, already dropping just before the election, is likely to decline even further, especially if success in the Chechen War eludes Russian forces. It is by no means clear that the centre can develop the infrastructural means to be able effectively to assert its control over the regions on a continuing basis, even if Putin is able to bring the present governors to heel. Indeed, Putin's failure to prevent the re-election of the mayor in his own hometown St.Petersburg, shows that his power to control events outside Moscow remains limited. And it is not clear that, despite the apparent economic improvement in 1999-2000, the economy will expand and grow sufficiently fast to bring about the improved living standards and conditions which people crave and upon which political performance ultimately will be judged. - *nun ratn.*

But the real tragedy here is that there is not a vibrant civil society which can impose checks upon an ambitious political executive. Political parties remain weak and shallowly rooted in the Russian populace, the wide range of public associations exercise little influence in the political arena, and the vast mass of the Russian populace show no evidence of easy mobilisation into political life. Political life does not exist in a vacuum, but nor is it soundly rooted in an engaged and organised citizenry who see their part as full involvement in the governing of their society. This situation is a result of the stalled nature of the Russian transition. Rather than moving on from Soviet authoritarianism to a vigorous and viable democracy, Russia has become stuck in a situation in which political actors wield far too much power and civil society far too little. This is a function both of the circumstances of the fall of the communist regime and the sort of political system built by Yeltsin. It is this which Putin has inherited and, at least at this stage, he shows no signs of seeking to tackle this most basic of problems: how can a viable and strong civil society be encouraged in Russia? What is clear is that if this does not develop, the authoritarian, militaristic outcome which many have associated with Putin will be a likely result of his attempt to strengthen the Russian state and the Russian presidency.

Notes

1   For an argument that the popularity of the institution of the presidency is rooted in Russian political culture, see Ryabov, 1999, pp.1-2.

2   For the classic typology of authority, see Weber, 1978, vol.1, chapter 3.

3   The Communist Party of the Russian Federation did seek his impeachment in early 1999, but this failed (Gill and Markwick, 2000, pp.202-3).

4   The basic charge was that Russian oil revenues had been diverted to pay for renovations to the Kremlin, that large bribes had been paid to officials including members of the 'Family', and that Yeltsin and his family had had the use of foreign credit cards paid for by the Swiss construction firm, Mabetex. For one report, see *Nezavisimaya gazeta*, 27 August, 1999.

5   Skuratov was finally removed by the Council at Putin's urging on 19th April 2000.

6   For example, see *Nezavisimaya gazeta*, 19 August, 1999.

7   This phenomenon was widely commented upon in the Russian press. For one interesting discussion, see *Obshchaya gazeta*, 22-28 July, 1999.

8   For example, see the vague discussion in Duparc, 2000.

9   *Izvestia*, 4 December, 1999. For a survey of the stances taken by various media outlets, see *Izvestia Media*, 1, 29 November, 1999.

10   For a discussion of this, and the war more generally, see Kovalev, 2000, pp.4-8.

11   *Obshchaya gazeta*, 16-22 September, 1999; *Izvestia*, 18 September 1999.

12   In September 1999 4% of voters supported Putin; by early March 2000 that figure was 59%. *Russian Election Watch*, no.8, 15 March, 2000, p.1.

13   *Izvestia*, 16 November, 1999; *Kommersant*, 25 November, 1999.

14   For a discussion of this, see G.Gill, 2000, p.9; *Russian Election Watch*, no.9, 7 April, 2000, pp.5-6.

15   *Nezavisimaya gazeta*, 20 January, 2000.

16   For his speech, see *Rossiiskaya gazeta*, 5 January, 2000.

17   For the broad coalition which formally nominated Putin, see *Nezavisimaya gazeta*, 13 January, 2000.

18   The description is Kovalev's. He also provides information as to the constitution of the party (Kovalev, 2000, p.8 n.3).

19   For example, for Putin's support for a market economy with substantial state involvement, see the statement he issued on the eve of becoming acting president (Russian Government, 1999). This is discussed in *Nezavisimaya gazeta*, 30 December, 1999.

20   *Izvestia*, 21 June, 2000.

21   For an early statement of this, see his speech before the Duma on 16 August 1999. *Rossiiskaya gazeta*, 17 August, 1999.

22   For the powers of these representatives, see *Rossiiskaya gazeta*, 16 May, 2000. For a discussion of the reorganisation, see Arkhangel'skaya, 2000, pp.53-6. The representative was to be formally on the staff of the Presidential Administration and was therefore directly answerable to the President.

23   These representatives were: former head of operations in Chechnya GeneralViktor Kazantsev in the North Caucasus, first deputy interior minister Petr Latyshev in the Urals, former commander in Chechnya (1994-96) Lieutenant General Konstantin Pulikovskii in the Far East, CIS affairs minister Leonid Drachevskii in Siberia, former KGB officer and presidential representative to Leningrad oblast Georgii Poltavchenko in the Central region, FSB first deputy director Viktor Cherkesov in the North-west region and head of the Union of Rightist Forces Sergei Kirienko in the Volga.

24   *Kommersant*, 12 May, 2000.

25   *Izvestia*, 14 June, 2000. This also seems to be evident in Putin's earlier prevention of Gusinsky from selling Most-Bank in order to raise capital to meet his debt commitments (Hoffman, 2000, p.A21).

26   *Moscow Times*, 1 June, 2000.

27   For Putin's comments about the need 'mercilessly to fight' oligarchs who seek to redistribute state resources in their own favour, see his interview with 'Welt am Sonntag' reprinted in *Rossiiskaya gazeta*, 14 June, 2000.

28   This is sketched in Putin's statement of 28 December 1999, 'Russia at the Turn of the Millennium' (Russian Government, 1999).

References

Arkhangel'skaya, N. (2000), 'Vertikal'naya Rossiya', *Ekspert*, no.19, 22 May, 2000, pp.53-6.

Berezovsky, V. (1994), 'Dva politicheskikh lagerya federal'noi elity Rossii', *Svobodnaia mysl'*, no.9, June, pp.82-3.

Duparc, A. (2000), 'New light thrown on Vladimir Putin's past', *The Guardian Weekly*, 1-7 June, 2000.

Gill, G. (2000), 'The Russian Duma Elections of 1999: The Main Game?', *Russian and Euro-Asian Bulletin*, vol.9, no.1, pp.1-9.

Gill, G. and Markwick, R. (2000), *Russia's Stillborn Democracy? From Gorbachev to Yeltsin*, Oxford University Press, Oxford.

Hoffman, D. (2000), 'Putin's Actions Seem to Belie Promise on Tycoons', *Washington Post Foreign Service*, 7 May, 2000.

Holmes, S. (1993-4), 'A Forum on Presidential Power', *East European Constitutional Review*, vo.2, no.4, Fall 1993, and vol.3, no.1, Winter 1994, pp.36-9.

Huskey, E. (1995), 'The State-Legal Administration and the Politics of Redundancy', *Post-Soviet Affairs*, vol.11, no.2, pp.115-43.

Kelley, D.R. (1994), 'Yel'tsin and Russo-Gaullism', *The Soviet and Post-Soviet Review*, vol.21, no.11, pp.44-55.

Kovalev, S. (2000), 'Putin's War', *The New York Review of Books*, 10 February, 2000, pp.4-8.

Kubicek, P. (1994), 'Delegative Democracy in Russia and Ukraine', *Communist and Post-Communist Studies*, vol.27, no.4, pp.423-41.

McFaul, M. (2000), 'Russia's 2000 Presidential Elections: Implications for Russian Democracy and US-Russian Relations', *Testimony before the Committee on Foreign Relations*, US Senate, 12 April, 2000.

Russian Government (1999), 'Russia at the turn of the Millennium', *www.pravitelstvo.gov.ru/english/statVP_engl_1.html*.

Ryabov, A. (1999), 'Politicheskaya stabil'nost', institut prezidenta i raskol vlastnykh elit: est' li u Rossii shansy izbezhat' politicheskogo khaosa?', *Brifing moskovskogo tsentra Karnegi*, vol.1, no.4, April, pp.1-2.

Thornhill, J. (1999), 'Vladimir Putin: The Family's Sinister Son', *Financial Times*, 14 August, 1999.

Weber, M. (1978), *Economy and Society. An Outline of Interpretive Sociology*, University of California Press, Berkeley, (eds G.Roth and C.Wittich).

White, S. (1997), 'Russia: Presidential Leadership under Yeltsin', in R.Taras (ed.), *Postcommunist Presidents* Cambridge University Press, Cambridge, pp.38-66.

Willerton, J.P. (1998), 'Post-Soviet Clientelist Norms at the Russian Federal Level', in G.Gill (ed.), *Elites and Leadership in Russian Politics*, Macmillan, Basingstoke 1998, pp.52-80.

Zotov, V.B. (1998), *Kak mer Luzhkov upravliaet Moskvoi (materialy lektsii)*, IM-INFORM, Lyubertsy.

3 Nationalism and Democratisation in Post-Communist Russia

DAVID W. LOVELL

Introduction

The transition from communism, in its most general aspects, is widely—but in an important sense, unfortunately—described as democratisation. What makes this description 'unfortunate' has to do with the complexity and extent of the changes (which are far broader than political), and with easy assumptions about the intrinsic merits and success of their destination. Nevertheless, we must play with the hand we are dealt. This paper therefore stresses the breadth of the changes of this democratisation—political, economic, social, and in some cases national—and the drag of the communist legacy which influences its progress and affects its outcomes. It examines, in particular, the role of nationalism in affecting the process of democratisation in Russia: partly because nationalism has played a major role in short-term political affairs, notably the recent and decisive election of Vladimir Putin as Russia's President; and partly because it provides an indication of the type of society that will emerge from the transition. Furthermore, the case of nationalism highlights a central problem of the Russian transition: a lack of leadership.

In March 2000, in the third election to the Russian presidency since the collapse of communism, Vladimir Putin was elected comfortably in the first round of voting. To democratic eyes, what was curious about Putin's election campaign and subsequent victory was both the lack of an explicit platform, and the desire by most of his competitors to be seen as his allies. Putin's success had a great deal to do with his ability to project himself as a decisive leader, especially in his prosecution of the war in Chechnya. Putin may not have engineered the war, but he profited from it. His actions appealed strongly to Russian nationalism and to Russians' wish to find a leader who will re-establish order and stability in their state and lives. Putin has consequently put an emphasis on reinforcing rules: strengthening the state's administration and reforming the tax and legal systems.

Perhaps Putin's greatest challenge is to curb the power of the financial oligarchs who control much of the economy, and who have siphoned money out of the country instead of productively reinvesting it. It is widely accepted that these people most threaten Russia's transition to democracy and free markets. There have been symbolic changes since Putin was made acting President, upon the resignation of Boris Yeltsin at the end of 1999. Yeltsin attracted suspicion that his administration was corrupt, and that his circle was unduly benefiting from his rule: his family, including especially his daughter Tatyana Dyachenko, and his major financial backers, including Boris Berezovsky. (A former Prime Minister, Yevgeny Primakov, launched a corruption investigation against Berezovsky which, when it seemed about to achieve results, led to the investigator being disgraced by a personal scandal.) Putin has distanced himself from Dyachenko, but whether this is a full-scale attack on corruption and on the growing gulf between elite and masses is doubtful.

The economic situation of Russia is difficult. There seems to be widespread system breakdown. Pensions are not paid; wages are not paid; and other government creditors (including international loan agencies) are not paid. Taxes are evaded. Russian industry and commerce are characterised by corruption, cronyism and inefficiency. Attempts by international agencies, such as the International Monetary Fund, to assist have been undermined by high-level corruption, as billions of dollars of aid money and loans have been channelled out of the country into private, 'off-shore' bank accounts. Nevertheless, a 1998 survey found that the vast majority of Russians—though many are not paid regularly—do not go without necessities such as heat and electricity, and were seldom short of food or clothing ('Can't Pay', 1998).

The transition from communism was never going to be easy. As citizens of the communist system learned to their disappointment, the absence of communism does not mean the immediate end to their problems. There has been a political settling-in period in many of the East Central European parliaments, and there remains political instability in those states that took a presidentialist path. In August 1999, for example, then-President Yeltsin nominated his fifth prime minister in 18 months. The inability of government officials to deal with corruption, lawlessness, and cheating, and their apparent cooperation in them, fuels a deep distrust of politics and administration. In the economic sphere, there is substantial uncertainty about job security, and people on fixed incomes such as pensions have been stunned by rising prices for food, housing and other necessities.

The transition from communism has seen the establishment of the formal institutions of democracy, while the attitudes and values of political and economic elites, and of citizens themselves, are struggling to adapt to their requirements. Russia, for example, has been called an 'incomplete' democracy (White, 2000). The notion that cultural development lags behind structural change has long been accepted; it is even basic to the early policies of most revolutionary regimes, which try to escape quickly from the drag of the past by changing personnel and eliminating opponents. The problem in postcommunist states, therefore, is a sub-set of a larger question about political institutions, and what makes them work the way they do. How can the democratic institutions established in postcommunism become strong, responsive and effective? Part of the answer can undoubtedly be found in the design of the institutions themselves (and especially in the distinction between presidential and parliamentary governments, already mentioned). A significant part of the answer can also be found in changing the culture within which these institutions operate.

The political culture of postcommunism is a complex construction of traditional and communist legacies. It sets a framework of habits and expectations. While it differs from country to country, there is an emphasis on order and stability. Disorder is indeed a problem in Russia. It is manifest in increasing crime and corruption, but also more insidiously in the absence of a properly functioning state—one that cannot police its laws, collect its taxes, administer its departments, and handle the physical infrastructure for which it is responsible. Such disorder is, in brief, symptomatic of a weak state. But the yearning for order which has accompanied this situation threatens to undermine the quest for freedom which was the impulse for the demise of communism. The diversity of freedom, and especially the responsibilities that underlie it, are at risk from order seen as imposed uniformity. And one of the dimensions of this order is a homogenous ethnicity which underlies the prevailing notion of nationalism. This is why attitudes have become so important when assessing democratisation.

Civil society—the sphere of multiple, independent associations and a diversity of ideas—underpins a mature democracy. The further progress of democratisation depends on the health of civil society. In Russia, civil society begins from a weak base; it conflicts with the people's continuing belief that to achieve their goals they should look first to the state. A major source of the disjunction between attitudes and aspirations, on the one hand, and behaviours on the other, can be found in the legacy of communist times. Furthermore, the attitudes of postcommunist officials and citizens can best be brought into line with the institutions and behaviours of postcommunism to produce a liberal democracy by way of developing a civil society. In that development, the role of leadership (particularly political leadership) is crucial.

This chapter focuses on nationalism's role in building a civil society both because national identification is a foundational task of democratising societies, and because nationalist issues continue to reappear in postcommunist Russia. Russian ethno-nationalism presents a danger both because its main aspect is illiberal and conformist, and because nationalist passions are readily manipulated by short-sighted politicians. Stoking the fires of Russian nationalism does not assist the development of a civil society that can act as a check on government power. Indeed, it exemplifies the approach of many Russian politicians who mistake populism for democratic leadership.

Democratisation and Civil Society

Postcommunism has been seen as another case of democratisation, as part of the 'third wave' of democratisation begun in 1974 in Portugal (Huntington, 1991, p.3). This view, however, obscures the particular features and problems of democratisation in postcommunist countries, as opposed to other types of authoritarian systems, and it obscures the problems in individual postcommunist countries which arise chiefly from their histories and cultures. Postcommunist states have had to confront not just political tasks, but also the dismantling of command economies and, in some cases, the redefinition of national boundaries. It is not simply a question of changing the political system, but also of a new socio-economic system, and in important cases (the USSR, Yugoslavia, and Czechoslovakia especially) a question of identity.

While substantial changes have been made on the institutional side, there remains significant work to be done. Parties may have been formed, electoral laws changed, and parliaments given a genuine say in discussing and approving laws. But change in the state's administrative apparatus has been much slower. A specialist writing in 1999 argued that Russia's bureaucratic transformation was 'still to be addressed' (Nunberg, 1999, p.3), including important issues in the areas of structure and processes of government, of the dimensions of government, and of professionalism in the civil service.

Institutional questions, of course, are important in themselves, and some analysts caution against the perils of presidentialism in consolidating democracy (Taras, 1997). The Russian Constitution adopted in December

1993 gives the president enormous powers vis-à-vis parliament. We may question the particular balance of powers that has been struck in Russia, and we may wonder at whether elections display a genuine will of the people. Nevertheless, democracy can have many institutional forms, and there are other factors to be considered when assessing its prospects: the state of economic development, the role of the military, the emergence of a stable middle class, the existence of some of the institutions of civil society (Diamond et al, 1997). A framework of new institutions—constitution, parties, free elections—is relatively easy to construct. But the assumptions and behaviours of the people who operate within their framework and give these institutions their full meaning cannot be changed overnight.

The task for postcommunism now is aptly described as 'consolidation': as bringing together institutions and the behaviour and attitudes appropriate to them (Plasser, Ulram and Waldrauch, 1998, pp.3-56). Offe has argued that this is the key measure:

> The gauge by which we measure success is the concept of consolidation ... implicating such basic (though hard to individualize) pre-constitutional ingredients as a balance of conflict and consent, of particularism and common good orientation, and of self-interested competitiveness and trust (Elster, Offe and Preuss, 1998, pp.271-2).

This is not just a question of ensuring the stability of the democratic institutions already created and their ability to withstand changes of parties in government, but also a question of acknowledging the rule of law and constitutionalism, and the effectiveness of government. These considerations have vital links to a diverse and tolerant society which looks to its political institutions to resolve its inevitable disputes with the minimum of violence.

Democratic consolidation requires development in three areas (Linz and Stepan, 1996): behavioural, attitudinal and constitutional. Behavioural consolidation means that no significant actor attempts to achieve their goals by creating a non-democratic regime. Attitudinal consolidation requires the majority of the population to believe in the appropriateness of democratic resolutions of conflicts, and in their own political efficacy (the notion that their political voice counts). Constitutional consolidation requires that all parties accept democratic procedures and that attempts to subvert them will be costly and ineffective. Consolidated democracy is 'routinised and deeply internalised in social, institutional, and even psychological life, as well as in calculations for achieving success' (Linz and Stepan, 1996, pp.5-6).

Consolidation means ensuring that democratic norms are respected, even in difficult times. It does not mean measuring postcommunist systems against Western liberal democracies, because those systems are diverse and they have their own problems with deep cynicism about politics and politicians. It means entrenching the institutional, legal and cultural foundations necessary for a society that respects both majority rule and minority rights (in other words, constitutional government and the rule of law).

The strong state of Soviet times—though perhaps not as strong as we once imagined—has collapsed, and a weak state has replaced it. But a strong society has not stepped in to take up the regulation of social, commercial and ethical life. Corruption and unchecked lawlessness are major problems in some postcommunist states (Galeotti, 1997, p.16), especially as they lead to a downwards spiral in confidence in the political system, as people look to their own resources for solving problems of personal security and contract enforcement. They give rise to private security forces (and thus opportunities for gangsters), to a fortress mentality, and to the carrying of weapons for self-defence. In the presence of an ineffectual state, Galeotti argues, 'the *mafiya* may be the only means of recovering a debt or enforcing a contract. Increasingly, organized crime offers one of the few reliable means of bringing order to a dangerously anarchic economic and legal system' (Galeotti, 1996, p.9). In some postcommunist countries, notably—but not only—in Russia, the so-called 'mafiya' is a significant problem, controlling large parts of the economy and receiving protection money from other businesses.

Liberal democracy and a market economy rely on building new relationships between people, especially relationships that put a premium on trust. This is where the concept of civil society become important. Consolidating democracy is bound up with building civil society, which may be based on the market, but is characterised chiefly by relatively autonomous associations and by ideological diversity.

The Legacies of Communism

The legacies of the communist era are key barriers to building civil society. The extent and depth of those legacies is in dispute; some of them may be more lightly shrugged off than others. Robert Tucker, Zbigniew Brzezinski, Richard Pipes and others have insisted on the importance of traditional culture in connection with Russia, as does Timo Piirainen, who argues that much of what was characteristic of Soviet society was actually 'traditionally Russian', and who makes a similar point about Eastern Europe (Piirainen, 1994, p.6).

To say that the problem is cultural, however, is not necessarily to allude to Slavic recalcitrance, or to insist on underlying and inescapable parallels with the political systems of earlier Russias: the system of internal espionage under Peter the Great; the 'dead souls' of Gogol; the lack of depth of liberal values and insistence of a higher spiritual unity of Russians that the Slavophiles championed in the nineteenth century. It is, rather, to refer to political habits of the Soviet regime, some of which may have had parallels with Tsarist practices, but most of which received their ultimate expression during the stagnation of the Brezhnev years and remained.

There are three legacies of communism that are central to the current condition of postcommunism. First, there is an underdeveloped public, or political sphere, and thus a discomfort with procedures in which conflict can be openly expressed and resolved. There is a corresponding emphasis on vertical control mechanisms, especially rule by law (as opposed to the rule of law). Second, there is a general lack of trust due to the systematic corruption and surveillance of populations under communism. And third, there is the prevalence of close networking, or *blat*, to oil the wheels of the economy in the command-administrative system. These legacies combine to impoverish social capital from which strong, effective and rule bound government can emerge. They prevent, or at least hinder, the development of the horizontal forms of organisation which are so important to the development of trust, norms of reciprocity and networks of civic engagement—that is, to civil society.

Bowser (1999) has argued cogently that despite the communist legacy of corruption, and continuing corruption in the former Soviet Union in particular, corruption is not a matter deeply ingrained in Russian culture. The real problem is the communist legacy of unaccountable government, which did not distinguish between the public and private interests of the officials. Incentives to corruption were increased by the relative poverty of the system, and remain because of continuing poverty. The arbitrariness of communist government, and the degree of discretion given to officials, meant that the people used any means to try to influence decisions in their favour. 'Corruption was a very personal form of contact with the bureaucrats and was very closely linked to friendships and the social networks that made life liveable in the USSR' (Bowser, 1999, p.4). This heritage has served to 'criminalise' Russia's postcommunist political elite (Coulloudon, 1977).

What are the prospects for changing political culture such that (on the part of citizens and officials alike) there are high expectations of government and low tolerance of incompetence, dishonesty and inefficiency? Can postcommunism break out of the culture of arbitrariness? Studies of political culture are divided on the issue. Some suggest that culture is a trap, and that Russia remains beholden to the tradition of centralisation, arbitrariness, and internal surveillance that it has endured since the time of Peter the Great. Others argue that the long-term operation of democratic institutions will induce the emergence of a civic culture appropriate to it. The problem is whether postcommunism, and Russia most particularly, has the luxury of time.

The development of a civil society is a good indication of the development of a political culture where trust is paramount. The institutional and ideological pluralism of civil society is not in contradiction to strong government, indeed it exists in the framework provided by strong government and the rule of law. The proliferation of autonomous organisations will ultimately change the way that people relate to each other. Civil society puts a priority on civility, trust, respect and tolerance in relations between people (though it doesn't always achieve them). These characteristics developed at a local level flow through to expectations about treatment at higher levels, especially by government. How can civil society be developed? There are no easy answers (Krygier, 1996), but the undoubted growth of independent associations in politics, economics and society is a necessary first step.

Robert Putnam's work on civic traditions in Italy, and how they affect the functioning of democratic institutions is instructive in understanding contemporary Russia, but offers little hope of a rapid change. Putnam insists that the social context within which institutions operate is crucial. Comparing the functioning of democratic institutions across different regions of Italy, he argues that those institutions work best—responsively and effectively—in regions which have higher quality civic life, the roots of which go back nearly a millennium to the division of Italy into monarchies in the south, and communal republics in the centre and the north (Putnam, 1993, pp.15-16).

The important element of civil society here is the character, or quality, of the social networks which people are accustomed to forming. The way liberal democracy functions in much of the West is based on a certain sort of society: one in which individualism is supreme, but also in which contacts are diverse and there is a correspondingly high level of anonymous trust in commercial and other transactions. By contrast in Italy, and especially southern Italy, 'amoral familism' has underpinned the centrality of the Mafia as a mechanism for organising society, resolving disputes and enforcing contracts, and thus the relative irrelevance of the state in these areas. In Russia, social networks—*blat*—of the old period remain crucial to the environment in which democratic institutions must operate. The continued existence of *blat*, reinforced by the same elites who have survived and prospered under postcommunism, remains a problem. In Russia, and despite the formal success of privatisation (Boycko, 1995), economic power remains highly concentrated and apparently well connected to the political elite.

Nationalism and Civil Society

Nationalism is a foundation issue for political communities based on popular sovereignty. Eugene Kamenka explained that 'modern political nationalism arises in the course of stabilising or making possible the transition from autocratic to democratic or at least popular government. It is a re-casting and re-formation of communities and of political boundaries in circumstances where the old basis of the polity has been radically undermined' (Kamenka, 1975, p.15). And while Kamenka's point is a historical one that seeks to explain the emergence of political nationalism in the late 18th century from the less focused senses of national consciousness—proto-nationalism—that had emerged in Europe from around the 12th century, it nevertheless reinforces the point that political nationalism is the first item on the democratic agenda.

In Russia, popular sovereignty has replaced the rule of the party and its historically ordained mission. For the new political institutions to gain legitimacy, for a significant level of trust and acceptance of laws and law-making to emerge, there must be some attention to 'the people' who are to be sovereign. As an individual confronted by this circumstance might reasonably ask: are we sufficiently similar for me to put my fate into the collective hands? Do we, in both literal and metaphorical senses, 'speak the same language'? In some states this understanding of 'the people' was achieved culturally before the development of popular sovereignty and representative government—France and England are obvious examples. Elsewhere, there was great turmoil in trying to define the nature of the community that was to exercise sovereignty.

Nationalism is not a simple phenomenon. It can serve for many as a liberating experience; for others, it has been a source of hatreds and divisions. In the latter case, nationalism is a zero-sum game, exciting hatred of 'outsiders' and attempting to gain at their expense. The experience of fascism means that this conception of nationalism dominates reactions to it, even though nationalism has been a sub-text of many left-wing issues and campaigns (from nineteenth century campaigns for Poland, to contemporary campaigns against imperialism and globalisation). But nationalism has also served to give identification and solidarity to people within a political system, and a basis for cooperating with others outside that system. The Young Italy and similar movements in Europe in the nineteenth century were of this sort. The danger arises when nations are interpreted as organisms that subordinate individuals to a mystic destiny.

Nationalism has a poor reputation, especially among intellectuals, and not just because of its fascist connections. Many see its chief characteristic (and failing) as its mythical quality, its selective forgetting of history. They believe, along with the philosophers of the Enlightenment, that people can live their lives according to abstract principles, and feel at one with an abstract, cosmopolitan community. But intellectuals also see nationalism as an inappropriate or unedifying basis on which human communities should be built: it is particular rather than universal; and it appeals to characteristics that are secondary, or inessential to the true nature of humans. Nationalism tends to eschew complexity; it appeals to emotions. Some believe, consequently, that nationalism is past its historical use-by date. Even if it were appropriate in the nineteenth century, it is now backward looking and reactionary.

What is perhaps so disturbing about nationalism is how easily political leaders are able to define and manipulate it for their own ends. Nationalism is even used in order to suffocate or deny critical analysis of it. External, or 'foreign', condemnations of it are merely grist to its mill. Nationalism can channel hopes and fears; it identifies those who are to be blamed for current problems. Yet the inescapable fact is that nationalism continues to have major social traction for populations in the modern world. It is preferred to most other forms of identification for the purposes of defining a political community. It supplies an answer to a basic question of democratic systems: with whom do you find it most comfortable to make collective decisions, in which you may sometimes lose, but where the community generally has your interests at heart? As the democratic theorist, Robert Dahl, once asked: 'which demos?'. Or: whom do you trust?

Nationalism is used by Russian politicians to help supply an answer to the quest for social order which characterises postcommunism in general. Calls for 'order' tend to blur the difference between two basic conceptions of social order: unitary and diversified. The unitary conception embraces the idea that social order is achieved by conformity of views and standards. It is influenced by the assumptions of the communist period, and is reinforced by the Slavophile-Orthodox view. By contrast, the diversified conception lies at the heart of civil society, where order is achieved through processes and rules designed both to recognise the legitimacy of diverse views and interests, and to conciliate them if and when they come into conflict. The goal is not uniformity, but harmony. The yearning for order in postcommunist states arises from a fear of diversity. It is part of the current appeal of Russian nationalism that it insists on a deeper unity between Russians than simply adherence to the rules of the political game. If, on this view, there is difference and conflict, it comes from outside, from other nations. Thus, organised crime is typically presented as a 'Caucasian' problem; the bombing of Moscow apartment buildings in 1999 was immediately blamed upon Chechens, with little if any evidence.

Nationalism is not necessarily incompatible with civil society. But civil society requires a particular sort of nationalism: easy, confident, tolerant. Maley (1991) distinguishes usefully between two ideal types of nationalism: communitarian and extended-order nationalisms. The societies in which communitarian nationalism flourishes are largely traditional, and in these 'custom remains an important mechanism of social coordination', including religious customs. Extended-order nationalism, by contrast, is characteristic of diversified societies with complex production and exchange based chiefly on contract, and an individualistic and pluralistic culture (pp.184-5). It is the latter type of nationalism which is far more conducive to the flourishing of civil society.

Both types of nationalism existed in the former USSR, with the Baltic states being representative of the extended-order nationalism, and the Transcaucasian and Central Asian republics being representative of communitarian nationalism. As to Russian nationalism, Maley concludes that although it is a complex phenomenon, it shows distinct traces of communitarian nationalism, in virulent anti-Semitism and in the demands of the *Pamiat* group for the re-establishment of the Russian Orthodox Church as a state church. Which way this develops, he argued in 1991, would depend a good deal on the political leadership of postcommunist Russia. Some of the evidence is now available, and it is not encouraging.

Russian Nationalism

Nationalism has had an interesting career in Russia. In the nineteenth century, it found major expression in Slavophilism. The Slavophiles believed that 'backward' Russia was different from the West and, in important ways related to the expression of community sentiment, superior. They further believed that Russia could preserve the traditional community because it was 'not encumbered by the heritage of rationalistic Roman culture' (Walicki, 1980, p.109). The Bolshevik Revolution of 1917 brought to power a group whose official line was cosmopolitan, but whose instincts for political survival meant using nationalism as a tactic (Smith, 1999). The Bolsheviks became nationalists to survive. Szporluk, who argues more generally that socialism and nationalism are responses to the same sorts of questions arising from modernisation, declared that 'Marxism won in Russia … but it did so only by becoming a nationalism' (Szporluk, 1991, pp.230-1).

The Bolsheviks drew on the Slavophile sentiment that Russia's destiny was to show the way forward to the decadent West; they also drew heavily on nationalism in the defence of the motherland during the so-called Great Patriotic War (1941–45). The USSR, formally declared in 1924, was technically a confederation of states with their own administrations, but it was led by its largest state, the Russian Federation, and Russian interests predominated. Pipes (1964) argues that Soviet borderlands were brought under control with a sympathetic nationality policy. Yet Russia was the only nation that had a branch of the Soviet Central Committee devoted to protecting its interests. The twists and turns of Soviet nationality policy need not detain us here. The major point is that the Russian nation held sway, and that it led to simmering discontents in other nations of the USSR. Obolonsky has argued that in the USSR, 'The party attempted to keep the numerous ethnic groups within the USSR hostile to one another, drawing on unsettled scores between non-Russian nationalities, especially in such tense and potentially explosive multinational regions as the Caucasus and Central Asia' (Obolonsky, 1995, p.15).

It is not surprising that a resurgence of nationalism should be part of the collapse of communism, because Soviet domination of much of Eastern Europe deliberately suppressed nationalist expressions and denied nationalist memories. Thus the collapse of communism there was both anti-communist and anti-Russian: 'double rejective' as Les Holmes has put it (Holmes, 1993). Consequently, postcommunism has had to deal not just with political and economic restructuring—difficult enough by themselves—but also with re-establishing the bases for political legitimacy and political boundaries (the classic grounds of nationalism's appeal).

By contrast to other postcommunist states, nationalism in Russia was taken largely for granted by Russians themselves. The anti-Russian sentiment released by the collapse of communism and the decline in world status suffered by the Soviet state thus produced a surge in defensive (but no less ugly, or assertive) nationalism. There was significant 'Russian' disappointment at the end of communism: Russia was no longer a great power; its citizens felt a loss of national pride; and they worried at the 'loss' of (Soviet) territory.

The Orthodox Church has had a major revival since the collapse of communism, with just over 50% of Russians declaring themselves Orthodox, and with political figures wanting to be seen as close to the church. The communists did not neglect to use Orthodoxy, after their initial anti-religious drive. The Orthodox Church received a boost in the Great Patriotic War; thereafter, it was tolerated only in so far as it was useful to the state. Orthodox priests often informed on their parishioners to the State Security Service. But since 1990, thousands of parishes have been re-established, hundreds of monasteries re-opened, and thousands of clergy given official posts. Patriarch Alexy II was present at the inauguration of Putin as acting President.

The resurgence of Orthodoxy gives some indication of the predominant character of Russian nationalism. Liberalism has never been strong in Russia, with its stress on procedures and limits to authority, on individual liberty and initiative. The Orthodox Church, drawing on the Slavophile inheritance and the profound differences between Eastern and Western Christianity, does not support liberalism: it supports powerful authority and moral community.

The fear that Orthodoxy may turn from persecuted to persecutor has, to some extent, been confirmed by a law passed in the Russian Parliament in 1997, 'On freedom of conscience and religious associations'. Despite its title, the law recognises a special role for the Orthodox Church, and sets stringent conditions for the legal existence (and concessions) of religious organisations, including that they must prove they had existed on Russian territory for at least 15 years. Many religions that rushed into the country in search of converts (such as Mormons, Seventh Day Adventists, Scientologists, and Rev Moon's Unification Church, among others) have no official status. Such organisations had to re-register with the state by the end of 1999, in order to be legally allowed to worship in public, hold property, have bank accounts and engage in missionary and charitable work.

In seeking to strengthen its links with the state, Orthodoxy might help to undermine one of the mainstays of a civil society: diversity and tolerance of beliefs. For the Orthodox Church works on the assumption that the stronger the faith, the stronger the society. But this is incompatible with civil society which looks to maintain coherence along with diversity. Even Vladimir Putin has argued that 'It will not happen soon, if it ever happens at all, that Russia will become a second edition of, say, the US or Britain in which liberal values have deep historic traditions' (Russian Government, 1999). But while a Russian way may be politically palatable to Russians, what is of more concern is that the values Putin identifies as traditionally Russian—'statism', 'patriotism', 'belief in the greatness of Russia' and 'social solidarity'—lay their emphasis on order as uniformity.

The type of nationalism which thrives in Russia today is based on the image of an idealised community which achieves harmony through its national and religious symbols and aspirations, not through the just application of rules. It is anti-liberal. It thrives in part because of the short term political advantage sought by political leaders in appealing to it. They have created enemies defined in nationalist terms. They draw on an uneasy feeling that has existed for some years about the southern regions of the former USSR, with its Muslim population: fear of fundamentalist Islam taking root and presenting political problems for Moscow; and fear of rapid population growth among Islamic peoples.

The focus of Russian nationalism has recently become Chechnya. In 1994, Russia stopped an attempt by Chechnya to become an independent republic. At stake was independence for Chechnya, and oil for the Russians. The Chechens were repaying a debt to the Russians incurred during the 1940s, when they were removed from their lands. The Russian military effort was abysmal in design and execution. The result was humiliation for the Russians, and lawlessness for the Chechens. After Vladimir Putin was named Russian Prime Minister in August 1999, he escalated the war in Chechnya, and by early 2000 had brought it to an indecisive conclusion. (Chechen 'rebels' continue to mount attacks on Russian forces.) Putin's success was to link his political career to the successful prosecution of the war.

Putin is not the only Russian political leader to claim the mantle of nationalism. But Putin's nationalist credentials have been cemented by actions, not words: especially his actions in Chechnya. Nationalism is such a powerful force for political legitimacy and popularity, and Putin is regarded as such a strong embodiment of it, that almost all parties and interests in the recent Russian presidential elections scrambled to ally with him. Most political leaders believe that nationalism is at least of short-term political advantage. Thus the Mayor of Moscow, Yuri Luzhkov, is a leader of the 'Fatherland-All Russia' party.

This type of nationalism has obvious short-term advantages. It can boost political careers; it can divert attention away from other problems, especially corruption. But it carries two sorts of risks. In the short term, military reverses can lead to disaster. The bellicose expression of nationalism can produce humiliation, political ruin for individuals, and further reduced trust in the political system that wastes Russian lives for no gain. In the longer term, it must seek new campaigns to revive its passions.

Conclusion: Democratisation at Risk

The extent of change in Russia over the last decade, and the achievements so far, have been impressive. And the direction of change—despite reservations—is still positive. Russia has survived a coup, in August 1991, and a bloody clash between executive and legislature, in September-October 1993; it has had a number of parliamentary and presidential elections: all without relapse to authoritarianism. About three quarters of the economy is in the non-state sector. But the problems, too, are obvious. In the governmental sphere, there is endemic corruption, ineffective government, and substantial practical limits on the free flow of political information. In the economic sphere, the people feel insecure: lacking job security; unused to paying market prices for the necessities of life, and justifiably fearful of being cheated.

There are three issues that I shall raise by way of conclusion. Each one is speculative, and none can be fully answered by the analysis that has gone before. First, it is worthwhile asking the standard political science question: *cui bono?* (who benefits?). Who stands to gain by the use of Russian ethno-nationalism, for use it surely is. In the short term, the beneficiary is Putin. But—in some ways more importantly for Russia and its future—the beneficiaries are the financial oligarchs, who seem to be supporting Putin for their own benefit.

The single most important thing lacking from Russia today is leadership. Leadership means putting the national interest ahead of self- or partial-interest, and even if Putin wants to do that, it is unlikely that he will be able to. As part of Yeltsin's circle for the past few years, he doubtless has debts to the financial oligarchs. The surging popularity that saw him elected as President may be a useful counterweight to their influence, but it seems to have been bought with the oligarchs' support.

Second, and again firmly within the political science tradition, we know that interests are important, but also that political movements and ideas have a logic of their own. So the question is: whither ethno-nationalism? Will it lead to fascism in Russia? It is impossible to rule out such an option, but at present it seems unlikely. Fascist movements tend to prosper in times of uncertainty, particularly political and economic uncertainty, to rely for their support on an appeal to stability and solidarity (usually based on a restrictive conception of community as nation), and to blame 'outsiders' and 'traitors' for undermining the community. The popular passions, and particularly the intolerance, it has unleashed, make it a malignant form of political expression quite alien to a healthy civil society. The instability of Russia has some parallels with Weimar Germany, and Vladimir Zhirinovsky—leader of the Liberal Democratic Party of Russia—comes closest to a Hitler, both in his hysterical nationalism and in the demographics of his support. But Zhirinovsky's nationalist thunder seems to have been stolen by Putin.

Third, what does the resurgence of Russian ethno-nationalism mean for the consolidation of democracy? The prospects for tolerance and diversity are not bright in view of the Chechnya experience. Illiberal nationalism has deep roots in Russia; it was tapped by the communists when required; and it is currently being tapped by postcommunist politicians for short-term advantage. Populism—the politics of blame—has been exploited by President Putin.

'Democratisation' is not a guaranteed process; nor is its end point predetermined. We have no cause to be disappointed if the outcome is dissimilar, in significant ways, to Western models of democracy (which have their own problems). But there are certain minimum requirements that must be met for the consolidation of democracy, Russian or not. Institutionally, government must fairly accurately reflect their citizens' views and demands, be accountable to citizens for their actions, and uphold the rule of law. More broadly, citizens must have confidence that their government is effective, and their own political efficacy is high. They must also accept the reality of politics as a continuing conflict of interests and views, and thus develop a tolerance of diversity. Nationalism—and particularly the illiberal ethno-nationalism which is prevalent in Russia—will be a major factor in the outcome.

Instead of confronting the enormous economic, social and political difficulties of the transition, many Russian politicians use nationalism to identify enemies and assign blame. The danger of this approach is not just further bullying of marginal national groups within Russia, but the continuing instability of democracy at best, or the rise of fascism at worst. Either way, attempting to manipulate the powerful emotions of nationalism means putting democratisation at risk.

References

Bowser, D. (1999), 'Corruption in Post Soviet States: A Question of Cultural Identity?', unpublished paper given at the Fourth Annual ASN Conference, New York.

Boycko, M., Andrei, S. and Vishny, R. (1995), *Privatizing Russia*. The MIT Press, Cambridge MA.

'"Can't Pay, Don't Need to Pay": How Russians view Taxation' (1998), *www.strath.ac.uk/Departments/CSPP/nrb7pr.html* (accessed 26 April 2000).

Coulloudon, V. (1997), 'Crime and Corruption after Communism: The Criminalization of Russia's Political Elite', *Eastern European Constitutional Review*, vol.6, no.4.

Diamond, L., Plattner, M.F., Chu, Y. and Tien, H. (eds) (1997), *Consolidating The Third Wave Democracies: Themes and Perspectives*, Johns Hopkins University Press, Baltimore.

Elster, J., Offe, O., Preuss, U.K. (1998), *Institutional Design in Postcommunist Societies: Rebuilding the Ship at Sea*, Cambridge University Press, Cambridge.

Galeotti, M. (1996), *Mafiya: Organized Crime in Russia*. Jane's Intelligence Review, special report No 10. Jane's Information Group, Coulsdon.

Galeotti, M. (1997), *Policing Russia: Problems and Prospects in Turbulent Times*. Jane's Intelligence Review, special report No 15. Jane's Information Group, Coulsdon.

Holmes, L. (1993), *The End of Communist Power: Anti-Corruption Campaigns and Legitimation Crisis*, Melbourne University Press, Melbourne.

Huntington, S.P. (1991), *The Third Wave. Democratization in the late Twentieth Century*. University of Oklahoma Press, Norman.

Kamenka, E. (1975), 'Political Nationalism—The Evolution of the Idea', in E.Kamenka (ed.), *Nationalism: The Nature and Evolution of an Idea*. Australian National University Press, Canberra, pp. 2–20.

Krygier, M. (1996), 'The Sources of Civil Society', Second Richard Krygier Memorial Lecture, 29 August 1996, *http://abc.net.au/rn/talks/bbing/stories/510754.htm*.

Linz, J.J. and Stepan, A. (1996), *Problems of Democratic Transition and Consolidation: Southern Europe, South America and Post-Communist Europe*, Johns Hopkins University Press, Baltimore.

Maley, W. (1991), 'Ethnonationalism and Civil Society in the USSR', in C. Kukathas, D.W. Lovell and W. Maley (eds), *The Transition from Socialism: State and Civil Society in the USSR*, Longman Cheshire, Melbourne, pp.177–97.

Nunberg, B. (1999), *The State After Communism: Administrative Transitions in Central and Eastern Europe*, World Bank, Washington D.C.

Obolonsky, A.V. (1995), 'Russian Politics in the Time of Troubles: Some Basic Antinomies', in A. Saikal and W. Maley (eds), *Russia in Search of its Future*, Cambridge University Press, Cambridge, pp.12–27.

Piirainen, T. (1994), 'Introduction', in T. Piirainen (ed.), *Change and Continuity in Eastern Europe*, Dartmouth, Aldershot, pp.1–9.

Pipes, R. (1964), *The Formation of the Soviet Union: Communism and Nationalism, 1917–1923*, (revised edition), Harvard University Press, Cambridge MA.

Plasser, F., Ulram, P.A. and Waldrauch, H. (1998), *Democratic Consolidation in East-Central Europe*, Macmillan, London.

Putnam, R.D. (1993), *Making Democracy Work: Civic Traditions in Modern Italy*, (with R. Leonardi and R.Y. Nanetti), Princeton University Press, Princeton.

Russian Government (1999), 'Russia at the turn of the Millennium', *www.pravitelstvo.gov.ru/english/statVP_engl_1.html* (accessed 26 April 2000).

Smith, J. (1999), *The Bolsheviks and the National Question, 1917–23*, Macmillan, London.

Szporluk, R. (1991), *Communism and Nationalism: Karl Marx versus Friedrich List*, Oxford University Press, New York.

Taras, R. (1997), 'Separating Power: Keeping Presidents in Check', in R. Taras (ed.), *Postcommunist Presidents*, Cambridge University Press, Cambridge, pp.15–37.

Walicki, A. (1980), *A History of Russian Thought from the Enlightenment to Marxism*, Oxford University Press, Oxford.

White, S. (2000), *Russia's New Politics*, Cambridge University Press, Cambridge.

4 Just the Rhetoric of Reform? The 'New Planning' in the Politics of the Yeltsin Era

ANTHONY PHILLIPS

One of the most enduring themes in Russian studies has been that of Russia's historical continuity. This theme is one that identifies a significantly enduring Russian culture and notes the way in which the patterns of this culture, in terms of behaviour and ways of thinking, keep reasserting themselves. However there is another side to this continuity: it is that Russian history has been a continuous struggle between what is seen as a particularly Russian way of being and the modernising impacts, influences and attractions of the West upon Russia. In many ways this dialogue between Russia and the West has been the defining context in which Russian social and economic change takes place. From the emergence of the Russian state, with the dissolution of the Mongol empire in the 16th century, through to the 21st century, Russia has co-existed and interacted with the (evolving) Western state system and the ideologies and discourses thrown up by this civilisation. From this perspective the transition embarked upon in 1991, towards a market economy and a developed democracy, was yet another chapter in this long procession.

The initial impetus for this article arose from a fascination with instances where Russian continuity reasserts itself over attempts to alter Russian life into Western patterns. This can happen in a number of manners, and to a number of degrees, and the process is of course not unique to Russia. Cultural cross-fertilisation is a staple of human existence, in the modern era made more obvious by the pervasiveness and pace of globalisation, led by capitalism and the increasing technological capacity for cultural transfers. Such cross-fertilisation can be as simple as the transfer of foreign terms into everyday language to create a new idea. Or it can be the seizure of an idea and practice, like take-away food franchises, which then complexly transform the structure of the economy, change lifestyles and even undermine traditional diets and the cultural authorities and inter-relational structures associated with them.

However, in Russia, such adaptations and resistances seem both more obvious and more significant, probably because of the importance the

West/Russia nexus has historically had in Russia. Communism itself can be seen as an historical compromise with this nexus and also as a continuation in the traditional manner of how Russia has dealt with Western incursion. Communism, after all, began as a claim to inherit an endpoint of Western culture and development: in theory it was to be the Westernisation of Russia par excellence. In Communism's practice a political culture unfamiliar with rule of law, and the importance of the democratic process, played an important part in returning/continuing Russia as a despotic nation fiercely concerned with regulating its citizens' access to the West, and seeing itself as alternate modernity in competition with the West. Thus, for much of its history, the Soviet Union's engagement with the West appeared little different to Custine's (1991, p.102) description of Russia in the 19th century, interaction with the West was in order 'to take advantage of the administrative progress in the European nations in order to govern [over two hundred] sixty million people in the oriental manner.'

When examining the Russian 'transition' of the 1990s, so fraught with problems, failures and setbacks compared to its Central European neighbours, it seems not unreasonable to expect political culture to play a part. Indeed the disputes over 'Who lost Russia?', which erupted among US policy-makers and academics in the wake of the August 1998 Russian debt crisis, often revolved around claims that it was principally the fault of culturally blind economic ideologues who hubristically assumed that their 'one size fits all rational individualism' could be easily slipped over the shoulders of the eager Russian customer. However, it was argued, Russian patterns of thought and behaviour that did not distinguish between the political and the economic, did not have faith in the continuity of government or law, and that were accustomed to the interaction of patronage and personal capital to solve problems, acted to undermine the macroeconomic prescriptions and expectations of the Western oriented Russian policy-makers and their Western advisors.[1]

That political culture can play a dead hand in the process of social change is quite a reasonable proposition, but why this has been so strong in the Russia of the 1990s is a particular question. This chapter is, in a manner, a case study of one aspect of this - namely the degree to which the old culture of planning, so pervasive in the Soviet system, found its way into the Russia political culture of the 1990s as a key term of discourse, and perhaps a key approach to policy. 'Plans' and 'programmes' abound in any survey of political pronouncements about Russia during the

Yeltsin period. The only word that could be confidently asserted to appear more often is 'reform'. Those taking part in any policy debate in Russia in the 1990s could almost certainly be expected to describe their policy as either, 'a reform', 'part of the reform process' or part of a 'reform plan' or 'programme.'

But what was meant by these 'plans' and what can they tell us about continuity between the Soviet system and the new Russia? Were they merely rhetorical devices, containing echoes of the old discourse to camouflage the introduction of new ways of thinking and doing, or were they Trojan horses by which the old ways of thinking and doing could stealthily propagate themselves in the 'new order'? Moreover to what extent were these 'plans' ideological and to what extent were they technical? By the former, I mean were they intended to act as rallying points for political actors with like interests and mind? By the latter I mean, were they actually intended or expected to solve practical problems?[2]

The approach taken in this chapter has been to examine the origins of these plans in three aspects. First in terms of which actors put them forward: second in a comparative light, in order to examine how *sui generis* they are, and how much are they a reasonable approximation of Western practice; and third to look at their accord with the actual material demands being put forward by the political economy of Russia. Such an examination should suggest how much these plans were/are (a) just rhetorical devices, (b) real policies, (c) reliable as ideological positions either put forward by existing actors, or functioning as poles around which political actors might coalesce. From this point we should be able to make some comments on degrees of continuity. As a precursor to the chapter a compilation of plans and references to plans in Russia was made using an electronic database of news agency stories for the last 10 years including Reuters, Itar-TASS, RIA-Novosti and Radio Liberty, and through selective browsing of the Russian press.

Originators and the Sources of Policy

The original plan of reform, the first new-style plan if one likes, was the '500 days' plan, also known as the Shatalin plan, which surfaced in 1990.[3] It had a number of features which were new but also clearly grew out of a culture of 'planning'. It assumed that rational and step-by-step actions could be taken which would remake the command economy into a market economy in less than two years. The plan was specifically revolutionary in its intent, scale and proposed speed of transformation, though it still placed itself inside the 'discourse of reform' that has been a primary feature of political rhetoric in Russia from Gorbachev in 1986 to the present day. It is worth noting that the key term has always been reform, rarely revolution, or even change.

The scale of the plan was highly radical. It foresaw sweeping changes in an extremely short time to patterns of Soviet economic behaviour and to Soviet institutions. It was also radical in its expected social impacts: its proposals for privatisation and the abolition of industrial ministries could be expected to change the class composition of society, and in its ideological underpinnings it owed much to liberal economics. The '500 days' emerged in reaction to political pressure, had a specific constituency, and, in a mutated form, was adopted as a rallying point by the emergent political coalition of the President of Russia, an institutional and charismatic political actor, and Democratic Russia, a genuine social movement. In these senses it was nothing like Soviet 'planning', which was a series of output targets allocated by a technocratic institution (Gosplan) to economic units in the Soviet economy. Moreover, while Gosplan both produced policy proposals and responded to policy demands generated by the Politburo, the Secretariat and the Soviet Council of Ministers, its planning was not overtly political. Its role was integrated into a larger ideological discourse and its main purposes were technical. Gosplan's role was to stimulate and co-ordinate economic production in the USSR.

The Shatalin plan was a plan about ending such planning. It came from, and was supported by, social and political elements and it became an ideological tool as much as a series of policy proposals. It entered the policy making process of the USSR because it had a powerful political backer in Yeltsin but it also served as a manifesto of the opposition. The importance of having an 'economic plan' in Russian politics, as opposed to policies of economic reform (e.g. *perestroika*) can be dated from this era as well. One moment illustrative of this happened in the wake of the furore around the Shatalin plan when the influential economist Oleg Bogomolov moved across to the Yeltsin camp and called for Gorbachev's replacement by someone with a 'coherent economic plan'.[4]

What is also notable about the '500 days' plan is that it was predominantly a domestic production, the influence of Western economics upon it was undoubted, but in rhetoric, structure and creative thought it was Soviet/Russian. It should also be observed that it did not, however, find its way into much policy implementation. Having first been politically pressured to take it up Gorbachev was then effectively forced to abandon it under duress from conservatives. The Russian republic's president, Yeltsin, never got much beyond threatening to apply a form of it when the coup of 1991 interrupted.

Following the collapse of the Soviet Union some of the content of '500 days' was reborn in the programme pursued by Yegor Gaidar. However there was a split between its originators. Some who had supported it were happy to go along with the politics that had dissolved the Soviet Union, the task being to adapt its features to a new plan for Russia. Others, of whom perhaps the most notable was Grigory Yavlinsky, argued that the success of the plan relied precisely upon the Soviet Union remaining a unified political and economic space.[5]

If one evaluates the nature of this first plan in terms of continuity with Russian tradition it is unsurprisingly at variance in both its content and intent. This plan was actually a political blueprint for radical change, it sought to create a new economic system rather than to manage an existing one. What continuity it had with Soviet tradition was in its ontological and epistemological presumptions, it still espoused the Soviet faith that radical change could be foreseen and predicted 'scientifically'. Moreover, such change could be managed by experts and specialists. From the point of view of hindsight '500 days' was highly hubristic. However its presumptions were by no means exclusively Soviet and nor were they given up on in the history of plans for Russia to follow.

Yeltsin's first plan

Russia's move into independent transition in 1992 was overseen by Yegor Gaidar, an economist in his thirties, who had served as Vice Premier of the government of the Russian Federation in 1991. Gaidar was later described by Vice-President Aleksandr Rutskoi as one of the Bolsheviks in short pants, and the tag has tended to stick.[6] The reference was to Gaidar's revolutionary and state directed political and economic aims and to his relative youth. His first programme was the highly detailed and grandly named 'The Memorandum on the Economic Policy of the Russian Federation'.[7] The detailing of the plan actually came after many policy decisions it advocated had already been implemented. It set forth a series of sequenced steps and policies to move Russia quickly to a market economy. Its key features were a commitment to balanced budgets, price liberalisation, including in foreign trade and foreign exchange, and macro-economic stabilisation. It had much in common with the Balcerowicz plan earlier implemented in Poland and, more pertinently, with the general prescriptions being laid down by the International Monetary Fund (IMF) and the World Bank for countries in transition. Indeed the key elements of Gaidar's plan quite deliberately matched the major conditions for Western credit to Russia.[8] The origins of the plan lay not just with Gaidar but also a number of Western advisors: in October 1991 Yeltsin had specifically called upon the World Bank and the IMF for help. In later years the proposals and priorities made in Gaidar's plan would become known as part of the 'Washington consensus'.

Gaidar's plan was highly focused on policy outcomes and can be read as a response to economic pressures. However it also served political purposes – as rhetoric to win approval, and as ideology to organise and mobilise support. Overall the plan can be understood as effecting four purposes.

First, having dissolved the Soviet Union and severely curtailed the power of the Communist party, Yeltsin's policy goals and objectives were to a degree unfocused. He identified himself as a democrat and, along with many in his entourage at the time, saw Russia's future as part of the West. However, the steps necessary to move Russia in this direction were not elucidated. Gaidar recalls Yeltsin's instructions to him as being that the transition (to capitalism) should simply be 'quick and beautiful'.[9] In this sense Gaidar's plan was a stand-in manifesto for the new order.

Second, Gaidar himself had strong revolutionary aims. He was an intelligent and convinced liberal democrat and at least in part the purpose of the plan was to dismantle what remained of the command economy so thoroughly that it could never be put back together. With the command economy's infrastructure and property system destroyed, the basis for communism would be abolished. As Rutskoi implied, like any good Bolshevik Gaidar believed that if the economy changed the political superstructure must follow (Desai, 2000, pp.15-16).

Third there was the pressure of looming economic catastrophe. Piecemeal reform and political struggle had reduced the command economy to a disarticulated and barely functioning hulk. The pressures of autarky flowing from the political dissolution of the Soviet Union threatened to create shortages unseen since the end of World War Two

(Gaidar, 1999, pp.185-6).[10] Some way to re-coordinate production and consumption had to be found.

The fourth purpose was to gain access to Western funds for alleviation of short-term adjustment problems and longer term investment and restructuring.[11] Having entered negative growth the year before, and with hidden inflation, a falling rouble, and the consequences of years of reduction in investment becoming manifest, an injection of outside capital appeared vital.[12]

Thus the Gaidar plan can be seen as mostly, but not entirely, a Russian creation. It was addressed in part to the general public but its other constituencies included the President, the parliament, those running the economy, and international financial institutions and investors. It was both an ideological blueprint but also a concrete policy document demanding implementation. Like a Soviet planner Gaidar was still setting out to co-ordinate and order the economy but like a Soviet revolutionary he was also planning to re-order the entire political economy. That said it must be remembered that in practice the plan was quickly mangled by the political and economic realities of Russia at the time.

Plans on the landscape through to 1993

The main actors advancing plans through to 1993 were those within the government or those seeking to be the government. Many of these plans had their first glimmerings as objections to the existing reform programme, which was itself vanishing as a coherent programme as its policies met political resistance from economic and political actors in industry, the Russian Central Bank and the parliament. The most common pattern was for the production of alternate programmes by academics or groups of academics and then their adoption and publicising by interest groups or political coalitions.

The basic historical pattern of the period can be sketched thus: as early as April 1992 the Russian parliament declared its support for the reform programme while at the same time making a series of amendments to legislation that effectively gutted it. The president and government responded by continuing as well as possible with the programme outside of the needed legislation. A new government reform plan was issued in June, and in July a coalition around the governor of Sakhalin and the hard-line conservative Viktor Aksyuchits claimed to be putting together an alternative plan. Later that year at least two other new plans appeared, from the industrial grouping Civic Union and from the Economists Association; both advocated the state boosting production via active intervention. Both advocated policy changes and the former served as an ideological rallying point for an important opposition grouping.

In September the speaker of the parliament, Ruslan Khasbulatov, admitted there was no agreement between parliament and the government on its reform programme. By the end of the year the parliament had rejected Gaidar's second programme of reform and then succeeded in obtaining his removal from the government. In 1993 the struggle over reform continued between parliament and government but the main source of plans was the government, often at the urging of, or in collaboration with, the IMF and World Bank.[13]

Plans during this period can be characterised as being primarily political in nature. Production of them served political as much as economic or policy purposes. The government continued to pursue policies that were in line with the aims established in its first reform plan. However, these were met with resistance and, particularly in the case of the Central Bank, directly countervailing policies of extended credit and loose money. Moreover, criticism of existing policy and advancing alternative policy does not appear to have been enough for those in opposition. Having a plan was a key to claiming a legitimate right to comment or alter policy. The make-up of the government was changing through this period and specific sectors of the economy were also coming under immense pressure. Hardest hit were the state-owned industrial sector and especially the military industrial complex. Plans supported by these actors frequently centred around calls for production and production capacity to be given priority. Such calls can be seen as masking cries for a continuation of subsidies, and to position the industrialists advantageously in the battle over privatisation. Furthermore, in advancing plans both interest groups and political parties can be perceived as staking claims for inclusion in the government itself or, in the case of Yavlinsky, and in 1993 his party Yabloko, laying claim to the title of opposition government-in-waiting.

For the analytic purposes of this paper these plans can still be classified as serving political ends and primarily originating from Russian roots. They were serving rhetorical and ideological purposes but they also actively sought to influence or change the course of policy through the political appeal provided by offering a legitimate policy response to genuine problems.

Plans post 1993

The advancement of plans and programmes in the period 1994-96 was mostly a government affair. This was hardly surprising since much of the political debate in the new political-economic environment was within the government. Under the new constitution the State Duma and the Federation Council were even further removed from policy-making than parliament had been before. Their main concerns, except at election times, were to cut deals on specific policy and to criticise government plans and policy. Mentions of, and proposals for, economic plans and programmes chiefly came from ministries within the government or from academic outsiders. These then presented their plans to the economic ministers as alternative directions for policy.[14] The government itself seemed to be addressing its plans as much to the international credit organisations as to the parliament or public at this time. Indeed approval of plans by foreign institutions was frequently held up to the electorate or parliament as proving the worth of reform course. In this sense the government was getting domestic political, as well as economic, credit from its foreign constituency.

Two other aspects of plans at this time are worth noting. First, plans and programmes became closely linked to budgets. Indeed in 1995 and 1996 the two are almost indistinguishable and mutually reinforcing. The logic ran along the lines that 'the budget is good because it is part of the plan and the need to follow the plan justifies the budget'. Second, the content and language of plans and programmes could be said to have reached a consensual plateau amongst those producing them. What I mean by this is that the language used and the mechanisms appealed to were more or less the same regardless of who was producing them. For example the plan put forward by the communist leader Zyuganov in his campaign for the 1996 election could have been expected to be radically different from the neo-liberal, one eye on Geneva and Washington, productions of the government at the time. But in fact it was only mildly different and was described by some commentators as basically Keynesian.[15] In this sense a hegemony of liberal capitalist thought might be said to have established itself in Russia, at least at the rhetorical level of acceptable political debate.

The other point to note with regard to the sources of plans is that as time went on between 1993 and 1999, particularly after the profits of privatisation were frittered away on recurrent expenditure in 1995-96, foreign financial institutions became the major players in agenda-setting and target definition for government economic plans.[16] Under Russian conditions this IMF style of macro-economic target setting had become absolutely central to plans and programmes of transformation. The process had begun as early as 1992 but by 1999, in the wake of the rouble crisis of 1998, the economic plan had become a detailed set of primarily macroeconomic targets that fitted IMF concerns. Russia's letter of intent of July 1999 can be read as an extreme example of the power of the IMF as a constituency. It explicitly builds, and appeals to, earlier plans lodged with the IMF. It comprises fifteen pages of policy targets, covering fiscal and taxation policy, including specified targets for growth in GDP and changes to tax collection and tax rates, and foreshadows structural reform in banking, bankruptcy law and non-payments.[17] The plan followed an agenda that international officials had been publicly urging for at least six months[18] and came on the heels of the sacking of Prime Minister Primakov in May 1999. Primakov had ridden out the 1998 crisis from September without a plan, the only Russian Prime Minister to do without one in the 1990s.[19] Primakov had also stated in January 1999 that Russia could not meet the conditions of the IMF.

Summary of originators and the sources of policy

An analysis of just where plans and programmes were coming from in the Yeltsin period reveals changes over time that have disturbing implications for the fate of democracy and sovereignty in Russia. The table 4.1 below, while not fully adequate to the complexity of the history, reflects a trend away from the debate of policy in the Russian public sphere and an interaction between society and state in the formation of policy. The table casts the sources of plans into three categories across four eras based on my examination of the electronic database and samplings of Russia's major central newspapers.[20]

What can be observed from this is a gradual confinement of planning to bureaucratic institutional politics and thus, given the importance planning had in the Russian context, policy-making generally. To a degree this pattern could be interpreted as a reconstitution of the political culture of the Soviet Union and its restriction of the sphere of politics and policy making. This is not to make the argument that Russia has returned to the Soviet era. Rather it is to point out that, in one aspect of Russian political culture at least, a general pattern appears to have been reasserting itself under Yeltsin.

Table 4.1   Basic summary of key groups originating and supporting reform plans and programs

Years	Central	Main Opposition/ Agenda-setting	Peripheral
1990-92	Central government; Communist party; government departments	Different levels of government; social movements and organisations; experts	Western organisations
1992-94	Central government; different branches of government (e.g. Central Bank, Supreme Soviet)	Industry groups; political parties; expert institutions; Western lending agencies	Experts; expert institutions, political leaders
1994-98	Central government; Western lending agencies	Government or semi-government or aspiring government members; some political parties/ groupings, groups of experts	Industry groups; government departments, regional governments (NB: Moscow/Petersburg perhaps in adjacent column)
1998-99	Central government; Western lending agencies		Groups of experts; some political parties and leaders; regional governments (NB: perhaps Moscow in adjacent column)

In the lead up to the collapse of the Soviet Union the political system continued to privilege state institutions but the initiative in agenda-setting and policy proposals was gradually escaping into the preserve of other institutions and into society generally. This enlargement of the political sphere, starting with the right to speak and extending gradually to voting choice and policy input, was the primary process of Gorbachev's time. The most important institutions in the process were of course the Union republics and the new Congress, but social movements, led by the intelligentsia, were providing most of the impetus, working through these institutions to advance their aims. Defined plans came late in the glasnost process but once institutions had been captured by oppositions there was an obvious need for plans and programmes. Plans functioned both to organise and orient policy and as ideological weapons in the quest for public and staff support.[21] I have listed Western organisations as present but peripheral during this period since they had little in the way of formal links into the Russian political economy. However, they exercised an important hegemonic role as 'the West' came to replace the image of communism as Russia's future.

The early period of the most revolutionary reform also sees the greatest amount of plurality in sources of plans. The government, and groups in and out of parliament, are all using plans to stake a place in the political spectrum and advance their claims on policy-making. The constitutional framework dispersed power over policy creation and implementation, with institutional struggles taking place between the centre and the regions, and between parliament and the government. Moreover, the arrival of fully-fledged electoral politics had encouraged the beginnings of party formation. Political leaders seeking social or interest group support were using 'plans' to attract it. At the same time the dispersed power worked against plans being unreservedly and fully implemented.

After the new constitution of 1993 the battle between institutions became less and the parliament in particular assumed more of a tribunate role, suited better to criticism or the alteration of specific policies. It was precisely discouraged from formulating (or taking responsibility for) the larger picture. The struggle over the direction of policy now moved much more into the government itself. One function of plans in the new ensemble was to play off the different interests and ministries within the government against one another,[22] or allow those outside the government, but with hopes of joining it, to advance their claims. International institutions are the other group that gains more real power to influence, formulate, and judge plans. Their conditional lending regime, combined with the trend that began in the late 1980s of Russian politicians openly claiming support from the West to legitimate their actions, gave these institutions leverage into the centre of Russian politics.[23]

The period 1998-99 is harder to categorise. The aftermath of the August 1998 crash did see a brief rash of plans, including one by the government, but almost nothing came of any of them. Western institutions were full of advice before and after the crash, and were instrumental in the formulation of the grand plan that is the Letter of Intent. This was signed in July 1999 and opened the way to more loans and loan disbursements. The regions of Moscow and Nizhni Novgorod could perhaps be promoted to the classification 'main opposition/agenda setting' at different times between as early as 1996 through to 1999. This is because both were led by politicians with an eye on high Federal positions. Moscow's Mayor Luzhkov was at one point a serious contender for the presidency and Boris Nemtsov could advance claims to the premiership on the basis of the 'successful' plan of reform carried out when he was governor of Nizhni Novgorod (Dikun, 1997).[24] However the latter was not a plan for Russia, merely a testament to Nemtsov's capabilities in carrying out a liberal plan. Luzhkov's Moscow planning more resembled the old Soviet planning, since he ran his city as an integrated enterprise (Hoffman, 1997). In this sense at least his 'plan', which was really more an example, was at variance with the dominant form of planning for Russia.

However, what is most significant about the period through to the end of 1999, and apparently continuing under Putin, is that planning became mostly the preserve of the government. Little in the way of plans or programmes has been adopted by credible oppositions, they have mostly confined themselves to addressing specific policies. Further, no plans from outside the government and Western lending agencies have been able to impact upon the political and policy-making agenda.

This examination of the sources of plans has suggested that, while plans continue to survive as an important rhetoric of legitimacy in Yeltsin's Russia, the plurality of actual policy-making in Russia has shrunk. At the beginning of the Yeltsin era plans served not just to stake legitimate claims to policy-making, they also influenced the policy process. Moreover, their sources were primarily indigenous. By the year 2000 the central government and Western institutions had the planning field almost to themselves. This would seem to suggest not just a continuity of rhetoric from Soviet times but also of a continuity of restricted institutional politics. It also means that the questions posed in the introduction: to what extent were plans merely rhetorical devices to garner legitimacy; intended as real policies; and reliable indicators of ideological positions; is somewhat blunted.

The continual use of plans by most political actors up until 1999 suggests they were important for credibility. However the extent to which they became real policy becomes a moot point as political power is internalised within government circles. Responsibility for plans being implemented diminishes as the responsibility of the government is weakened and the opposition marginalised. The opposition struggles to hold the government to account and, being so far removed from power, it has little need to present itself as an alternative government. However, better answers can be found to questions of whether plans were more than rhetoric, and the extent to which they constituted ideological positions, when they are examined in a comparative and historical context. This I propose to do briefly in the next two sections.

In the Light of Comparison

Russian economic plans and programs can be fruitfully examined by two contrasts. The first is with the Western policy process; the second is by comparison with the other transitional states of post-communism. In this section I will make some general points about the former and make some brief comparisons with experiences in Poland and Hungary.

Russia and the West

The most obvious reason for contrasting Russia's plans with plans, programmes and policy making in the West is to get a sense of the depth of difference. Do Russians just prefer the term 'plan' or 'programme', where a Western politician or specialist would reach for 'policy', or does the different term actually represent a real difference of approach? Moreover if there is a difference of approach is it shrinking? Inasmuch as Russia is embarked upon a transition to Western 'normality' it would be expected that plans were actually playing a role similar to that of policy in the West, or were fading away in favour of 'policies' (as perhaps the work in the section above suggests). The degree to which this was so would provide an indication of progress in transition. In this sense the content and intent of plans are critical.

Turning first to Western experience it can be said that plans do not play a very central role in Western policy making, especially in those countries that have embraced neo-liberalism. Apart from having their own Cold War resonances, plans suggest a more integrated and long-term predictive capability than Western policy makers feel capable of making about their own market economies.[25] Plans are acceptable in specific policy areas, and programmes and plans are quite acceptable for specific government activities in particular spheres of activity. Planning for the whole economy, with its hosts of actors, is a more dubious proposition. This is not to say planning does not happen. 'Targets' and 'profiles' are frequently set, especially as part of election platforms, which perforce are tempted to pretend to grasp the big picture, but the plan generally takes a back seat to more circumscribed policy.

In general the key concepts and building blocks of Western policy making are policy principles and objectives, and policy programmes. In theory the political masters enunciate the former and gather with them sufficient votes to govern. Then a disinterested public service puts together programmes to accord with, or to realise, said principles and objectives. Where macroeconomic management is concerned the principles will be translated into objectives and then targets. At the microeconomic level specific programmes will be implemented. In the actual practice of policy the situation is far more ad hoc: much Western policy is simply a continuation of existing practice, adjusted where possible to changing circumstances, or a (usually politically inspired) reaction to actual or perceived crises. Plans, inasmuch as they exist, are just one part of policy making as described in the theory. And the theory by no means dominates actual policy practice. A grand plan in the Western context is unlikely to last long if it attempts to match its logical and rational rhetoric with an unyielding practice of implementation. It will be defeated by both economic and political reality as the feedback mechanisms of market and democracy kick in. This seems to be tacitly accepted by all political players. Grand plans normally serve alongside policy principles and objectives as orientative of policy practice and are often primarily rhetorical (we have a plan/policy so we deserve the right to govern) and/or ideological (we have this type of plan/policy so you should support us if you share this type of vision or values or interests).

It can already be concluded from the above that Russian plans and programmes have shared a similarity with Western policies at the rhetorical level. This in itself is a shift away from the primary form of

Soviet legitimation, which was based on an ontological claim to know the future, to one based on a promise to act and deliver. For those outside of government, and some of those inside, we have also seen plans working ideologically, supporting or underpinned by a particular vision of what's best for Russia, and attempting to organise supporters around their articulation of this. However there are three key aspects of Russian plans that have made them quite different from those of the West.

Transformative not managing

Despite being couched within a rhetoric of reform, plans in Russia have been about quite radical change. The entire political economy of Russia was altered substantially under Yeltsin. The economic programmes advanced by both the government and other groups have been explicitly about creating that radical change. The goal of most plans has been to replace state-directed change with a market economy that by definition constantly begets change. Thus, as noted earlier, they have been revolutionary. At the same time, as changes have occurred, plans have also been about managing change, change they have directed and change generated by the market processes they have unleashed. The progress of transition could be charted at one level by examining the degree to which *planned change* has been replaced by the *management of change*. This has clearly happened if we contrast early plans concerned with elaborating steps of government action (the liberalisation of prices and the process of privatisation) with later ones where concerns are with meeting specified targets and indicators. However, the restructuring of the Russian economy was still far from over when Yeltsin left office, and the plans of the entire period reflect a concern with the nature, speed and direction of transformation, rather than maximising outcomes in a given political economy.

Technocratic rather than political

The modern origins of 'the plan' lie almost entirely in economics and thus its predisposition is toward what Habermas has called instrumental rationality (Held, 1980, pp.251-7). Planning privileges a top-down approach to social change, prodding those subject to it to behave in a 'rational manner' that equates with conforming to the plan. This form of rationalisation meets mixed results in the real world since its predictive capacities are not equal to the task of calculating everything and it has to substitute by ad hoc interventions. At the most abstract level this was the fate of Soviet planning. It is also a reason why planning and democracy had so much trouble co-existing in the Soviet Union. This tendency to flight from democratic politics was arguably repeated in Russia under Yeltsin as the government, frustrated by the failure of its planning, and also its inability in a democratic environment to implement all aspects of the plan, distanced itself from the evidence of its failure and the source of its inabilities, namely democratic politics. This is not to say democratic politics disappeared in Russia but it can be clearly seen that the logic of planning worked against the logic of democratic expansion and development. Moreover, the hold technocratic thinking had on Russian politics was actually reinforced by the IMF. Its stipulations of plans and programmes had the same political effects as the Russian reformers own adherence to plans. The IMF used its economic leverage to become a second, and perhaps more powerful, Russian government constituency and sought to lock the government into a specific set of measures regardless of domestic opposition.[26]

Means become ends

The net effect of the above process has seen Russia pushed, by the force of economic and ideological powers outside itself, back into a culture of economic policy as specific, technocratic, targets and goals. These goals have been delivered from what was the new utopia on Russia's horizon, 'the West'. The thinking goes: the West, made incarnate in the IMF and the World Bank, surely knows best how to turn Russia into the West, and sets forth the commandments to do so. Unfortunately, within a context of shrinking political space and debate, there has been a tendency for the means to replace the ends among the Russian political elite. Having a plan and following a plan became the way to nirvana, or at least the next loan disbursement. The original, and much more multi-faceted, end of a Western-style economy and standard of living gets lost. In the early part of Yeltsin's presidency the end of a Western standard of living and way of life was justifying the means (and the pain). As the processes I have mentioned took hold it became the case that the means were replacing this end as ends in themselves. The shock of 1998, for both the Russians and the IMF, may have gone some way toward correcting this trend. The appointment of Primakov as Prime Minister meant a temporary abandonment of planned policy for ad hoc policy making and the international financial organisations began a round of navel gazing regarding the fitness of their advice (Stiglitz, 2000; Bruszt, 2000).

In summary it can be said that Russian plans were more comprehensive, rationalising, and therefore demanding, than the domestic approach to policy in Western countries. Moreover, their orientation of transformation as opposed to managing makes them both broader and more contentious in their aims and effects. Paradoxically all this acts as an incentive to remove plans and their effects from scrutiny and accountability. By nature of their comprehensiveness, plans demand to be implemented in full and democratic responses to their effects can make this difficult, so democracy becomes a problem, a barrier, or even an enemy.

The new plans do also echo the redemptorist Soviet Marxist project in both their mission of transformation and their tendency to substitute means for ends. However, their indicators, targets and language are mostly derived from liberal economic discourse. In this sense at least they are ideologically captured and the 'new planning' is clearly a political-ideological break with the Soviet period.

Russia and other post-communist countries

With regard to the experience of other transition states, a cursory overview points to Russia's strongest similarities being with other post-Soviet states. These states inherited the language of reform extant at the collapse of the Soviet Union and it is often tied into their justifications of statehood: they were not only asserting national sovereignty but also beginning a journey West. Economic collapse and a shortage of capital has also made them partial to Western largesse and thus they have had to accept the demands for plans and programmes that have come with it.[27]

In central Europe a more mixed experience is found. Post-communist Poland has a history of plans and received considerable Western assistance in both forming them, and because of them, in the early stages of its transition. The most famous of these was the Balcerowicz plan of shock therapy, held up by influential Western experts as an ideal model. The immediate effects of this model, and the strength of the Polish democratic system, led to the defeat of the government implementing it. Successive political infighting in the early 1990s meant that while plans were formulated for rhetorical and ideological reasons, actual policy making was more ad hoc. This appears to have worked quite well, perhaps because a combination of internally agreed principles, reinforced by European and international lender norms, kept policy aims and targets within a liberal economic framework. The shock itself may have cleared away many of the transformative tasks early on as well.

A form of plan that at first seemed to hark back to communist times was accepted by the Polish government in May 1994. It was a genuine four-year plan, called a 'strategy', which predicted high growth rates, a lowering of inflation and a rise in real wages. Poland also set up an Economic Strategy Council. Poland's economy did experience a boom over the next four years, growing at between 5 and 7% per annum. The degree to which the strategy retained its plan-like features is however debatable. It appears to have mutated into a Western style set of principles and targets as early as July of 1994.[28]

By comparison, in Hungary planning had been well and truly discredited by its associations with communism. Moreover, the political discourse of reform communism that post-communist Hungary inherited was imbued with a preference for ad hoc approaches to specific problems. Under IMF scrutiny the ex-communist government did produce a four-year economic plan in 1991. It sketched a timetable of changes culminating in 'rising living standards' in 1994. However by 1992 such pretensions had been swept away, the plan of 1991 having had no detail added. Hungarians dismissed the idea of a plan, stating that observing and following Western examples would be enough (Okolicsanyi, 1991).

A brief examination of the fate of plans in post-communist countries suggests that in general, and quite ironically, they are as much a product of Western pressure as communist hangover. Moreover, the plan as an approach to policy has survived best where it has been least subject to the pressures of democracy, though possibly for varying reasons. For example in Russia, where Western demands and elite conceptions have favoured plans, and democratic resistance is weak due to economic depression and institutional bias toward a strong presidency, their mixed outcomes have not led to their rejection. In Belarus, where the opposition is weak, and the communist political culture still buttressed by a conservative government, plans have been offered up to the IMF but funds have not been forthcoming since the plans appear primarily rhetorical in form. There appears more than a hint of the Soviet political culture of 'appearance over substance' about them.

The Proof of the Pudding

In this section I will look at just what role plans and programmes have played in Russia since 1992. Are they just rhetoric? The point here is that for a plan to be more than rhetoric it really needs to be implemented. Thus it is difficult to judge the non-government plans in relation to this question. To a limited degree we can say that many were not just rhetoric in that they (a) did attempt to address a constituency in specific fashion or (b) attempted to hold together logically and move into credible detail. However, much of the role they were playing, with the possible exception of programmes advanced by Yavlinsky and the Communists during presidential campaigns, where making a credible claim on government was also at stake, was that of criticism. In this sense they are not very different to opposition policies in Western politics, which need to be more rhetorical.

However, where Russian plans and programmes show some difference is in their political flavour. By the late 1990s there was little that was addressed to particular social groups, that is worked as ideology, and, precisely because the political sphere was so limited, little that attempted to actually make a legitimate claim to government. In the presidential election of 2000 issues of state power and patriotism raised by the second Chechen war, and accompanied by the 'charisma' of a young leader, managed to push economics to one side. Lack of plans was the notable and, in the case of Putin, deliberate feature of the 2000 election campaign.[29]

What of the government's various plans throughout the Yeltsin period? Were they just rhetoric to satisfy domestic and international demands? The answer to this must be no, since the evolution of the plans and their function in providing accountability measures for the IMF and Western investors meant that they had a real influence on the shape of policy, including the detail of policy itself. Very few plans promised to the IMF appear to have been carried out in full and both the IMF and the Russians have been quick to find excuses for this. Notwithstanding their limited implementation plans were doggedly pursued. The targets they did meet formed part of the basis for renewed claims for loans by the Russian government. In this sense the IMF, and the other international lending and investment agencies that follow its lead, have been a constituency that could call the Russian government to some account.

In summary it can be stated that the plans weren't just so much rhetoric designed to legitimate the government or claims to government.

Plans had real policy agendas and real addressees. However, over time it did appear that the government's main constituency was first and foremost international. The government's domestic audience was either addressed with specific policies or policy promises (much closer to Western practice) or in non-economic ideological terms such as rhetorics of nationalism, culture and state power. The appeal of the approval of international institutions as a way of garnering domestic support inverted over the period as economic conditions worsened. The predominant pattern by late 1999 had become one of blaming foreigners by virtually all opposition groups, and using them as an excuse for policy failure, and also policy continuation, by the government.

Overall it can be said that plans were related to real policies, they were not just rhetoric. The other question is whether they represented reliable ideological positions? That is did they represent social actors or function as poles around which social actors could group and become politicised. To some extent this did happen, especially in the early periods of Yeltsin's presidency when the struggle was over the exact nature and pace of transformation. However, inasmuch as the origins of the plans and programmes were tied to the IMF and World Bank, which are themselves founded on strong ideological principles of economic liberalism, it is tempting to say that Russia's plans and programmes most reliably represented world capital rather than domestic actors. If they had an ideological barrow to push it was much closer to that of groups outside the country.

If this is true it has a number of grave implications for the future of democracy in Russia. Modern Western democracies are supported by pluralist civil societies which throw up a variety of ideological positions, usually manifested as values and policy positions. Economic and social policy positions are central to political contests and debate. While it can be argued that there is a broad capitalist/liberal democratic, ideology/consensus which overdetermines most debate in Western societies, it cannot be denied that myriad important policy positions, including some which subvert it, exist within this consensus. The health of both the democracy and the market can be measured by the ability to produce ideology.

In terms of Russia's transition it is therefore worrying that economic policy, in the shape of a concern with planning in the form it has taken so far, actually serves to disenfranchise the Russian people in the most crucial area of satisfaction of their wants and needs – economic policy. While it might be argued that the building of a sound economy and the attendant sacrifices mean that too much democracy could be a problem, the danger of minimising political debate about economic policy is that politics becomes a realm of other more divisive and ultimately anti-democratic debates such as identity politics.

Conclusion

My original presumptions were that continual reoccurrence of plans and programmes of reform throughout the 1990s in Russia were symptomatic of two things. The first was that these plans and programmes were primarily rhetorical. They were window dressing of the old Potemkin kind, designed primarily to fool outsiders and domestic critics. They had no roots in real forces in Russia's political economy nor any concerns with the real problems of Russian transition, hence their failure to address the real problems such as crime, corruption and the non-money economy. The second was that they would prove a good example of the resilience of political culture in Russia, whereby the new would be re-subordinated to preferred habits of mind and action.

However, my investigations have lead me to conclude that these presumptions not entirely correct. Plans and programmes advanced in Russia have been more than rhetoric. They have come from a variety of social actors, have served as ideological rallying points and claims to legitimacy, and more crucially have formed platforms and agendas for policy. Aims and targets of plans have been met, fiscal rectitude and large-scale privatisation sourced from plans has taken place.[30] In light of this we may assume that demands made in the 1999 Letter of Intent were meant, and indeed we can already see that much of the economic policy agenda under Putin has revolved around them. However, that one major root of Russian planning is from non-democratic technocratic institutions based in the West is potentially disturbing for the fate of Russian democracy and Russia's place in the world economy.

As to the assumption of the importance of cultural continuity to post-Soviet Russian politics, in terms of planning it could hardly be said to arise from any particular 'Russian essence'. If anything the continuity of a preoccupation with planning can be seen as arising from a particular aspect of the culture of modernity, namely a technocratic faith in the economic. It was Marxism-Leninism's fetishisation of this that led to planning in the

Soviet Union, happily marrying itself to a state-centred authoritarian culture. Modern day Russia's desperate demand for capital, combined with an unfortunately incomplete democratic revolution, has placed it in the hands of technocratic economic liberalism. This discourse can be viewed as Marxism-Leninism's twin (both are progeny of modernity's fascination with rationalism) and its truimphalism has been feeding off the carcass of its brother since 1989. The fetishism of market rules and plans that informs IMF policy has perhaps made a new happy marriage, or at least found fertile ground, in the Soviet political culture that also assumed that the administration of 'scientifically given' and 'universal' principles couched in a plan could produce predictable and desirable results.

If there is a basic lesson in all of this it is probably that poli*cies* (emphasis on the plural) are symptomatic of a more healthy polity and economy than plans. Russia's economy performed better without a plan under Primakov, Hungary did well and so has Poland. Policies imply competition and democracy; policies get modified in the face of electoral opinion and the experience and urgencies of government. Moreover, policy-making ideally connects principle to programme. Plans, on the other hand, will tend to demand the world adapts to them, they freeze out competition. In a context that gives them free rein they incline to the tyrannical. If we examine the fate of planning in Russia it primarily serves to highlight Russia's economic dependency and the weakness of its democracy. Thus one positive sign that Russia is moving out of 'permanent transition' might be when all the 'planning' disappears.

Notes

1   Contributors to the debate include Buzgalin, 1998; Gaddy and Ickes, 1998; Glinski and Reddaway, 1999, esp. pp.23-7; Lloyd, 1999; Wedel, 2000; various authors, 'Tainted Transactions: An Exchange', *The National Interest*, no.59, Spring 2000; Goldman, 2000; Soros, 2000.

2   It should not be thought here that these two purposes are mutually exclusive, parties contesting elections in the West would reasonably be expected to put forward policies intended to do both. As a general rule we might expect that the ideological purpose would predominate pre-election and the technical come to the fore in government.

3   This was the most popular name it was given, however it was also closely linked to Grigory Yavlinsky and indeed had its origins in a 400 days programme he came up with in May 1990.

4   *Radio Liberty Daily Report*, 30 November, 1990.

5   For this and an overview of his criticisms see Yavlinsky, 1992. See also interview with Yavlinsky in *Moskovskaya Pravda*, 23 April, 1993.

6   The original phrase, used in December 1992, was 'young boys in pink shorts with red shirts and yellow boots'. For one of the earliest academic elaborations of this idea see Tsipko, 1993.

7   *Nezavisimaya gazeta*, 1 April, 1992, p.2.

8   An earlier version of the memorandum was submitted to the IMF in February 1992.

9   Yegor Gaidar, public lecture at the University of Melbourne, 3 April, 1996.

10   For more of the flavour of political urgency in the 1992 programmes see also Chubais, 1995, esp. pp.55-6.

11   The IMF executive board met on 30th March 1992 and praised the Russian programme. Managing director Michael Camdessus stated that 'if fully implemented it will lay the foundation for an economic programme the IMF could support...' (*Interfax*, 31 March, 1992). The IMF went on to allocate US$3 billion to Russia.

12   In April 1992 David Roche of Morgan Stanley estimated that Russia needed an injection of between US$76 and US$176 billion a year if reform was not to be abandoned (*Financial Times*, 6 April, 1992).

13   For example, World Bank President Lewis Preston said the IMF and the Bank could not continue to loan money to Russia until they [again] produced an 'acceptable reform plan' (*Radio Liberty Daily Report*, 26 March, 1993). In August such a plan was produced and Prime Minister Chernomyrdin was at pains to stress Russia's adherence to it at the World Economic Forum in Davos in early 1994 (*Delovoi mir*, 13 August, 1993; *Radio Liberty Daily Report*, 31 January, 1994).

14   For example *Izvestia* (29 January, 1994) reported a new 'gradualist' programme put together by economists from ten institutes.

15   F. Weir, 'Evaluation of Zyuganov's Economic Programme', *Johnson's Russia List*, 27 June, 1996.

16   For example, the Russian government signed detailed agreements with the IMF in 1995 and 1996 setting targets for fiscal policy. The aid package for 'reform' on the table in 1996 was worth just over US$10 billion, to be disbursed as the IMF deemed targets were being met. In April 1997 U.S. Treasury Deputy Secretary Lawrence Summers called for the World Bank to follow the lead of the IMF and greatly increase its role in Russian reforms, particularly in the areas of fiscal management, social protection and sectoral restructuring. In June 1997 the World Bank announced a new strategy for Russia and approved loans worth US$884.6 million. The loans were justified on the basis of reform programme targets already met and those foreshadowed in Russia's current economic reform plan. The strategy recommended expanding assistance to the value of US$2-3 billion annually if the Russian government delivered on its planned structural reforms. IMF director Michael Camdessus informed a press conference in Washington in April 1998 that he had raised concerns about Russia's programme of reform with President Yeltsin at a US-Russia business council meeting and got from Yeltsin a commitment to a new programme. Camdessus stated that a programme for 1998-99 was then worked out *between the IMF and Russia* that would allow a continuation of disbursements of the US$10 billion loan [my italics]. (United States Information Agency, 1 April, 1997 and 6 June, 1997; *Radio Liberty Daily Report*, 3 April, 1998).

17   Russian Federation Letter of Intent of 13th July 1999, www.imf.org/external/country/RUS/index.htm (accessed 30 November, 1999).

18   IMF managing director Michael Camdessus in February 1999 restated the IMF's importance to setting Russian policy: 'There are voices in Russia that say you must

reject co-operation with the IMF, cut yourself off from the rest of the world, and proceed along some kind of traditional-for-Russia "own way"...Practice shows it would be a mistake' (*Novye izvestia*, 16 February, 1999). Later in the month he told the Institute of International Bankers that Russia would not receive further credits until it produced a credible economic plan. First deputy Prime Minister Maslyukov went on to call IMF pressure on Russia 'indecent' (*Interfax*, 2 and 3 March, 1999).

19   It should be noted that a highly conservative plan was foreshadowed by Prime Minister Primakov's economics chief Yuri Maslyukov late 1998, but was still being drafted when Primakov was removed from office in May 1999. The Primakov government did present budget plans to the IMF when seeking US$2.5 billion aid in October 1998.

20   See page 54.

21   Staff here is meant in its Weberian sense of the people who run the system. In nearly all of the revolutions against communism it was the collapse of staff morale, and the staffs subsequent switching of sides that was decisive.

22   The most obvious cleavage has been between the economic and power ministries. The latter are far less inclined to worry about the niceties of liberal thought and frequently advocate more Soviet style feudal grab and mobilise policies. An excellent example of the power approach was the 'economic programme' put forward by Minister of Internal Affairs Gen. Anatoly Kulikov in February 1996. Among his suggestions were the partial nationalisation of the banks and commercial structures with monopoly positions and issuing a decree that all individuals must declare their sources of capital on pain of confiscation of it. Nothing came of this proposal as the economic ministries continued their dominance in the area, for the most part the power ministries have been left to pursuing their ideological inclinations in the realm of civil rights and conflict resolution ('What is General Kulikov Proposing?', *Argumenty i fakty*, no.7, February 1996).

23   Note that the importance of the latter could be said to be waning while the former was waxing. Russia's sovereign debts grew to about US$155 billion by 1998 and disbursements from the IMF were just over US$15.5 billion between 1992-98. The economy's lack of success was lessening the domestic legitimation effects of Western approval but also making Western lending more crucial. That said the most important part of this trend, the change in the language of economic policy to liberal economics as the only legitimate term of reference was well bedded in for all but a few actors, see footnote above (figures from IMF website www.imf.org/external, accessed on 10 and 18 October, 2000).

24   The plan itself was authored and overseen by Yavlinsky in 1992 and was also used by him to advance his claims on government.

25   They seem to feel more hubristically confident with regard to plans for others. Perhaps the feeling of superiority that comes from subscribing to a worldview that sees the West as more developed makes predictive planning for these countries a more confident activity. After all they are following in the West's historical path. Like the Soviet Marxists the liberal transitologists and their political backers know what should happen next. For elaboration on this critique see Anthony Phillips, 'Changing Characterisations of the Roots of Russia's Problems: A Look at the Virtual Economy Thesis' *Russian and Euro-Asian Bulletin* Vol.8 No.3 March 1999 pp.3-4.

26   A variation of this point was made forcefully by the former Chief Economist at the World Bank, Joseph Stiglitz, in April 2000 (Stiglitz, 2000). Similar thinking is evident in European Bank for Reconstruction and Development's report for 1998: '[W]hether

crisis leads to renewed reforms or to backtracking depends in part on the functioning of democratic institutions and the constraints they place on interest groups and on policymakers'. Executive summary of the report available through www.ebrd.org/english/Public/index.htm (accessed 2 March, 1999).

27 This process is of course by no means confined to post-communist states. Indeed they are arguably replicating a pattern familiar to third world countries. See Payer, 1989, esp. pp.14-16.

28 *Radio Liberty Daily Report*, 14 July, 1994.

29 Putin's approach was to avoid detailing any plans but at the same time foreshadow a grand 10 year plan that was to be announced in the future. The Gref plan did arrive, though not in full, in mid-2000 and immediately became a site of squabble. It was said to be accompanied by over 500 pages of notes making it perhaps a 500 pages plan! (Proskurnina, 2000). For an overview of the plan see 'Russia's New Economic Program: Does "Putinomics" Mean a Slimmed but Muscular State?', *Transition Newsletter*, vol. 11, nos.3-4, May- July 2000.

30 It might be noted though that the second stage of privatisation that involved 'loans-for-shares' was not sourced from a plan. It came as an ad hoc response to fiscal crisis and the particular urging of small group of Russian interests.

References

Bruszt, L. (2000), 'The Russian Lesson: A Market Economy Needs an Effective State', *Transition Newsletter*, vol.11, nos.3-4, May-July, pp.21-2.

Buzgalin, A. (1998), 'Russia: "Capitalism's Jurassic Park"', *Prism*, vol.4, no.15, part 4, July.

Chubais, A. (1995), 'The Results of Privatisation in Russia and the Tasks of the New Stage', *Problems of Economic Transition*, vol.38, no.1, May.

Custine, de, M. (1991), *Letters from Russia*, Penguin, Harmondsworth, 1991.

Desai, P. (2000), 'A Russian Optimist: an interview with Yegor Gaidar', *Challenge*, May-June, pp.15-16.

Dikun, Ye. (1997), 'A Profile of Boris Nemtsov', *Prism*, vol.3, no.5, part 2, April.

Gaddy, C.G. and Ickes, B.W. (1998), 'Russia's Virtual Economy', *Foreign Affairs*, vol.77, no.5, September-October.

Gaidar, E. (1999), *Days of Defeat and Victory*, University of Washington Press, Seattle WA, 1999.

Glinski, D. and Reddaway, P. (1999), 'The Ravages of Market Bolshevism', *Journal of Democracy*, vol.10, no.2, April.

Goldman, M. (2000), 'Reprivatizing Russia', *Challenge*, vol.43, no.3, May-June.

Held, D. (1980), *Introduction to Critical Theory*, University of California Press, Berkeley.

Hoffman, D. (1997), 'The Man who Rebuilt Moscow: Capitalist Style Could Propel Mayor to National Power', *Washington Post*, 27 February.

Lloyd, J. (1999), 'The Russian Devolution', *The New York Times Magazine*, August 15, p.34.

Okolicsanyi, K. (1991), 'Hungary: the Nonexistent Long-term Economic Plan', *Radio Liberty Research Report*, 18 December.

Payer, C. (1989), 'Causes of the Debt Crisis', in B.Onimode (ed.), *The IMF, The World Bank and African Debt: The Social and Political Impact*, Zed Books, London.

Phillips, A. (1999), 'Changing Characterisations of the Roots of Russia's Problems: A Look at the Virtual Economy Thesis', *Russian and Euro-Asian Bulletin*, vol.8, no.3, March.

Proskurnina, O. (2000), 'Missing Points from Strategic Development Plan', *gazeta.ru*, 14 June.

Soros, G. (2000), 'Who Lost Russia', *New York Review of Books*, April 13.

Stiglitz, J. (2000), 'What I Learned at the World Economic Crisis', *The New Republic*, 17 April.

Tsipko, A. (1993), 'Democratic Russia as a Bolshevik as well as a National Party', *Nezavisimaya gazeta*, 9 April, p.5.

Wedel, J.R. (2000), 'Tainted Transactions: Harvard, the Chubais Clan and Russia's Ruin', *The National Interest*, No.59, Spring.

Yavlinsky, G. (1992), 'Spring '92 Reforms in Russia' (Report from the Centre for Economic and Political Research), *Moscow News*, Nos.21-22.

5 Farewell to the Oligarchs? Presidency and Business Tycoons in Contemporary Russia

YURI TSYGANOV

Despite claims recently made by some observers[1] suggesting that the role of clan politics in Russia is of small importance, particularly in relation to Russia's major social and economic problems, the developments of the last few years have yet again demonstrated that not only does the problem exist, but that it also affects many areas of contemporary Russian development. The roots of the problem go back to the start of the Russian reform in the early 1990s. At that stage Russian politics were often seen as a struggle between a small group of reformists who were determined to pursue changes, and a vast majority of conservatives, most of whom were a part of the previous Soviet *nomenklatura*. However, as recently noted by Sam Vaknin, the motivations that formed the background of policies pursued by these Russian reformists were far from altruistic.

> With very few exceptions, they [reformists] were out to enrich themselves by all means, fair and foul. The kith and kin of Chubais and the Chubais-like were as ruthless and iniquitous as any Russian gangster. A lot can be explained by attributing the worst of intentions to this lot. The haste in privatising state assets and lifting price controls afforded them with the touch of a Midas and the wealth of a Croesus. A mobsters' pact divvying up territory led to the rising political fortunes of the regions. The illicit nature of the ruling classes is the parsimonious explanation to recent Russian chronicles.[2]

But what is even more important than the selfishness of the Russian contemporary political class which has rejected any form of social paternalism that could have smoothed the path of transition, is the fact that Russian social and economic life continues to be easily manipulated by a relatively small group of people who form the ruling elite. After 1996 the so-called political technologies, i.e. the arts of manipulation, have developed rapidly in Russia. The last parliamentary election saw these arts at their best, when one political group (the so-called 'Family') systematically crushed all competitors in an attempt to secure another decade of political life. Political manipulation had to a large extent pre-determined the results of the parliamentary election of 19 December 1999 as well as the outcome of the 2000 presidential election. The main emphasis of this manipulation was to encourage so-called 'negative selection' by the electorate, while the main emphasis of the election campaign was on the weaknesses and possible implications of the election of an opponent rather than on the strengths and advantages of your own candidate. This phenomenon of Russian politics was widespread under the communist regime and often ensured election of the most malleable (and often the least capable) candidates to bodies of power. As a result, the ruling group became overloaded with politicians most of whom might be regarded as political nonentities lacking positive experience in politics, but who, whenever required, will act as loyal 'soldiers of the party'.

Andrei Piontkovsky, a Russian political commentator, described the December 1999 election in terms that leave little to add:

> A crook despised and hated by the entire nation, but close to the extremely unpopular presidential family, travelled across the country and talked governors into creating a new pro-Kremlin party just several months before the election. He managed to persuade three or four of them, including those most famous for corruption scandals and the one who is suspected of organising the murder of an opposition journalist. Two months later this 'party' gained a remarkable victory at the parliamentary election. What happened during these months and why was the famous crook so prudent as to invest in an undertaking which seemed to be so hopeless? [3]

The 'crook' alluded to in this quotation is apparently one of the so-called 'oligarchs', Boris Berezovsky, while the artificial party Piontkovsky speaks about is the new political movement Unity, which comprises middle-rank *nomenklatura* and was set up to fill what has long been the vacant place of the 'party of rulers' in Russia.

Vladimir Putin: Another Virtual Strong Man

Answering to the question that Piontkovsky asked above, an observer would note that the Kremlin group managed to use the events preceding the election with a high level of efficiency. I would like to remind the reader of three major events that greatly increased Putin's chances of election. These were: the Chechen incursion into Dagestan, the explosions that demolished two apartment buildings and killed 200 people in Moscow, and the beginning of a new war against Chechnya. Regarding Chechnya, I wish to point out that in my considered opinion the reasons for the outbreak of the second Chechen War were nothing to do with the real or false existence of terrorist groups in this breakaway republic. The need to bring Russian military forces into action, including massive bombings and artillery strikes, emerged from the decay of police force structures and, more generally, of all security services. In post-Soviet Russia police functions were de facto privatised, in a growing number of cases policemen were in fact no longer working for society, but instead serving their own clans and groupings. Such a police force was unable to deal with the numerous criminal groupings that emerged after the first Chechen war. Military units sent to Chechnya with the officially proclaimed goal of fighting terrorists disguise the fact that a vast part of the Russian state machine can no longer act efficiently due to corruption and decay.

As there is not enough evidence, I do not intend to discuss the role of the successor to KGB, the Federal Security Service (FSB), in the above events. However, it is important to note here that Vladimir Putin served in both secret agencies, a fact that undoubtedly has facilitated his way to the top office in Russia. While the latest Chechen War has left more questions than answers, its one major outcome is obvious. It is well known that the war enormously increased Putin's rating and indirectly played a crucial role in the rise of the Unity political movement, which from the start was endorsed by Putin. In the months leading up to parliamentary and presidential elections a wave of patriotism swept the country. The largest media companies came under the control of the ruling group. As a result, about 60% of the population supported Putin as Premier and three months later 52.94% voted for him as the new President.[4]

I would divide Putin's electorate into three main groups: those who always vote for authorities (about 20% of the population); a very significant section of voters who really felt grateful to Putin as he personified the end of the 'Yeltsin epoch'; and of those who long for a 'strong hand' in Russian politics and favour re-establishment of a Stalinist-type regime. In modern Russia advocates of authoritarian rule can be found everywhere; even some well-known former liberals today prefer to be counted among the neo-Stalinists (see Tretyakov, 1999; Belotserkovsky, 2000).

Paradoxically, in the wake of the elections and during the first months of Putin's rule, very few asked the question just who this man was who, only eight months before his election, was absolutely unknown to the public. This seems to be a very important question, although its answer proves rather discouraging. The peak of Vladimir Putin's career with the KGB was in the 1980s when he held the insignificant position of KGB major in charge of Friendship House in the former German Democratic Republic.[5] In the early 1990s he worked in the Administration of Mayor of St.Petersburg, Anatoly Sobchak, and at the time was accused of shady dealings in the barter of oil products.[6] When in mid-1990s Sobchak was not re-elected as mayor, Putin left the administration but later managed to move to Moscow and was appointed to a middle-ranking post within the Presidential Administration (Golovkov, 2000). He soon replaced Nikolai Kovalev as the Director of the Federal Security Service (FSB). According to Kovalev, this was done in order to close criminal cases that had been launched by the FSB against several persons close to the Presidential Administration (Voschanov, 2000). In 1999 Putin played a very active role in ousting Yuri Skuratov from the office of Prosecutor-General. This happened after Skuratov sanctioned investigations into several corruption cases involving high-ranking officials, the 'oligarch' Berezovsky among them (Golovkov, 2000). Later in the year Putin portrayed himself as a hard-liner in the escalating Chechen conflict and in August was promoted to the office of Premier. Finally, in March 2000, this middle-level bureaucrat completed his four-year ascent to the top when he was elected by an absolute majority of voters into the position of Russia's new president.

In my view, the rise of Putin can be explained by an symbiosis between the centuries old Russian tradition of favouritism and the modern achievements of 'political technologies',[7] which are more known. The result of this symbiosis was another 'virtual' leader, one created in accordance with the same scenario that was earlier invented and successfully used in Yeltsin's case. 'Virtual' Yeltsin appeared in Russian politics on the eve of the 1996 presidential election. In late June, between the two rounds of elections Yeltsin suffered a massive heart attack and was set to lose the election race. However, he chose to hide his illness and instead presented himself as a healthy and strong leader, capable of leading the country. It was at that time that Yeltsin's 'virtual' image was created through the staging interviews that the President never even held, through to the introduction of weekly pre-recorded radio addresses to the nation, etc. Valentin Yumashev, a professional journalist who until early December 1998 was the Head of the Presidential Administration, had re-arranged the work of the Administration around public relations and was the driving force in making 'virtual Yeltsin' a real political figure at a time when

Yeltsin himself often had a very dim idea of who he was and where he was (Timakova, 1998).

Since the autumn of 1997, when it became clear that neither real nor 'virtual' Yeltsin had any chance of winning a new presidential election, the Kremlin group, or the so-called 'Family', became engaged in the search for a successor to Yeltsin. One of the first choices of the group was a young 'reformist', Boris Nemtsov, who for a short period became widely acclaimed by the mass media but soon proved to be incapable as a statesman. The next attempt, which also failed, was the appointment of Sergei Kirienko as Russian Premier in March 1998. At the time he was presented as another 'young reformist' who was capable of implementing unpopular, but necessary, measures in order to promote Russian reform. However, very soon Kirienko demonstrated a low level of professionalism and a high level of dependency on those political leaders who played behind the scenes. Following the August 1998 financial crisis Kirienko was ousted from office and transferred to a 'reserve force', while Yeltsin and the 'Family' tried to bring the former Premier, Viktor Chernomyrdin, back to power. The attempt to re-appoint Chernomyrdin was undermined by the combined efforts of Yuri Luzhkov and the Communists (Tsyganov, 1999, pp.278-9). In a compromise move Yeltsin appointed Yevgeny Primakov as the new Premier. Primakov turned out to be too independent from the Kremlin and eight months later he was replaced by the former head of the FSB and then Interior Minister, Sergei Stepashin. However, Stepashin, who shared responsibility for the First Chechen War of 1994-96, refused to support the start of the second war and eventually lost his position, seen by the Kremlin as too soft a leader.

During the crisis of August 1998 the first attempt was made to create a new power centre in Russia that could parallel the official presidency. Chernomyrdin tried to unite the 'business *nomenklatura*' (which he himself represented), regional leaders (governors Lebed and Shaimiev) and some of the few surviving oligarchs (first of all, Berezovsky). This was a chance for the post-Soviet *nomenklatura* to consolidate its position under Chernomyrdin's leadership and to weaken the 'new generation' of Russian managers and politicians. At that time Chernomyrdin also had the best chance among Russian politicians of succeeding Yeltsin as the new president. Ironically, it was the most offended *nomenklatura* group, the one that was united around the Communist Party (KPRF) that played the crucial role in undermining Chernomyrdin's chances. This group was supported by Moscow's mayor, Yuri Luzhkov, who at that time decided to make public his own presidential ambitions (Tsyganov, 1999, pp.278-9). It was not long before it became clear that neither Luzhkov nor Primakov were acceptable to the 'Family' as Yeltsin's successors. This started a new round of power struggles in the Kremlin, which eventually brought Vladimir Putin to the forefront.

The real success of the 'Family' efforts might be the creation of a 'virtual strongman' image for Putin. This was done with the use of intensive, communist-style, propaganda methods. Throughout the second half of 1999 and in early 2000 Vladimir Putin was frequently shown by the media visiting troops in combat; flying a jet fighter, sailing in a submarine. His specific use of language dotted with criminal slang added to this image and his promise to 'slaughter terrorists even in the shithouse' became a sort of electoral slogan for his campaign. A significant part of the population was confirmed in the view that Russian problems could not be solved on the basis of liberal values and that only a 'strong hand' could put the country in order (Roitman, 2000). Apparently, this illusion was successfully exploited in Putin's campaign. It is worth mentioning that Yeltsin's own success in defeating the August 1991 coup was largely ensured by a popular perception of him as a strong man, which became especially evident in comparison with Mikhail Gorbachev, who failed to control his closest appointees during the days of the coup.

There is evidence that Yeltsin's inner circle tried to use the image of a 'tough politician' on the eve of the 1996 presidential election (Porfiriev, 2000). To this end, a special plan was elaborated. According to the plan, Yeltsin would exchange his democratic image for that of the 'strong man' in order to keep the power and prevent property redistribution. However, Yeltsin, being seriously ill, rejected the plan. It was General Lebed, who in the second round transferred his support to Yeltsin, who successfully filled in the 'vacancy' of strongman during the crucial 1996 presidential election. In 1999-2000 this experience was used again to put Yeltsin's successor into Russian politics. The major task that the successor was expected to fulfil was the same: keeping power, preventing property redistribution and suppressing alien clans.

On the last day of 1999, when Putin had successfully adopted his new hard-line image, Boris Yeltsin made a spectacular move. Yeltsin, who at the time was moving and speaking with great difficulty and in appearance was the twin brother of his late party comrade Leonid Brezhnev, announced his voluntary resignation from the post of president. Although the possibility of such a decision had been discussed for several months (Babasyan, 2000), it was the outcome of the December 1999 parliamentary elections that prompted him to take the final decision. According to

Mikhail Gorbachev (2000), it was the 'Family' that persuaded Yeltsin that it would be the right step to make Putin an Acting President, thus utilising his high rating in the most efficient way. Yeltsin himself eventually closed the last 'page' of his eight-year unchallenged rule that had started with an unscrupulous continuation of the August 1991 coup and the ousting of Gorbachev from the presidential office. Yeltsin's retirement put an end to 'Yeltsinism' as a specific form of rule that had emerged in the early 1990s.

Unity: a New 'Party of Rulers'

It was the August 1998 crisis that marked the collapse of Yeltsin's political regime. This regime was established under the 1993 constitution, which was drafted in a situation of acute struggle for power inside the group that had come to power in Russia back in 1991. The constitution was designed to enshrine political power in the hands of Yeltsin and the 'reformists'. It gave vast rights to the President in the areas of executive and even legislative power and formed the basis of a 'superpresidential system' in Russia. At the centre of this system was an extraordinarily strong, nearly authoritarian, presidential position, which was described by many observers as a nouveau 'tsarist rule'.[8] This system also brought to life the phenomenon of favouritism so common to tsarist times. Moreover, Yeltsin himself often encouraged the struggle between different groups of his supporters, each aspiring to gain ultimate influence over the President. In the end, the actions of these groups balanced each other, allowing the President to stand aside from political struggles and act as a supreme referee.

This was the general framework of 'Yeltsinism', a specific political system that emerged during the chaos of the Russian transition.[9] Inside this system a version of the democratic principle of 'checks and balances' emerged. It substituted for the counterbalance between different branches of power a system of struggles between rival cliques. This arrangement became deadlocked when the referee (the President) failed to play his role, mainly because of the poor condition of his health. This situation was further complicated by the loss of popular support for the regime. By the mid-1990s it was clear that seven years of 'radical economic reforms' had destroyed all of the 'credit of trust' that the Russian people had initially awarded Yeltsin. In 1997 Russia again found itself ruled by a weak leader who was surrounded by rival political groups, each seeking to promote their own goals and displaying little care for the common people and the future of the country. The regime was clearly politically weak and incapable of solving the grave problems the country faced.

Another distinguishing feature of 'Yeltsinism' was the lack of normal political parties. Decades of suppression of any individual initiative, and the elimination of elites that could not be integrated into Communist party structures, had predetermined the development of a post-Soviet situation where Russian political circles would fail to establish normal political parties that could protect and promote the interests of various elites and social groups. There are no consolidated elites in modern Russia, and there are also no mature legal political structures. In such a situation only clan- or mafia-type formations can survive. In contrast to traditional political parties, these groups are based on a sense of common origin or on a common aspiration to dominate other groups. Among the two hundred parties and political movements that have been registered in Russia only a few have known leaders and practically none of them has adopted a programme that clearly states plans and programmes for solving Russia's problems. Following this trend Vladimir Putin, in the course of his presidential campaign, having said that he wanted to avoid possible criticism, continually rejected requests to reveal his views on the economy or to produce an election programme (Sharyi, 2000). However, this in no way complicated his accession to the highest office in the country.

It appears that many of these so-called parties and movements are just tools used by their leaders to obtain power. On this point, Unity is just following the pattern: a political leader – in the case of Unity there was a 'division of labour' between Vladimir Putin as the presidential candidate and Sergei Shoigu as the direct promoter of the movement - who manages to secure political financing and strong support from part of the mass media, campaigns in the regions to attract local political aspirants, who make up the body of the political formation. The only distinctive feature of Unity was that, in contrast to earlier political struggles with their epicentre in Moscow, this time the ruling group put its stake directly upon the provinces, targeting middle level local *nomenklatura*. Very few local politicians in Russia would pass up an opportunity to join the top-level political game.

In 1995-97 a particular version of the two-party system emerged in Russia, one which united the so-called 'party of rulers' against the so-called 'systemic opposition' (Tsyganov, 1999, pp.261-2). At the time the 'party of rulers' was based on the Russia is Our Home (ROH) movement that was created in 1995 by then Prime Minister Viktor Chernomyrdin. All major political groups that supported the President and the federal government joined this 'party'. It was a rather flexible coalition that attracted a large number of minor parliamentary factions and groupings, as well as some democratic and reformist parties and movements that lacked parliamentary representation. On the other hand, KPRF formed the basis of 'systemic opposition'. However, in practice it often turned out that the confrontation between the 'party of rulers' and the 'systemic opposition' could easily be bridged. In many instances both sides managed to cooperate, including on such major issues as the adoption of the state budget, changes in taxation policy, etc.

In March 1998 the sacking of Viktor Chernomyrdin from the post of Prime Minister destroyed this system. At first, following the resignation of its leader from the top government position ROH immediately lost its attractiveness to regional leaders and the federal bureaucracy. Later, in August 1998, the federal government lost all of its earlier political support in the Parliament when it became obvious that no parliamentary faction was prepared to support the 'young reformist' Prime Minister Sergei Kirienko. Thus, the federal government remained as the only basis for the 'party of power'. In September 1998, Yevgeny Primakov's appointment to the post of Prime Minister gave the 'systemic opposition' hope that it could transform itself into the 'party of rulers'. However, a strange impeachment attempt in May 1999 ruled out all such hopes. The 'Fatherland' movement launched by Moscow mayor Yuri Luzhkov was the next to try to occupy this vacated political space. Under the circumstances the 'Family' saw the task of another Prime Minister Sergei Stepashin and then Vladimir Putin (as the former failed) as the destruction of that movement. The latter was successful with the 'Family's' support, and now Unity incorporating the remains of ROH and 'Fatherland's' former ally 'All Russia' has become the new 'party of rulers'.

It appears that very few of the national political collisions that drew public attention in Russia in the period after the summer of 1999[10] – the Kremlin-Luzhkov conflict, the establishment of Unity, the two election campaigns – were a reflection of the real processes that were driving the political establishment. The political parties that are represented in the current Russian Parliament (Duma), such as Unity (also known as *Medved'* or the Bear party), SPS (Union of Rightist Forces), the Liberal Democratic Party of Russia, 'Yabloko' and even a significant part of the 'Fatherland' movement, are all fingers on the same hand of behind-the-scenes manipulators. Very often they have the same sources of political financing. Being ideologically neutral they can easily achieve compromises with each other. Despite recent changes in the leadership and in the names of some parties, they still represent the same old 'party of rulers' and the same old 'systemic opposition' of Yeltsin's Russia. In the course of recent years these two groupings have developed a variety of mechanisms that now allow them to peacefully coexist. During the 1999 parliamentary election campaign they did not fight each other; it was rather the party of rulers that was suppressing an 'uprising' inside its loose formation. This was Luzhkov's attempt to create an electoral bloc, which was effectively destroyed by a broad attack through the mass media.

Russia's 'Clan-Corporate' Capitalism and Its Crisis

This specific 'two-party' system is the tip of the political iceberg of Russia's 'clan-corporate capitalism' as developed during the last decade. The first symptoms of this development were already visible during the Brezhnev period. This development has its roots in the legacy of the command economy – now a number of small management pyramids have emerged from the collapse of the central, authoritarian, bureaucratic government. In addition to Soviet roots these pyramids have also been based on emerging capitalist relations and have incorporated traditional forms like semi-feudal clan relations which existed in Russia in various forms since Tsarist times. Privatisation of state property has completed this process, leading to the emergence of the so-called 'oligarchic' groups. Even before privatisation became an official state policy, various political groups were already actively privatising state property. The result of this process was the emergence of the so-called 'oligarchic' groups.

Specific features of the Russian economy, like its monopolistic and highly centralised structure, have greatly facilitated the process of development of 'clan-corporate' capitalism in Russia. In Russia 80% of all taxes in the federal budget are paid by just 50 companies. At the same time, just 2% of companies account for 80% of the share market (Novoprudsky, 2000a). Such a high level of centralisation of wealth in the economy means that there is a very narrow circle of executives and property owners controlling the bulk of the Russian economy. This, together with the existing strong links between business and the government, has created fertile ground for the rapid development of oligarchic structures in post-Soviet Russia.

Another important factor that played a crucial role in the development of oligarchic relationships within contemporary Russia was the former Soviet *nomenklatura* system, which largely has managed to retain its control over the post-communist management system. In 1992 Dmitri Yuriev argued that the *nomenklatura*, as a special group of administration professionals united by common political and economic interests, managed to preserve 80 to 90 percent of Soviet positions at all levels of government in the areas of economic and land management.[11] The emergence and growth of the oligarchic groups in Russia was based upon their connections to Russian officials who in the early 1990s were substituting for the former USSR's apparatus. In contemporary Russia the level of proximity to federal or regional authorities became one of the most important determining factors of the influence of any particular group. On the other hand, as became evident at the 1995-96 elections, the state authorities in turn had become dependent on the oligarchs.

However, it is necessary to note that the formation that is usually called 'oligarchy' includes a variety of financial and political groupings which often have different agendas. In the strict sense of the word, this formation does not even deserve the term. It is rather common for an oligarchy to be an extremely amorphous entity with its various groups engaged in continuing struggles with each other. There are serious policy and economic interests that divide the oligarchs, for example the issue of economic protectionism. At the same time one of the major conflicts that divides the oligarchy is the conflict between the bureaucracy and the new manager-bankers: these two groups coexist, but they do not merge. In his recent study on the 'new Russian corporatism' Sergei Peregudov (1998, p.114) points to the dispersed and chaotic character of interaction between oligarchic groups and official authorities in Russia, which eventually forces elites to pursue mere egoistic and short-term goals.

Following Yeltsin's re-election in 1996 the oligarchs started to publicly demand 'rewards' for the support they had provided during the election, including provision by the state of unrestricted access to the property that still remained in the state ownership. These favours did not come automatically and in reality many oligarchs had to fight for them. The situation was further complicated by Yeltsin's health problems; this was when power in Russia became mostly concentrated in the hands of one political group within the Presidential Administration, i.e. the notorious 'Family'. Only one of oligarchs managed to get into this group: Boris Berezovsky (Dikun, 1999).

The August 1998 crisis was the last straw that broke the political and economic might of the Russian commercial banks controlled by oligarchs. For several months before the crisis the Kirienko government was making attempts to protect the rouble from devaluation, supporting bankers and helping them with their repayments on international borrowing.[12] The government was successful in securing an enormous amount of funds from abroad and in the 2-3 weeks before the crisis a significant part of this new credit (more than US\$ 6 billion) was sold by the Russian Central Bank to commercial banks in order to prevent these banks from going into liquidation. However, by mid-August the state currency reserves were exhausted and the government was forced to undertake a devaluation of the rouble. But this devaluation was carried out with little planning and even less responsibility; its immediate effect was chaos in the entire Russian economy. However, massive sales of currency by the Central Bank in the days preceding the crisis helped the oligarchs to at least save their own personal assets. Kirienko's government did nothing to protect individual customers, who lost access to their savings (only comprising 7% of total bank assets), which rapidly depreciated following the devaluation of the rouble. The crisis demonstrated that by the end of the 1990s Russia's oligarchic businesses had failed to become self-sustaining and could not survive without continuing governmental support.

Thus, it would be right to say that most of the recent discussions about the overall dominance of oligarchs in Russian political and economic life have not been well grounded. In practice, their influence has turned out to be much more limited than was thought at the time. In the late Yeltsin period the oligarchs were a small group of seven people, all of whom had made a large part of their fortune through the servicing of state accounts in the commercial banks they controlled. However, with the collapse of the system of Russian commercial banks in 1998, a majority of the oligarchs failed to recover much of the economic control and political influence they had earlier enjoyed.

Oligarchs Come and Go

In this section I will examine more closely what happened to the businessmen who used to be called oligarchs. On the of the seven oligarchs, Vladimir Vinogradov, who used to be the head of one of the largest commercial banks in Russia, Inkombank, was ousted by his partners from business, while in 1999 the bank in which he personally held 8% of shares was declared insolvent.[13] SBS-Agro, a bank headed by another oligarch, Aleksandr Smolensky, was also declared bankrupt. Smolensky, however, managed to preserve control over several companies that were earlier controlled by his bank. Russian state authorities recently opened a criminal investigation into Smolensky's activities.[14]

Boris Berezovsky was the only one of the oligarchs who was not engaged in the commercial banking business on a large scale. In 1999 he was sacked from his post as Executive Secretary of the Commonwealth of Independent States (CIS).[15] Later he was accused of breaking the law while pursuing business activities, including money-laundering operations that used the money and accounts of the Russian national air carrier, Aeroflot.[16] But in the last months of Yeltsin's rule Berezovsky managed to secure the support of the Kremlin grouping, the 'Family', and expanded his influence in the mass media. He established his control over the *Kommersant* newspaper and channel 'TV-6'. Criminal proceedings against him were stopped and in the December 1999 parliamentary elections he was even elected to the lower house of the Russian Parliament (the State Duma) as a representative of a tiny Caucasian republic of Karachaevo-Cherkessia. In recent months Berezovsky has announced that he is creating a new Russian media holding.[17]

Another oligarch, Vladimir Gusinsky, had established one of the most powerful media holdings in Russia, 'Media-Most'. This controls the only national independent TV channel NTV. With the help of the Moscow government he managed to save his Most-Bank from bankruptcy in 1998. When he later became involved in the power struggle between the Kremlin and Moscow mayor Luzhkov the state-owned Vneshekonombank refused to restructure Most-Bank's debts of US$42.2 million. This was followed by a series of other state actions against his holding, including a search of 'Media-Most' headquarters in May 2000 by a joint team of investigators from the FSB, the Procurator-General's office and the Taxation police.[18] In a court ruling later these actions were characterised as illegal. That, however, did not stop the state authorities from applying further pressure. In June 2000 Gusinsky was himself arrested and put in prison. He was released three days after without any charges being laid.

According to some observers, there are grounds for believing that the entire operation undertaken by the state against Gusinsky and his 'Media-Most' holding were aimed at transferring the control of his NTV channel to the state. At the time of writing, in September 2000, the state-controlled gas monopoly Gazprom was in possession of 14% of 'Media-Most' shares. However, in addition to that, the gas-producing giant also controlled two packages of shares equal to 40% of Media-Most. Gazprom received these packages as collateral for loan guarantees that it provided on behalf of 'Media-Most' to Credit Swiss-First Boston bank. Thus, in practice a total of 94% of shares of Gusinsky's media holding were controlled by Gazprom and its Chairman, Rem Vyakhirev. Moreover, 'Media-Most' itself owes US$211 million to Gazprom.[19] It is no surprise that the state, which owns Gazprom, has attempted to convert these 'Media-Most' debts into a real influence over the holding. In September 2000, at the time of writing, Alfred Kokh, the head of the 'Gazprom-Media' company which was specifically created with the task of managing media assets that belong to Gazprom (including the NTV channel and 'Media-Most' shares), was engaged in a series of negotiations on the issue of transferring part of 'Media-Most' shares in repayment of the media holding's debt.

The criminal case against Gusinsky was closed on the 26th July 2000. Six days before that it was announced that an agreement had been signed between Alfred Kokh and Vladimir Gusinsky, under which Gazprom had de facto established its control over 'Media-Most'. The Russian Press Minister, Mikhail Lesin, personally supervised this deal and also provided guarantees to Gusinsky that no further legal action would be taken against him.[20] But when on 9 September Vladimir Gusinsky publicly announced that he viewed the deal as one made under pressure, it became clear that he was not going to fulfil it. The criminal investigation against him was immediately reopened, while the Procurator's office put an arrest on the stocks of 'Media-Most' and its affiliated companies. While at first sight this story looks like a struggle for property control between a private company and the state, some observers emphasize that this is in fact a political issue. There is plenty of evidence pointing to direct pressures coming from the Kremlin, as the 'Family' attempts to effectively destroy the independence of Gusinsky's media holding in an effort to prevent any further criticisms of the Kremlin grouping (Bovt, 2000).

The fifth oligarch, Vladimir Potanin, was one of those closest to reformists who had been in the Russian government and was himself part of the government in 1996-1997. During the 1998 crisis Potanin's Uneximbank transferred a large part of its funds to an affiliated Rosbank, leaving only the shell of the business. In mid-2000, after the Russian Central Bank restored its banking license, Uneximbank announced its merger with Rosbank through an exchange of shares with Rosbank shares.[21] Potanin's banks also managed to maintain their control over the largest group of companies in Russia. These include the 'Norilsk Nickel' joint stock company, the Novolipetsk Metallurgy Plant and the 'Perm Motors' joint stock company. These three companies together have a combined share of about 7% of gross Russian exports. It seems that

Potanin's holding will also be able to retain its control over the ailing oil company Sidanko (Pravosudov, 2000).

Despite the fact that the 1998 crisis only marginally affected Potanin's business interests and influence, in the attack on oligarchs launched from Kremlin in 1999-2000 Vladimir Potanin is often seen as the second target after Gusinsky. In July 2000 it was announced by the Office of the Procurator General that Alfred Kokh, the former head of the State Property Committee and an important member of the Anatoly Chubais 'team' in the Kremlin, had received bribes in relation to his organisation of the privatisation auction of 'Norilsk Nickel', the world's third largest producer of non-ferrous metals with a global market share of about 22%. The auction was organised in such a way that the Uneximbank-Interros financial group (controlled by Potanin) managed to establish its control over the company for an exceptionally low price.[22] According to the investigation team, the support from Kokh enabled Potanin's Uneximbank to obtain 38% of shares in the company at a price that was US$140 million lower than the market price. The Office of Procurator General demanded that this sum be paid back to the state budget.[23]

The sixth of the oligarchs, Mikhail Khodorkovsky, became prominent as the head of a large commercial bank Menatep. However, this bank did not survive the August 1998 crisis and went into liquidation. But an affiliated company of Menatep, the oil company Yukos, has continued its operations and is doing well, particularly because of the recent increase in world oil prices. In September 2000 Yukos finalised its takeover of the Eastern-Siberian Oil and Gas Company (ESOGC) through buying a 19.9% stake in it (Davydova and Manvelov, 2000). In previous months companies controlled by Yukos had already acquired a controlling share in ESOGC and by the end of 2000 the company should be fully integrated into the organisational structure of Yukos. ESOGC explores for and produces crude oil in the Yurubcheno-Takhomsky oil and gas zone of Krasnoyarsk region in Eastern Siberia. This zone contains about 700 million tons of oil reserves and has a significant amount of natural gas. The Eastern Oil Company, a Yukos affiliate, together with Slavneft are the main producers of crude oil in the area. A takeover of ESOGC will allow Yukos to significantly expand its influence in one of the most oil-rich areas of Russia, making Khodorkovsky one of the most successful Russian oligarchs in the post-crisis period.

The last of the former seven oligarchs was Mikhail Fridman, whose Alfa-Bank survived the 1998 financial collapse without many losses, mainly due to the fact that the bank was significantly less dependent on servicing budgetary funds than the other leading Russian commercial banks. In the post-crisis period Alfa-Bank received much broader access to state funds and with the election of the new Russian president the bank seems to have become the Kremlin's new 'court bank'.[24]

The last months of Yeltsin's rule and the rise of Putin were accompanied by the inclusion of new people in the oligarch group. For example, one newcomer is Roman Abramovich, who is Boris Berezovsky's partner in the oil company Sibneft. In early 2000 he was thought to have the same influence as Berezovsky. At the beginning of 1999 Roman Abramovich managed to organize a scheme through which Sibneft stocks were exchanged on a non-equivalent basis (one to four and one to eight) for the stocks of its affiliates. This 'technical' operation reduced the government share in Sibneft to less than 10%.[25]

The rise of Abramovich signifies an important development in the evolution of Russian oligarchic capitalism. If in the earlier years the Kremlin group was exercising its influence through the control or supervision of other business groups or individual oligarchs, in the early 21st century this group has started to acquire business interests of its own. This process was facilitated by the fact that Anatoly Chubais, leader of the 'reformist' group that virtually made-up the Russian government throughout the Yeltsin period, left the government in the late 1990s and transformed himself into a 'normal' oligarch. He did this by securing control over the Russian electricity monopoly, UES.

In the recent months there have also been two other newcomers to the group of Russia's business tycoons. These were Rem Vyakhirev of Gazprom and Vagit Alikperov of Lukoil. In previous years the two were never considered part of the notorious oligarch group of the 'seven bankers'. Moreover, Vyakhirev actually openly demonstrates his dislike for political struggles and has publicly proclaimed that the stable development of Gazprom is his only policy priority. These declarations, however, mask the fact that Gazprom brings in one-third of government revenues, which inevitably makes Mr Vyakhirev a very important figure in the modern Russian ruling elite. Recent moves by Gazprom towards increasing its control over the mass media, as described above, also contradict these statements. As in the case with Vyakhirev, the mere fact that Mr Alikperov heads Russia's largest oil company also makes him one of the leading players in Russian politics.

An updated list of the Russian oligarchs in 2000 can easily be compiled from their signatures on the letter published on 14 June that year and addressed to the Prosecutor General. The letter called for the release of

Vladimir Gusinsky from custody and the signatories included V.Potanin, A.Chubais, V.Lisin, M.Fridman, P.Aven, V.Vekselberg, K.Benukidze, M.Khodorkovsky, A.Karachinsky, A.Kokh, A.Mordashev, V.Yevtushenkov, V.Maschitsky, Ye.Shvidler, R.Vyakhirev and O.Kiselev. Understandably, the list did not include Gusinsky himself. While Sibneft president Yevgeny Shvidler did sign the letter, the two people who control his company, Berezovsky and Abramovich, were not among signatories. As was widely reported in the Russian press in mid-2000 it was actually Berezovsky who was considered to be the main initiator of Gusinsky's arrest.

Vladimir Potanin, Anatoly Chubais, Mikhail Fridman, Petr Aven, Mikhail Khodorkovsky as well as Viktor Yevtushenkov and Rem Vyakhirev are often mentioned in the Russian media as being among the leading 'oligarchs', either as members of the group of 'seven bankers' or just as having an equal influence. The other signatories included businessmen who are little mentioned in the mass media but who have significant political influence and can be included in the group of 'oligarchs'. These are, in particular, the Chairman of the Board of the Novolipetsk Metallurgy Complex V.Lisin; the head of the large aluminium producer, SUAL, V.Vekselberg; the General Director of the Urals Machinery Plant K.Benukidze; the president of the International Business Systems Group, a partner of Dell Computer Corporation, A.Karachinsky; the General Director of Vympelcom, a large company in communications, L.Zimin; A.Kokh of 'Gazprom-Media'; A.Mordashev, General Director of the Northern Steel Plant; the president of the Rosinvestneft Group, a crude oil-producing company, V.Maschitsky; and the president of Impexbank O.Kiselev. Although drawing up a full list of all Russian oligarchs is rather a difficult task, the above listing gives a picture of who some of the most important of these people are.

In general, the post-crisis developments in Russia over the last two years have lead to a significant decline in the almost absolute influence that the oligarchs had enjoyed during most of the 1990s. Five of the initial seven business tycoons are no longer actively engaged in politics. Moreover, if in the early years of Russia's post-communist development politicians were often seeking the support of the oligarchs, nowadays it is the oligarchs that seek support from the authorities and try to demonstrate their loyalty to the state. The explanation is simple: in modern Russia businesses continue to depend greatly on the state while their leaders are often afraid of authorities. This is because the economic environment in Russia is still more defined by the personal inclinations of the national leader and his appointees in the government, rather than by the rule of law. Even if they provide politicians with substantial funding Russian businessmen continue to be in an inferior position to state officials. In the words of one of Russian commentator, this new pattern of relations between the government and business that has emerged in 2000 can be summarised by the following phrase: 'What is good for Putin is good for business' (Novoprudsky, 2000b). Thus, the dominant role that was played by the state (in a direct or indirect way, legally or through breaking the law) in the creation and development of all large Russian businesses has lead to the appearance of a specific form of Russian capitalism and has prevented Russian businessmen from organising themselves into an alternative and independent source of power.

Consolidation of the Ruling Elite around the Kremlin Grouping

Despite the political weakness of the so-called 'oligarchs', Russia in 2000 did see a number of attempts aimed at consolidating the unity of its ruling elite. If successful, this process could lead to the creation of a real oligarchy in Russia, where several people determine all the major developments in the country. A major feature of this new development would be the desire and ability of a new oligarchic circle to absorb some of the most important representatives of the old *nomenklatura*, private and state-owned businesses, the secret services and the military. The main initiator of this process was the Kremlin's 'Family' and so far it has been quite successful in its attempt.

Although the notion of the 'Family' comes from the closeness of its members to the real family of Russia's first president, Boris Yeltsin, it is not made up exclusively of members of Yeltsin's household. Strictly speaking, Yeltsin's daughter Tatyana Dyachenko is the only representative of Yeltsin's family in the group. All the others are former favourites and colleagues of Yeltsin. It was reported that on some occasions Yeltsin's wife Naina interfered in decision-making, but apparently she always had a very limited influence; for a number of years Tatyana was the real leader of the grouping. Two other important members were Valentin Yumashev, who received the informal 'title' of Yeltsin's adopted son, and Aleksandr Voloshin, who joined the group in the late 1990s and who served as the head of Presidential Administration under Yeltsin and continued in the post under Putin. This 'trio' forms the basis of the 'Family'. Reportedly, all others depend on this trio. This includes Boris Berezovsky, who apparently lost his influence within the group because of the scandal involving Aeroflot, which is headed by Yeltsin's son-in-law Valery Okulov.

A new member of the 'Family' group is Roman Abramovich, who has managed to get a leading position within a very short time. In the spring of 1999, during the fierce struggles between the 'Family' and Procurator General Yuri Skuratov, who at the time was trying to pursue a criminal investigation into the activities of some of the members of the group, the 'Family' received its newest member, the then FSB Director and Secretary of the Security Council Vladimir Putin. At the time Putin was characterised as 'stubborn, purposeful and loyal to the team' (Dikun, 1999). Another member of the 'Family', Anatoly Chubais, had recently lost a lot of his earlier influence, but he remained a person whose advice was always valued by Yeltsin. Chubais was usually called to the scene in critical moments. Although in mid-2000 there were signs that his position as head of the UES electricity monopoly was coming under increased scrutiny, it was still too early to conclude that his political role has diminished.

It was President Yeltsin himself who drew the boundaries of how far the 'Family' could intervene in decision-making and in what areas. While the 'Family' had a very low influence in military or foreign policy-making, in economic issues the authority of the 'Family' easily competed with that of the Russian government.

The origins of the rise of this and other 'clan-type' political groupings in modern Russia can be traced back to the 1993 Russian constitution. This constitution was rather authoritarian in nature and was drawn up mainly as a tool for political struggle that Yeltsin could use against his current and future rivals. It gave the president wide powers and responsibilities, which inevitably had to be transferred to a third body. Memories of past confrontations and the fear of losing his grip on power discouraged Yeltsin from transferring part of his absolute power to the parliament, the government or the Constitutional Court. Instead, what appeared was the so-called 'collective Yeltsin' represented by the president himself, along with the inner circle of his favourites. At first these favourites included Burbulis and Poltoranin, then Korzhakov, Ilyushin and Barsukov. It was after the 1996 presidential election that the 'Family' finally replaced the previous groups of favourites. The names of the favourites might have changed but the nature of the phenomenon has remained the same.

From 1996 this Kremlin grouping was concerned with the need to find a suitable successor to the ailing Yeltsin. It was then that the 'Family' started to actively build up its financial base. A recent independent investigation has found, for example, that the mass capital outflow from

Russia is actually being controlled by a group of powerful Kremlin insiders.[26] Aleksandr Mamut, the head of the Board of MDM-Bank and also a member of the 'Family', is closely connected with Tatyana Dyachenko, Valentin Yumashev and Roman Abramovich, is playing a key role in capital export. Although he always keeps a low public profile, Mamut is considered a very powerful person. For instance, recently channel NTV revealed that it was Mamut who had initiated the removal of Dmitri Saveliev from the executive office of the Transneft, Russia's monopolist in the field of oil transportation. Aleksandr Mamut is a son of a professor at Moscow State University and is married to the ex-wife of Andrei Brezhnev, grandson of the late Soviet communist leader Leonid Brezhnev. MDM-bank, which Mamut controls, is a project financing company and supervises the allocation of World Bank funds. Mamut also controls another financial company, Sobibank. He is known to have close and friendly relations with Alfa-Bank, which is controlled by one of the seven oligarchs Mikhail Fridman. The three banks together - MDM-bank, Sobibank and Alfa-bank - have in their deposit accounts approximately half of the money belonging to the State Customs Committee. In addition to its ability to influence the appointment of the head of the Customs Committee, this direct control of the Committee's accounts gives the 'Family' a very strong lever of control over Russia's exports and imports.

It is in this context of the continuing struggles to control Russia's diminishing financial resources that one should view recent attacks against oligarchs. In July 2000 Vagit Alikperov was the third 'oligarch', following Gusinsky and Potanin, to find himself under pressure from the state. This time accusations of fraud came from the Federal Tax Police, they announced that Alikperov's Lukoil company was guilty of tax evasion and had not paid the federal budget dozens of millions of dollars. While some years ago Lukoil received an official title as a 'Good Taxpayer', and was even awarded a prize, the recent audit suggests that in 1998-1999 the company managed to evade taxes via receipt of value added tax rebates under the pretext of false export of oil products. [27]

Indeed, Russian business is known to be one of the most corrupt and probably the least law obeying in the world. On the other hand, the Russian state has to carry a great deal of responsibility for creating this criminal environment. It provides draconian, and at the same time contradictory and extremely obscure business legislation, as well as having corrupt and inconsistent practices in dealing with business. Moreover, in its attempts to implement justice the state has acted very selectively. While some 'oligarchs', who for this or any other reason have fallen out of favour, suddenly find themselves prosecuted by the state, others, still in favour, have enjoyed almost total immunity from the law.

In conclusion, I would like to emphasize that in my view it was not by mere chance that Yeltsin decided to appoint Vladimir Putin as his successor. In the post-crisis period all earlier candidates in this role had connections with the Russian or Soviet secret services. If Russian developments in the future were to take a critical turn, the ruling elite could easily sacrifice democracy altogether or whatever democratic façade Russia still has. Democracy, or rather Russia's pseudo-democracy, has performed its role in masking the real outcomes of privatisation, it has helped to exchange the political power of the *nomenklatura* for property rights and to establish oligarchic control over the economy. Now democracy is no longer needed. What Russia's real 'oligarchy' needs is safety and the security for its capital, and protection from the millions of frustrated people who were impoverished and deceived during the so-called 'reforms'. The very nature of the oligarchy, as an exploitative but not a development and asset-increasing force, is an obstacle to any further extensive expansion of new 'oligarchic' groups. This means that the current 'oligarchs' will inevitably continue to clash with each other in competition for scarce national assets. These groups will increasingly feel the need for a 'supreme referee' to whom they can appeal and who can guarantee a certain order within the country. Russian political commentator Boris Kagarlitsky (2000) argues that it is the possibility of the establishment of an oligarchic state through future reforms that poses the real threat to Russia's democratic development. While in the past many observers expected and feared a possible dictatorship in Russia coming from the 'left', as a result of the return to communism, it is the dictatorship of the 'right' that has more chance today of becoming Russia's next reality.

Notes

1   For example, Malle (2000, p.6) wrote: 'What is worrying is the perception among Russians that petty politics, the formation of inner circles of power and sordid alliances are the main causes of Russian problems ... In my view, these perceptions are highly questionable ...'.
2   *Central Europe Review*, vol.2, no.26, 3 July, 2000 (http://www.ce-review.org/00/26/books26_vaknin).
3   *Novaya Gazeta*, 22 December, 1999.
4   'Vybory Presidenta RF priznany sostoyavshimisya', *Elections.ru*, 5 April, 2000.
5   According to the last KGB Chairman, Vladimir Kryuchkov, this position was a mere sinecure, one of many others used by the KGB to provide its officers with sources of

additional income. Kryuchkov told a correspondent of *Moscow News* that Putin did not serve in the intelligence service and was an officer of other department (so-called the Department for the Security of the Constitutional Regime, which played the role of political police). This is why, upon returning from the GDR, Putin, who did not achieve any remarkable results, was removed from active duty and joined the reserve force of KGB (Nikitinsky and Shpakov, 2000).

6   'V 1990 godu Putin obvinyalsya v korruptsii', *Lenta.ru,* 13 January, 2000 (http://www.lenta.ru).

7   The Russian notion of 'political technologies' used in a political context refers to what is more commonly known in the West as 'technologies of political control'.

8   See for example Lidia Andrusenko, 'President ili tsar?', *Nezavisimaya gazeta,* 1 February, 2000.

9   For more on 'Yeltsinism' see Tsuladze, 2000.

10   For example, the conflict between the Kremlin and Moscow Mayor Luzhkov, the establishment and rapid rise to power of the Unity movement, the two election campaigns of 1999 and 2000.

11   *Rossiiskaya gazeta*, 4 March, 1992.

12   In my view, one of the best analyses of Russia's 1998 crisis is that was published recently by Andrei Illarionov, Director of the Institute of Economic Analysis and economic adviser to the President. See Illarionov, 2000.

13   Aleksandr Persikov, 'Kak rossiiskiye oligarkhi proveli 1999 god', *Komsomolskaya Pravda,* 25 December, 1999.

14   Alexey Zhuravlev, 'Pomenyaet li Aleksandr Smolensky zamok v Vene na kameru v "Matrosskoi tishine"', *Argumenty i fakty,* 14 April, 1999.

15   'Otstavka B.Berezovskogo', *Polit.ru Monitor,* 5 March, 1999 (http://www.polit.ru/ monitor/99/0399-1/050399-1.htm#snos3).

16   'Priglasheniye   na   kazn'',   *Profil',*   No.13   (135),   12   April,   1999 (http://www.profil.orc.ru/koi/archive/n135/hero.html).

17   Mila Kuzina, 'Berezovskomu ne dayut stroit Media Kholding', *Gazeta.Ru,* 27 July, 2000.

18   Pavel Zimin, 'Shagi komandora', *Utro.ru,* 6 July, 2000.

19   'Gusinskiy peredumal prodavat "Media-Most"', *Gazeta.Ru,* 9 September, 2000.

20   This was reported in 'Khronika tonuschego kholdinga', *Izvestia,* 20 September, 2000.

21   Nils Iogansen in *Izvestia,* 19 September, 2000.

22   'Prokuratura Moskvy osparivaet prodazhu Norilskogo Nikelya', *Lenta.Ru,* 20 June, 2000.

23   'Prokuratura sobiraetsya peresmotret' rezul'taty zalogovykh auktsionov', *Lenta.Ru,* 21 June, 2000.

24   '"Alfa" shturmuyet Kreml'', *APN.Ru,* 26 April, 2000.

25   The Joint Stock Company Sibneft was established under a 1995 presidential decree. At the time the controlling share of 51% was left with the government. The company consists of four oil-producing and oil-processing companies: Omsk Refinery, Omsknefteproduct, Noyabrskneftegaz and Noyabrskneftegazgeofizika. The major production unit is Omsk Refinery. In 1998 Sibneft produced 17.32 million tons of crude oil. On 1 January 1999 the Joint Stock Company Sibneft had 1837 stockholders, but just four months later, on 6 April 1999, the figure had already reached 5840. When, at the annual meeting of stockholders on 29 June 1999, government representatives were not elected to the new management board, the state totally lost its control over the company ownership. The major stockholders were the Financial Oil

Corporation Ltd. (46%), SINS Firm Ltd. (14%), Rifan Oil Ltd. (10%) and Dart Management (5%). However, despite this official listing of corporate control over its shares it is believed that the real owners of Sibneft are Roman Abramovich (who controls more than 40% of shares) and Boris Berezovsky (30%). The President of Sibneft is Yevgeny Shvidler and Chairman of Board of Directors is Konstantin Potapov (Politkovskaya, 1999).

26   This was a newspaper investigation based on information received from sources in the Government, the Presidential Administration, the State Customs Committee, and the Federal Tax Police. See 'Kto i kak organizovyvaet ottok kapitala iz Rossii?', *Gazeta.Ru*, 4 October 1999 (http://www.gazeta.ru).

27   *Lenta.ru*, 11 July, 2000.

References

Babasyan, N. (2000), 'Semiya otpravila Yeltsina v otsatvku', *Deadline.ru* (http://archive.deadline.ru/babas/bab991231.asp).

Belotserkovsky, V. (2000), 'Na kogo pokhozh Stalin?', *Nezavisimaya gazeta*, 29 January.

Bovt, G. (2000), 'Va-bank', *Izvestia*, 20 September.

Davydova, M. and Manvelov, N. (2000), 'Yukos idet na vostok', *Segodnya*, 25 September.

Dikun, Ye. (1999), 'Vsya kremlevskaya rodnya', *Obschaya gazeta*, no.29, 22 July.

Golovkov, A. (2000), 'Vtoroi president Rossii', *Nezavisimaya gazeta*, 28 March.

Gorbachev, M. (2000), 'Lyudi bez printsipov', *Nezavisimaya gazeta*, 15 January.

Illarionov, A. (2000), 'Mify i uroki avgustovskogo krizisa', *Polit.ru*, 13 and 19 April (http://www.polit.ru).

Kagarlitsky, B. (2000), 'Pereraspredeleniye mechty: pochemy oligarkhi budut zashishat' ne demokratiyu, a tol'ko sobstvennost'', *Obschaya gazeta*, 24 February.

Malle, S. (1999), 'Foreword', in V.Tikhomirov (ed.), *Anatomy of the 1998 Russian Crisis*, CERC, Melbourne, pp.1-8.

Nikitinsky, L. and Shpakov, Yu. (2000), 'Putin v razvedke: "zavklubom" ili "superagent"', *Moskovskie novosti*, 25 January.

Novoprudsky, S. (2000a), 'U nas vsyakii mozhet stat' Abramovichem', *Izvestia*, 27 April.

Novoprudsky, S. (2000b), 'Unizhayushiisya kapitalizm', *Izvestia*, 22 March.

Peregudov, S.P. (1998), 'Novyi Rossiiskii korporativizm: ot byurokraticheskogo k oligarkhicheskomu?', *Polis*, no.4.

Politkovskaya, A. (1999), 'Esli vraga nel'zya kupit', ego unichtozhayut', *Novaya gazeta*, 26 July.

Porfiriev, A. (2000), 'Pravilo silnoy ruki', *Segodnya*, 25 July.

Pravosudov, S. (2000), 'Hovard Mason: my ponimayem, chto biznes i vlast' v vashei strane tesno svyazany", *Nezavisimaya gazeta*, 20 June.

Roitman, L. (2000), 'Izbiratel' kak grazhdanin', *Radio svoboda*, 21 March (http://www.svoboda.org/programs/RT/2000/RT.032100.shtml).

Sharyi, A. (2000), 'Mozhno li provesti parallel' mezhdu Putinym i Leninym?', *Radio svoboda*, 26 March (http://www.svoboda.org/archive/elections2000/0300/ll.032600-22.shtml).

Timakova, N. (1998), 'Yeltsin vs. Yeltsin', *Intellectual Capital*, vol.2, no.46, 9-16 December.

Tretyakov, V. (1999), 'Stalin - eto nashe vsyo', *Nezavisimaya gazeta*, 22 December.

Tsuladze, A. (2000), 'Ot demokratii ostanetsya tol'ko forma', *Nezavisimaya gazeta,* 1 June.
Tsyganov, Yu. (1999), 'Political Background of the Economic Crisis in Russia', in
    V.Tikhomirov (ed.), *Anatomy of the 1998 Russian Crisis*, CERC, Melbourne, pp.259-94.
Voschanov, P. (2000), 'Yesli b Lubyanka mogla...', *Delovoi vtornik*, 21 September.

6 Russian Industrial Privatisation: Strategy and Outcome

STEPHEN FORTESCUE

Russia's industry is essentially privatised. Although the state retains a number of fully owned enterprises in particular 'strategic' sectors (the so-called 'unitary' enterprises) and not insignificant shareholdings in many other enterprises,[1] the great bulk of industrial assets are in private hands and the state is generally unable or unwilling to exercise even those ownership rights which it does possess (Fortescue, 1998b, p.2).

In this paper two major questions are posed: What sort of privatised industry is it? How is that outcome linked to the strategy and procedures followed in Russian industrial privatisation? To answer these questions involves an analysis of the privatisation programme, as well as an evaluation of the current state of Russian industry and its future prospects, particularly in terms of ownership and corporate governance.

What Sort of Privatised Industry Is It?

It would be hard to claim that Russian industry is performing well. The declines in output since the collapse of central planning have been spectacular, and any episodes of recovery weak and unsustained.[2] Although there has been a useful upturn since August 1998, there is considerable fear that it is an unsustainable consequence of the massive devaluation of the rouble that was part of the financial crisis of that month. Although explanations of poor performance can be found that are not directly related to privatisation - the abysmal state of enterprises and their product lines as they began transition, and poor fiscal and monetary conditions at the macro-level (Stuart and Panayotopolous, 1999; Slay, 1999) - problems of ownership and corporate governance have also been evident. Essentially, those who have found themselves in control of enterprises after privatisation have been unable or unwilling to adapt their enterprises sufficiently well to new conditions to provide significant growth.

To take the analysis further we need to bring a little more differentiation to our characterisation of Russian industry, necessarily brief here because of space and data limitations. The dismal national output figures can be put down to the very considerable number of enterprises which could be described bluntly as dysfunctional. Either they produce nothing and continue to exist purely on paper, or they produce minimal output and continue to exist thanks to indebtedness to the state, workforce and suppliers. [3]

Analysis of what determines whether enterprises fall into the dysfunctional category or not is a daunting but interesting task. [4] Sectoral and geographical location is very likely to play a role; chance, in the form of the qualities of owners and managers, is also likely to be a relevant factor. This author believes there is another factor, albeit one which at the moment cannot be claimed as much more than an unconfirmed hypothesis: that dysfunctional enterprises are likely to be owned or controlled by managers who have retained their posts from the Soviet period (for both biological and historical reasons they are likely to have gained their top-management positions under Gorbachev, rather than being the classic 'Red directors' of the Brezhnev period). They will have retained their places at the head of their enterprises through the privatisation process, with some sort of paternalistic 'social contract' with the workforce possibly being involved.

Such a hypothesis is supported on two grounds. Firstly, that Soviet-era managers are particularly unprepared to lead the adaptation of enterprises to new circumstances. Because Soviet-era managers remain in charge, enterprises are more or less doomed to failure in the market place. Part of the argument is that they are likely to be unprepared psychologically and in terms of training and experience, with their Soviet-era focus on production process and output being inappropriate in new conditions.

Beyond that, it is quite likely that a component part of their retention of control of the enterprise is a deal with or accommodation of the interests of the workforce and middle management. Option 2 privatisation, that form of privatisation that guaranteed workforces at least 51% of their enterprises, more often than not was implemented and manipulated by existing top management to their personal benefit. Nevertheless significant shareholdings were likely to be held by enterprise staff below the top management level, both rank-and-file workers and middle managers. These holdings are used to reinforce workplace relationships that were evident in the Soviet, particularly Gorbachev, period – low productivity work habits, employment security, and decentralisation of financial controls to middle management (Fortescue, 2000). None of these circumstances allow for the possibility of meaningful enterprise restructuring.

The second ground on which to suggest a link between retention of Soviet-era management and dysfunctional enterprises is that enterprises which have been left in the hands of old managers are likely to be enterprises in which no other investor has been able to recognise any potential. This is based on the author's belief, one which appears to be supported by the evidence, that no Soviet-era manager is able, over a period of time, to resist a challenger with a serious interest in the enterprise. In the end the old manager's political, financial and social resources are inadequate. This means that the dysfunctional enterprises are not just disadvantaged by having old managers in charge, but are probably also disadvantaged by the 'objective' circumstances in which they find themselves, whether it be sectoral or geographical location, age of plant, inappropriate product lines and technologies, etc.

The implication of the preceding discussion is that enterprises which are not controlled by Soviet-era managers are unlikely to be 'zombies'. The fact that someone else has gone to the trouble – usually considerable and even dangerous – to gain control indicates that the enterprise, in terms of the objective circumstances in which it is situated, has some potential for good performance. Further, it could be hypothesised that those new owners are likely to be more entrepreneurial and less wedded to old ways than their predecessors.

One would like to have quantitative data to support the claims made in the last few paragraphs. Unfortunately quantitative analysis of the link between enterprise control, ownership and performance is hard to come by and is fraught with a whole range of methodological and definitional problems. The initial focus in such analysis was on the comparative performance of state-owned and privatised enterprises. Although generally finding in favour of privatisation,[5] this does not address our concern, which is what form of private ownership has produced better results. One of the few surveys addressing that issue, of 321 enterprises across a range of sectors carried out by Earle and Estrin in 1994, found that although outsider-owned enterprises were more likely to restructure and enjoy higher productivity than worker-owned enterprises, management-owned enterprises performed even better (Earle and Estrin, 1996, p.15). That finding, as limited as it is, might appear to contradict our argument. In defence, the author can only point out that our immediate concern is not so much whether an enterprise is owned by managers or by outsiders and performs better or worse as a consequence,[6] but whether it is owned by Soviet-era managers or new owners. Some of the most dynamic industrial enterprises today are owned by their managers. However their youth and their method of gaining control ensure that they could not possibly be described as Soviet-era 'Red directors'. Indeed the role of such new owner-managers is a feature of post-privatisation developments well worthy of close attention (Fortescue, 1998a).

The Role of Privatisation: Strategy and Procedures

In the absence of applicable quantitative data, we have to rely on impressionistic evidence to support the suggestion that the retention of control of enterprises by their Soviet-era managers has not been beneficial for those enterprises in which it has occurred. Indeed many commentators believe the fact that so many Soviet-era managers have retained control to be one of the greatest failures of Russian industrial privatisation (McFaul, 1995). There is no doubt that the privatisation reformers were forced to allow workforce ownership as a concession to the management lobby. All early privatisation programmes, from Gorbachev's stillborn legislation, through the Shatalin-Yavlinsky '500 Days' programme, to the initial Russian legislation, had made no more than token gestures towards the workforce and management.[7] It was in the circumstances of 1992-93, when the management lobby was particularly powerful (not least because of the solid bloc of managers in the semi-freely elected Supreme Soviet), that Chubais was forced to include Option 2 in the privatisation procedures.

The original draft of the privatisation programme recognised workers' claims to ownership of the enterprises in which they worked in only a small way, granting workers 25% of shares, but non-voting shares, in their enterprise (Schleifer and Treisman, 1998, p.65). In the final legislation this was retained as Option 1. But the workers, and the managers who were taking their side on the matter, were not satisfied with a shareholding that would offer them no hope of control of or even a veto over corporate policy and therefore no guarantee that their jobs would be retained. They were able to extract from Chubais a major concession, a new privatisation option that allowed workers to forego the grant of non-voting shares and instead to buy at concessionary prices up to 51% of shares, with these shares having full voting rights.[8] It was clearly an option which offered workers full control of their enterprise, and one which over 70% of enterprise workforces took up (Blasi, Kroumova and Kruse, 1997, p.41).

The outcome was the management ownership that the critics of Option 2 had feared and predicted, often in the particularly damaging form of a 'social contract' relationship with the workforce.[9] Two comments are in order here. Firstly, the reformers ensured that, while they were forced into a tactical retreat in 1992-93, they retained the weapons necessary for a future advance, the most important of which was the full transferability of workforce shares. On occasions this meant that managers strengthened their positions by buying workers' shares; often it was outsiders who bought them. Determined outsiders could build up a good core holding by purchasing blocks of shares at voucher auctions and then through investment tenders. But they also had considerable success building those holdings to controlling levels by buying workforce shares, often by setting up vans outside factory gates.[10] That meant that enterprises in the second category identified above, those whose potential was recognised by outsiders, were not condemned to remain in management's hands, with in most cases a change in ownership control leading to the replacement of top managers (Fortescue, 1998b, pp.4-6).

The second point to be made is that the reformers could well have seen workforce/management ownership of enterprises in the first, dysfunctional category as a relatively desirable outcome. If it were recognised, as it surely was, that many Russian enterprises would not survive the market no matter who owned them,[11] then to leave them in the hands of those most directly affected by their fate, their workers and managers, was as good an option as any. The state would have more flexibility in the degree to which it provided or failed to provide 'socially oriented assistance' than if they remained in state hands, while it would be the market, not the fallible state, which would decide whether they would fall in the first or second categories. Under virtually all other approaches - reliance on greenfield enterprises, 'restructure before sale', and 'sell to the highest bidder' - those enterprises would have remained in state hands. They might not have been in any worse condition as a result, but the state would have been more responsible for them.

Russian industrial privatisation was a matter, therefore, of abandoning dysfunctional enterprises without potential to their fate. The strategy was based on a belief not just that many Russian enterprises were doomed under any circumstances but also that there was nothing the state could do about it. This belief was undoubtedly partly ideologically based; but it also had a degree of pragmatic realism about it.

Thus the state in effect abandoned a good proportion of Soviet-era industrial assets. Our focus in evaluating the privatisation programme therefore must shift to those enterprises in the second category, whose potential was recognised by new investors to the degree that they were prepared to engage in a struggle to gain ownership control. In a sense this is the true test of privatisation, because it is these enterprises that were seen as providing the basis for economic growth, at least from among existing industrial assets.

Ownership of these enterprises has been from the beginning and for many still is a matter of a struggle for control, the so-called *peredel sobstvennosti*. Initially that struggle for control took the form of a contest between old managers and newcomers, which as we have already suggested regularly ended in victory for the newcomers. The struggle usually took the form of attempts by managers to subvert the rights of outside shareholders, including those who had, or believed they had, majority or at least controlling holdings. The tactics included removing holdings from share registers, holding board or shareholder meetings without prior notice or having credentials commissions refusing to register shares for voting purposes, and pushing through new share issues to dilute opponents' holdings.[12] It should surprise no one that the same tactics are often used by new owners who have gained control against subsequent threats from newer challengers.

It was and is a situation in which there is very little room for a passive minority shareholder. Minority shareholders fear, with good reason, that they will not receive their fair share of the profits of the enterprise, because of asset stripping and dividend manipulation by those in control (Fortescue, 1998b, p.5). That is, an investor takes a minority interest only in the expectation of increasing it to a controlling level.[13] Those in control know that this is the intention of any outside investors and so do everything they can to frustrate them. The consequence is that owners are unable to use the equity markets to raise capital (share issues are not rare, but usually they are made to dilute the shareholdings of unwelcome investors rather than to raise capital) [14] and the share market is illiquid, undervalued and speculative.[15]

This has consequences for the type of capitalism that has been developing in Russian industry. The focus on corporate control and the consequent lack of access to equity markets for capital mean that on those occasions when enterprises look for outside investment, they look for a single strategic investor or debt financing. In the mid-1990s both were found at the same source, major financial institutions. These of course were not insurance companies, pension funds or even mutual funds; rather they were banks.

This was not what the designers of the privatisation programme initially wanted. They had demonstrated great suspicion of the involvement of financial institutions in the ownership of industrial assets, especially in conglomerate form, insisting on the break-up of the old industrial associations through production unit-level privatisation and the imposition of restrictions on the holdings of banks and holding companies (Fortescue, 1997, p.156). That suspicion was however almost certainly based on a fear of the resurrection of old Soviet ministry and *glavk*-type structures, not 'new' financial structures. When it became clear that a decentralised privatisation was not going to bring the investment and restructuring that Russian industry so desperately required, there was a ready willingness to turn to the 'strength in size' argument (Blasi, Kroumova and Kruse, 1997, p.74). It was a time of much earnest discussion in policy-making, lobbying and academic circles, both domestic and foreign, of the possibilities of the Japanese, Korean and German models.[16] Russian banks were building up considerable financial and political clout, not without the help and protection of the government.[17] As the rouble stabilised and their profit opportunities in currency transactions declined, the banks turned to industrial investment, a development the government welcomed even when it violated the restrictions on bank holdings.

The government's commitment to financial-industrial groups (FIGs) culminated with the shares-for-credit scheme of 1995, in which the state 'auctioned' its shareholdings in a number of major enterprises, mostly in the resource sector, in return for large credits. Although the shares were in theory to be held in trust until the credits were repaid, it was widely expected from the beginning and indeed occurred that the credits were not repaid and the shares were transferred to the full legal ownership of the credit providers. From the very beginning it seemed a bizarre procedure. When it became obvious that the 'auctions' were totally rigged in a most blatant way in favour of a very small group of highly favoured banks, the government's privatisation programme lost whatever remaining shreds of legitimacy it retained. An argument could perhaps have been made that it was necessary on economic efficiency grounds to transfer ownership to major commercial structures - the concept of 'financial-industrial groups' was in itself quite respectable at the time. However the blatant favouritism showed to particular groups within the commercial sector was hard to so justify. It is generally believed that the whole scheme, if not driven by purely corrupt financial motives, was essentially the purchase of political support by the presidential administration. It was a deal which led some of the most dedicated Western supporters of Russian economic reform to publicly express their disgust.[18]

One suspects that by this time the skin of Anatoly Chubais was thick enough to withstand the widespread condemnation of the shares-for-credit deal. But if he had any hopes of the deal beyond the purchase of political support, he must have disappointed by the failure of financial-industrial capitalism in economic terms. Indeed it would have to be described as one of the major disappointments of the privatisation programme as a whole, that new owners, particularly financial institutions, when they did finally gain control of Russian industrial assets, did not necessarily make better use of them than the old Red directors.

This is an issue that requires more detailed analysis than is possible here. But even before the August 1998 crisis there was considerable scepticism as to whether the Russian banks were strong enough to provide the required levels of investment to Russian industry. The situation obviously was not improved by the events of August 1998. There was no less scepticism with regard to the banks' strategic vision and managerial capacity (Fortescue, 1998a).

The failure of the FIG model exposed the almost total lack of an Anglo-US style institutional investor in Russia. The voucher investment funds were never a success (given the Czech experience perhaps thankfully), and there are simply no other institutions (Blommestein, 1998, pp.23, 30-1; Black, Kraakman and Tarassova, 1999, pp.57-63). For some privatisation insiders this has been seen as a crucial problem, and they call for priority to be given to the development of mutual funds and capital markets in general (Blasi, Kroumova and Kruse, 1997, pp.159-60).

Some non-FIG success stories can be found, although one has to be wary of the public relations expertise of the heroes of these stories. They range from such giants as Oleg Deripaska in the aluminium industry and Aleksei Mordashov in steel (Fortescue, 1998a), to smaller efforts such as the new entrepreneurs at the 'Vakhrushi' leather goods plant.[19] These are stories of entrepreneurs who have gained control of enterprises in their own right, not always in ways that would be approved of in corporate governance textbooks, but without relying on either Soviet-era stakeholder relationships or new financial structures. They have brought to their enterprises a tougher management approach, a degree of strategic vision, and even a degree of investment funding. For the moment this management-dominated form of capitalism, being a very different form of management dominance to that feared by the critics of Option 2, might be the best that Russia can hope for. It is after all not such a rare form of ownership in Western and particularly Asian capitalism, although it is admittedly one which raises major issues of sources of funding, succession, and controls over entrepreneurial owners when they reach the boundaries of good judgement.

Despite this possibly positive development, for this author it is one of the most telling outcomes of privatisation that a shift in ownership control from Soviet-era managers to new owners of seemingly quite different backgrounds and orientations has brought improvement but nothing approaching salvation. Some commentators express their disappointment in far stronger terms. Black, Kraakman and Tarassova, early supporters and indeed participants in the privatisation policy process, now describe it in the blackest terms, precisely because it is the new owners, not the would-be Soviet-era beneficiaries of the process, who have wrought such havoc. They note initial conditions that encouraged asset stripping by owners, including a confiscatory tax system and the separation of enterprise control and cash flow rights among many others, and then point out most tellingly that the behaviour becomes self-reinforcing. Enterprises are worth more to asset strippers, able and willing to extract 100% of the asset value of the enterprises for their personal benefit, than to honest investors wanting to run companies for the benefit of all shareholders. The dishonest investor is therefore prepared to outspend the honest one to obtain control, not just in terms of cash but also in terms of corrupt and even violent behaviour (Black, Kraakman and Tarassova, 1999, p.63).

Can or Should Privatisation be Reversed?

Russian privatisation has been subjected to extensive and bitter criticism. For this author, criticisms of the programme on the grounds that it handed control to Soviet-era managers and that it has failed to turn around the bulk of Russian industry are misplaced. Outsiders were able to gain control if they wanted to. It is unlikely that privatisation was ever expected or intended to turn around all Russian industry. More telling is the failure of new owners, taking over the most promising Russian enterprises, to achieve the desired results. Neither can one ignore that aspect of privatisation that has most cost it support among the Russian population - its all too obvious fraud, corruption and inequity.

Given the problems and controversies of privatisation, does Russia have the option of reversal? There are two arguments in favour. Firstly, that privatisation is inherently a bad thing, particularly in Russian conditions, and so the state should reassert its role in the ownership of industrial assets. Secondly, that privatisation in itself is not a bad thing, but that the Russian attempt at it was so botched that assets should be renationalised and then another attempt made.

One does not have to be an apologist for the Russian privatisation programme to find the first argument a worrying one. It would clearly represent a near total abandonment of economic reform. While the author is sufficiently reassured by President Putin's statements that privatisation will not be reversed not to feel that economic reform is under such fundamental threat, the techniques for the reversal of privatisation are there and being used, currently on an ad hoc basis. The first technique is the weakest. There have been constant calls, since privatisation first began, for the state to exercise more effective use of the ownership rights it still has through the possession of residual shareholdings in many enterprises. By now those shareholdings are too few and small to make much difference, but even so there is no evidence that the state and the agencies that represent it are in the slightest degree able and willing to play an effective ownership role.

That clearly raises big questions about how the state would cope with the governance of larger and indeed dominant shareholdings, if privatisation were truly reversed. Nevertheless there has been much talk, although relatively limited action, of having enterprises pay off their debts to the budget by transferring equity to the state (Nellis, 1999, p.10). Although that has not happened at federal level, there have been cases at regional level. Generally the greatest pressure for renationalisation has come at that level, with regional governments also using bankruptcy proceedings to get their representatives into enterprises as administrators.[20] They are then potentially in the position to take over the assets of liquidated enterprises.[21] They also simply apply crude administrative pressure to have enterprises cede them shares, whether in trust or full ownership.[22]

We have also seen in recent times an increased willingness of courts, presumably not acting purely on their own initiative, to reverse the privatisation of individual enterprises, on the grounds that correct procedures were not followed at the time of privatisation or that investment tender conditions had not been met. Often such court findings have involved the removal of major shareholdings from investors who were not involved in the original privatisation but had bought their shares subsequently. Clearly the scope for this form of re-nationalisation is enormous, since one imagines that a determined judge could find shortcomings in just about any privatisation that had ever occurred.

It should be noted, however, that the most notorious of these cases have been eventually reversed or some compromise arrived at.[23] Indeed one suspects that often the cases are more a Russian form of business negotiation than dedicated efforts at re-nationalisation.

Generally, it can be said that cases of re-nationalisation are scattered, usually controversial, and unlikely to lead to the sort of improved corporate performance that would encourage its wider application. To that extent, privatisation seems for the moment to be safe from reversal.

The cases of renationalisation just described are clearly not of the type that would be approved of by commentators such as Black and his colleagues, who call for the re-nationalisation and then prompt reprivatisation of some of the most corruptly privatised enterprises, accompanied ideally by some exemplary prosecutions. They do not sound, however, overly confident of the feasibility of their suggestion in current Russian conditions:

> [T]he reprivatization strategy makes sense only if the reprivatization will be more honest than the initial privatization and the new controllers will be more likely than the old ones to create value instead of strip assets. In Russia today, there is no basis for either of those beliefs (Black, Kraakman and Tarassova, 1999, p.69).

Questions need to be asked, moreover, not only about the ability of the state to find better new owners, but also about, firstly, the basis on which the re-nationalisations will take place, and, secondly, their effect on the psychological atmosphere among post-Soviet Russian capitalists. With regard to the first question, would firms be chosen for re-nationalisation on the basis of the degree of corruption involved in their privatisation or the degree of mismanagement and asset stripping since? Norilsk Nickel would appear to be a prime candidate on the first count, but perhaps not so under the second. The shares-for-credit deal that saw the nickel producer pass into the hands of Potanin's Interros group was one of the most notoriously rigged, yet the firm is clearly better run now than it was under its previous management. Black and his colleagues imply that they would not renationalise purely on the grounds of corrupt privatisation procedures. One of their key points is that the argument of the defenders of the shares-for-credit deals - that it does not matter how the enterprises were disposed of as long as they got effective new owners - is invalid. This is because the new owners are in fact ineffective. While there could well be a useful difference between illegal and incompetent running of enterprises, nevertheless to encourage the state to take over enterprises on the basis of poor performance appears undesirable, particularly in light of the outrageous abuse of existing bankruptcy procedures.

Black, Kraakman and Tarassova clearly have in mind selective re-nationalisations along with exemplary prosecutions, with it being made clear that they were not to be seen as establishing a general procedure to be used routinely. To the extent, therefore, that they would have an element of being 'for show', one wonders how much effect they would have on the business class. There is the added problem that no one in Russia today - probably in Russia ever - would believe that the selection of the victims was anything other than politically based. Even if the state genuinely searched for cases of gross corruption, asset stripping and incompetence, and renationalised and prosecuted on that basis, one suspects the popular reaction would be to assume that the victims had somehow fallen out of political favour and were paying the price, thereby reinforcing the view that the whole system is corrupt. Further, any move against even the most notorious of oligarchs is likely to raise fears of political repression among a sensitive population. A state genuinely following the advice of Black and his colleagues would clearly not choose Vladimir Gusinsky as its example. Nevertheless, the reaction to that recent case provides some clues to how even a better chosen example would be received.

The dangers of re-nationalisation, even of the carefully selected strategic kind recommended by Black, Kraakman and Tarassova, are considerable, and perhaps greater than are justified by the shortcomings, as real as they are, of privatisation. The condition of the major resource firms that were the main objects of the shares-for-credit deals is clearly a matter of major concern, not just, or so much, because of their relevance to our evaluation of privatisation, but because of their major place within the Russian economy. But their circumstances are very special, and perhaps should not be allowed to colour our evaluation of the privatisation programme as a whole. While privatisation has clearly had its ups and downs, the analysis in this paper suggests that it was a relatively well-thought out strategy, designed to drastically diminish the state's responsibility for the very many Russian industrial 'zombies'. It also provided the opportunity for enterprises with 'objective' potential to bring in new owners and managers and realise that potential.

The first task was always going to be, and is, a long and painful one. There are a large number of enterprises still owned by their workforce and management, primarily because no one else wants to buy them. They are generally moribund. The state has not abandoned them entirely: they still receive subsidies, albeit usually in the form of payments arrears to and subsidised prices from government instrumentalities, as well as tax arrears. The same subsidies are made available by regional governments, where there could also be more direct subsidies as well as assistance in arranging local sales and ensuring local inputs. But such assistance could be best described as a form of social welfare and certainly has no industrial development function. Occasionally an outsider suddenly recognises some potential in such a firm and moves in, by now usually without fuss; sometimes one is taken over by a competitor or link above or below in the input-output chain. But most will, one imagines, slowly disappear and as they do so each in their own small way contribute to the sectoral and geographical restructuring of Russian industry.

With regard to enterprises that have been taken over by new owners, as always one can find success stories and egregious failures. Generally, though, the outcome has been disappointing. While enterprises perhaps perform better than they would have if they had remained in the hands of the state or old management, clearly most do not perform well enough to bring Russia genuine growth and competitiveness, either in domestic or international markets. The reasons are myriad but include, beyond simple dishonesty, an orientation towards enterprise control which militates against the recognition of minority shareholder rights, a failure to attract foreign investment, and a consequent lack of investment funds and advanced management know-how.

Russian industry is still very unlike the Anglo-US model, lacking institutional owners and with no more than the glimmerings of a professional managerial class. The alternative FIG model never worked well and was struck a crippling blow by the August 1998 crisis. The most dynamic element of privatised Russian industry are entrepreneurs who find it in Russian conditions essential to hold tightly in their own hands both ownership and management functions. In those circumstances one can only hope that the quantity and quality of entrepreneurial owners and the ownership they exercise will improve.

Notes

1   For some data on the state's holdings, see Fortescue, 1998b, p.2.
2   For figures for January 1997 to September 1999, see OECD, 2000, p.47. Earlier data can be seen in OECD, 1997, p.29, and Tikhomirov, 2000a, p.221.
3   Daniel Treisman (1998, p.263) refers to 'zombies', 'inefficient enterprises, starved of cash or any long-term hope of improvement, somehow managing to hang on in a strange limbo.' It would appear that over half Russian industrial enterprises have negative cash flows (Djankov, 1999, pp.130-31; Tikhomirov, 2000a, pp.224-6).
4   The author has attempted to do so for the mining and metals sector in a paper, presented to the 6th ICCEES World Congress (Fortescue, 2000).
5   For a summary of panel data devoted to that issue, see Fortescue, 1998b, pp.8-9. To the surveys listed there can be added the extensive analysis in Brown and Earle, 2000.
6   By outsiders I mean investors from outside the enterprise, whether domestic or foreign. Given the general lack of foreign investment in Russian industry, they are highly likely to be domestic investors.
7   On the Gorbachev and early Russian legislation, see Fortescue, 1992, pp.33-9. The '500 Days' Programme is contained in *Perekhod k rynku*, Moscow, 1990.
8   Option 2 was described by Petr Filippov, one of the privatisation planners, as a concession that had to be made if privatisation were to proceed at all. Quoted in Nelson and Kuzes, 1995, pp.136-7.
9   Some commentators have seen the positive sides of such relationships, but their hopes have not been sustained in the long term. See Veronika Kabalina's (1996) account of management/workforce ownership of the Lebedinsk Ore Enrichment Combine, before the combine's performance deteriorated and the general director was replaced by a new owner, the bank 'Rossiiskii kredit'.
10   It should not be thought that *this* was an easy process. For an account of the adventures of the representatives of Kakha Benukidze's NIPEK as they travelled beyond the Arctic Circle to buy up the last shares needed to get control of an oil exploration enterprise, see *Kommersant*, 30 May, 1995, p.5.
11   For evidence that Chubais understood this, see Nelson and Kuzes, 1995, p.158. See also the comments of other privatisation insiders in Blasi et al, 1997, pp.177-8.
12   For references to a whole series of examples, see Fortescue, 1998b, p.6.
13   The first stage is to get 25%+1, which is sufficient to block amendments to the articles of association; the ultimate goal is 75%+1, in order to be able to make those

amendments without hindrance. For a summary of Russian corporate governance legislation, see Fortescue, 1998b, pp.6-7.

14   For examples, see Fortescue, 1998b, footnote 52.

15   For an account of how poor corporate governance practices encourage investors to work towards full control, with in the Russian case full control meaning a very substantial holding, see Aukutsionek, Kapelushnikov, Filatotchev and Zhukov, 1998, pp.498, 502.

16   Fortescue, 1997, pp.26-32; *Finansovo-promyshlennye gruppy i konglomeraty v ekonomike i politike sovremennoi Rossii*, Tsentr politicheskikh tekhnologii, Moscow, 1997. For a discussion of the desirability of bank equity holdings, see Dittus and Prowse, 1996, chapter 2. For a much briefer outline of the issues, see Fortescue, 1998b, p.8.

17   Such help took the form of restrictions on the activities of foreign banks in Russia, and the nomination of favoured banks as 'agent banks' through which the government's cash flowed.

18   John Nellis (1999, p.9) cites Jeffrey Sachs as declaring at a Washington presentation his belief that the Russian government should renationalise the resource firms that had been wrongly privatised. He clearly had in mind those privatised through the shares-for-credit deal.

19   *Ekspert*, 1 November, 1999, pp.32-6.

20   Often the enterprises' insolvency has been deliberately engineered, usually by having locally controlled utilities charge excessively high prices. Aman Tuleev, governor of Kemerovo region, used this approach in classic style to remove the Moscow investment bank MIKOM from control of the Novokuznetsk Aluminium Factory. *Kommersant*, 20 January, 2000, p.5.

21   If, after a period of external administration, the conclusion is reached by the court that the enterprise cannot be salvaged, it is liquidated, i.e. its assets are sold.

22   *Kommersant*, 10 September, 1998, p.4; *Profil'*, 12 October, 1998, p.32; East West Institute, *Russian Regional Report*, vol.4, no.3, 28 January, 1999.

23   One of the most notorious cases was the Lomonosov Porcelain Factory, in which the US investment group KKR was stripped of its shares. That decision was subsequently reversed. 'Foreign investors regain ownership of Lomonosov', East West Institute, *Russian Regional Report*, vol.5, no.9, 9 March, 2000.

References

Aukutsionek, S., Kapelushnikov, R., Filatotchev, I. and Zhukov, V. (1998), 'Dominant Shareholders, Restructuring and Performance of Privatized Companies in Russia: An Analysis and Some Policy Implications', *Communist Economies and Economic Transformation,* vol.10, no.4, pp.495-517.

Black, B., Kraakman, R. and Tarassova, A. (1999), *Russian Privatization and Corporate Governance: what went wrong?* John M. Olin Program in Law and Economics, Working paper No.178, Stanford Law School, Stanford.

Blasi, J.R., Kroumova, M. and Kruse, D. (1997), *Kremlin Capitalism. Privatizing the Russian Economy*, Cornell University Press, Ithaca and London.

Blommestein, E.T. (1998), 'The Development of Securities Markets in Transition Economics - Policy Issues and Country Experiences', in *Capital Market Developments in Transition Economies. Country experience and policies for the future*, OECD, Paris.

Brown, J.D. and Earle, J.S. (2000), *Privatization and Restructuring in Russia: New Evidence from Panel Data on Industrial Enterprises*, Working paper series No.1, Russian-European Centre for Economic Policy, Moscow.

Dittus, P. and Prowse, S. (1996), 'Corporate Control in Central Europe and Russia. Should Banks Own Shares?', in R.Frydman, C.W.Gray and A.Rapaczynski (eds), *Corporate Governance in Central Europe and Russia*, vol.1, *Banks, Funds, and Foreign Investors*, Central European University Press, Budapest.

Djankov, S. (1999), 'Enterprise Restructuring in Russia', in H.G.Broadman (ed.), *Russian Enterprise Reform. Policies to Further the Transition*, World Bank Discussion Paper No.400, World Bank, Washington D.C.

Earle, J. and Estrin, S. (1996), *Privatization Versus Competition: Changing Enterprise Behavior in Russia*, Discussion paper No.316, Centre for Economic Performance, London School of Economics.

Finansovo-promyshlennye gruppy i konglomeraty v ekonomike i politike sovremennoi Rossii, Tsentr politicheskikh tekhnologii, Moscow, 1997.

Fortescue, S. (1992), 'The Privatisation of Soviet Large-Scale Industry', in H.Hendrischke (ed.), *Market Reform in the Changing Socialist World*, Macquarie Studies in Chinese Political Economy, No.4, Macquarie University, Sydney.

Fortescue, S. (1997), *Policy Making for Russian Industry*, Macmillan, London and Basingstoke.

Fortescue, S. (1998a), 'Ownership and Corporate Strategy in the Russian Mining and Metals Sector', *Soviet and Post-Soviet Review*, vol.25, no.2, pp.163-80.

Fortescue, S. (1998b), 'Privatisation, Corporate Governance and Enterprise Performance in Russia', *Russian and Euro-Asian Bulletin*, vol.7, no.5, pp.1-9.

Fortescue, S. (2000), 'Enterprise Adaptation in the Russian Mining and Metals Sector', Paper presented to the 6th ICCEES World Congress, Tampere, July-August.

Kabalina, V. (1996), 'Privatisation and Restructuring of Enterprises under "Insider" or "Outsider" Control', in S.Clarke (ed.), *Conflict and Change in the Russian Industrial Enterprise*, Elgar, Cheltenham.

McFaul, M. (1995), 'State Power, Institutional Change, and the Politics of Privatization in Russia', *World Politics*, vol.47, no.2, pp.210-43.

Nellis, J. (1999), *Time to rethink privatization in transition economies?* International Finance Corporation Discussion Paper No.38, The World Bank, Washington, D.C.

Nelson, L.D. and Kuzes, I.Y. (1995), *Radical Reform in Yeltsin's Russia. Political, Economic, and Social Dimensions*, Sharpe, Armonk N.Y.

OECD (1997), *OECD Economic Surveys 1997: Russian Federation*, OECD, Paris.

OECD (2000), *OECD Economic Surveys 1999-2000: Russian Federation*, OECD, Paris.

Perekhod k rynku, Moscow, 1990.

Schleifer, A. and Treisman, D. (1998), *The Economics and Politics of Transition to an Open Market Economy. Russia*, Development Studies Centre, OECD, Paris.

Slay, B. (1999), 'An Interpretation of the Russian Financial Crisis', *Post-Soviet Geography and Economics*, vol.46, no.1, pp.24-33.

Stuart, R.C. and Panayotopolous, C.M. (1999), 'Decline and Recovery in Transition Economies: the Impact of Initial Conditions', *Post-Soviet Geography and Economics*, vol.40, no.4, pp.267-80.

Tikhomirov, V. (2000a), 'The Second Collapse of the Soviet Economy: Myths and Realities of the Russian Reform', *Europe-Asia Studies*, vol.52, no.2, pp.207-36.
Treisman, D. (1998), 'Fighting Inflation in a Transitional Regime. Russia's Anomalous Stabilization', *World Politics*, vol.50, January, pp.235-65.

7 Russia's Debt Problem and the Financial Constraints of Reform

VLADIMIR TIKHOMIROV

In the years that followed the collapse of the Russian bond and financial markets in August 1998, there was much speculation as to what future Russian economic policy would be. Despite some modest recovery through mid-2000, the Russian stock market has continued to be rather unattractive to foreign investors, who, on one day in August 1998, found themselves denuded of their investments by a Russian government that was *de facto* bankrupt. Many local investors also continue to have a sceptical view of investment prospects in Russia. The majority of small investors have seen a rapid depreciation of their real savings in the post-crisis period, while most of big investors, the so-called oligarchs, have lost significant parts of their fortunes as a result of the crisis. Those former oligarchs that have managed to retain control of a part of their wealth have preferred to invest it abroad. Some have moved openly into politics in order to protect themselves and their property, while others were trying to resist attempts by the state to take hold of their estates. Overall it can be stated that the investment sector of state economic policy in the post-August 1998 period so far was even less promising than in the hectic and disorderly first years of the Russian reform.

A similar veil of obscurity also largely covers the main objectives of current Russian economic policy. Indeed, since the August 1998 collapse every Russian Prime Minister has publicly stated his commitment to the general course of reform and assured local and foreign businesses that there will be no turning back to the Soviet days. However, under the cover of this pro-Western and pro-reform talk some fundamental changes in the government's economic policies have also taken place. Initiated by Prime Minister Yevgeny Primakov, who replaced Sergei Kirienko in the first post-crisis months, these changes have been targeted at increasing the state's power and control over general economic matters.[1] Due to the fact that the crisis was mainly a development in the financial area, changes took place mostly in the areas of currency regulation and banking. Within just 1-2 months after the crisis the Russian currency market was brought under the full control of the state bank (Matlack, 1998; Peach and Bivens, 1998). This was followed by a prolonged process of revaluation of Russian commercial banks, which eventually led to the reinstatement to primary position of the ex-Soviet, and still state-controlled, Sberbank (savings bank). The state policy of subsidising loss-making enterprises and sectors of the national economy, which was at the core of late Soviet economic mentality, was also reinstated, albeit in a significantly lesser form.

Although Primakov was in power only eight months, replaced in May 1999 by the short-lived government of Sergei Stepashin, his policies continue to remain largely in place. Vladimir Putin, who took over the premiership from Stepashin in August 1999, has continued, and even expanded, Primakov's economic policy.[2] Although Putin's preferred political method seems to be keeping his policy objectives as secret as possible, there has been a notable and remarkable difference between his proclamations and his practice ever since the time he took power. This pattern has continued into his Presidency. This new 'double-speak' was very reminiscent of the Soviet period.

Putin's stated aim in the economic area has been for the continuation of the (market) reform process. He even went so far as to proclaim his support for such radical measures as the privatisation of land.[3] He presents himself as a staunch supporter of reforms, which he wants to see done in an orderly manner and in full compliance with the law. In fact, his general remarks have encountered very few criticisms from either the right or left opposition, simply because these remarks have been too general in nature.

Since Putin's inauguration as the new Russian President in May 2000 many observers have expected that he would finally reveal his economic plans in a more concrete and detailed form. At the time of writing this, however, has not happened and, in my view, cannot happen, simply because he does not have at hand any realistic recipes for solving Russia's economic problems. From his first initiatives as the new president it has been quite clear that Putin would like to see a much more stronger and orderly system of state power appear in Russia, possibly even more centralised than the communist system that existed in Soviet Russia.[4] Putin's first steps have also left little doubt that the new Russian president would like to establish more state control over the media and other channels of mass information.[5] Practical policies that were implemented by Putin's government during the late 1999 and early 2000 demonstrate that the new president was generally quite comfortable with a continuation of Primakov's economic policies. But at the same time he also attempted to give these policies a more 'respectable' and 'pro-market' look by appointing a few well-known economists as advisors or ministers.[6]

However, recommendations made by these economists since they were appointed have largely fallen on deaf ears.

While Russia's current developments provide fertile ground for a wide range of speculation on the issue of where Russia is heading and what the future of reforms will be, the aim of this chapter is to try to analyse the existing limitations to the reform process. These limitations - no matter what the future personal composition of the Russian government is - will largely frame and direct Russia's national economic policy. It is my view that most important among these limitations are the financial constraints on Russian reform. Whatever economic policy the Russian government might choose to implement, it will definitely need large amounts of capital to bring these policies into reality. For instance, the current Primakov-initiated policy was based on two major objectives: (1) *de facto* closure of the Russian internal market to foreign goods and (2) a significant increase in direct and indirect subsidies to local industry and agriculture. By 1999-2000 this policy had resulted in quite visible economic growth in Russia.[7] However, continuation of this policy in the future is certain to create increased demands for capital (both in the form of subsidies and investment) and eventually might lead to exactly the same problems as the ones that were experienced by the Soviet economy just one decade ago. On the other hand, promotion of further market-type reforms in Russia is unlikely to have any major effect on its national economy, unless they are accompanied by a significant flow of investment. This investment needs to be directed toward the modernisation and restructuring of those industries that can be modernised, or towards the creation of new jobs that will replace imminent job losses at those industries that need to be closed down.[8] Additionally, in any event Russia, given the size of its territory, will have to spend a significant amount of funds on the servicing, development and renewal of its massive and expensive transport infrastructure.

Thus, in the same way as its predecessors, from the very start Putin's administration was facing the acute problem of needing a dramatic and rapid increase of investment in the economy. This major financial constraint will dominate the prospects for the current or any future economic policy in Russia. If Russia is going to achieve a sustainable economic growth, it needs to ensure a continuing and growing capital flow into the national economy. However, the reality of the last decade has been quite different. The Russian economy continues to experience an acute investment crisis, probably the largest in its history. With the exception of the boom on the Russian bond market during 1995-98, investment in all

Table 7.1   Russian capital investment and foreign investment trends

7.1.1. Gross volumes of capital investment in Soviet Russia, 1980-91 (a)

	1980	1985	1988	1989	1990	1991
In constant roubles, bn (c)	83.5	98.2	122.3	127.3	127.4	107.7
In constant 1999 USD, bn (cde)	70.7	83.2	103.6	107.8	107.9	91.2
Year-on-year change, % (c)	...	3.4	7.7	4.1	0.1	-15.5
Dynamics, 1992=100 (cf)	128.5	151.3	188.4	196.1	196.3	165.8

7.1.2. Gross volumes of capital investment in Post-Soviet Russia, 1992-99 (a)

	1992	1995	1996	1997	1998	1999(b)
In constant roubles, bn (c)	64.9	39.3	32.2	30.6	28.5	28.7
In constant 1999 USD, bn (cde)	55.0	33.3	27.3	25.9	24.1	24.3
Year-on-year change, % (c)	-39.7	-10.0	-18.0	-5.0	-7.0	1.0
Dynamics, 1992=100 (cf)	100.0	60.5	49.6	47.1	43.8	44.3

7.1.3. Gross volumes of foreign investment in Post-Soviet Russia, 1992-99 (g)

	1992	1995	1996	1997	1998	1999(b)
In current USD, bn	0.2	3.0	7.0	12.3	11.8	9.6
In constant 1999 USD, bn (d)	0.3	3.2	7.3	12.6	11.9	9.6
Year-on-year change, % (f)	...	177.3	129.2	73.5	-5.5	-19.8
Dynamics, 1992=100 (f)	100.0	960.4	2201.5	3818.7	3610.2	2894.0

Notes:
(a) Combined private (company) and state investment.
(b) Preliminary data.
(c) In constant 1980 prices.
(d) Recalculated using United States GDP deflators (NASA GDP Deflator Inflation Calculator at http://www.jsc.nasa.gov/bu2/inflateGDP.html).
(e) Calculated using 1999 average official dollar/rouble exchange rate.
(f) In constant 1999 US dollars.
(g) All foreign investment in non-financial sector of the economy.

Sourced and calculated from: TsSU, 1984, p.365, and 1985, p.385; USSR Goskomstat, 1987, p.330, 1988, p.15, 1989, p.556, 1990a, p.535, and 1991, p.553; Goskomstat, 1992, p.531, 1993, pp.31-2, 1994, p.371, 1995, p.444, 1999, pp.529, 539, 2000c, p.3, 2000d, p.120.

other sectors of the Russian economy has remained at very low levels. In the real sector of the Russian economy capital investment [9] in constant US dollars had actually fallen from about $100 billion in the late Soviet period of the early 1990s to just over $24 billion in the late 1990s, or by more than three quarters (Table 7.1). Foreign investment has remained at almost non-existent levels, with the gross volume of money invested during 1992-99 by foreigners in all sectors, excluding financial operations, amounting to about 47.6 billion in constant US dollars or 17% of the total capital investment made from internal sources during the same period (Table 7.1.3).

It should be mentioned that the larger part of capital invested in the Russian economy during the 1990s originated exclusively from internal sources and, as a rule, was not linked in a direct or indirect way to the financial flows that entered Russia from abroad in the form of revenues from foreign trade or as credits received by the Russian government. Constantly falling returns from taxation and the shrinking reserves of Russian banks meant that both the government and the financial sector in general were able to invest less and less money into the economy.[10] This fact helps to explain negative investment trends presented in Table 7.1.

Figure 7.1   Net foreign currency inflows and capital investment trend (in billion current US dollars)

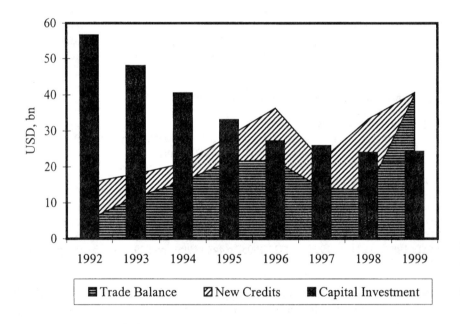

In Russia's official propaganda these negative investment trends are often linked to the critical state of the Russian economy. The continuing Russian economic crisis is seen as a result of inefficiencies, over-centralisation and anti-market attitudes of the Soviet past. However, if one compares net inflows of foreign currency into Russia during the 1990s (both through credit and foreign trade channels) with the capital investment trend, one striking conclusion that becomes apparent is the absence of any direct link between these inflows and general investment trends. On the contrary, as Figure 7.1[11] demonstrates, in the early 1990s Russia was investing more in its economy than it was receiving from credits and from maintaining a large positive trade balance. The larger part of investment was coming from internal sources (state and commercial credits, and company funds). However, in the late 1990s the situation changed when the combined revenues from foreign credits and foreign trade received by Russia were significantly higher than the total amount invested into its economy. This is striking given the fact that part of the foreign credits given to Russia was actually disbursed with the objective of increasing investment in its economy, as was the case with many of the World Bank and EBRD-funded projects.

One question that arises after analysing the data presented in the table and graph above is, where did all the money go that Russia received from foreign trade and foreign credits? If these funds were not invested in the Russian economy in direct or indirect ways (i.e. though the banking system), then where were they invested? One might suspect that in the months that preceded and immediately followed the August 1998 financial collapse in Russia a large part of this money was taken out of Russia by corrupt bankers and shady business people. But as Figure 7.1 shows, the discrepancy between investment trends and foreign cash inflows into Russia actually became sharper in the post-crisis period, e.g. during 1998-99.

According to some Russian officials, most of Russia's earnings and the credits it borrowed during the 1990s were used to repay the debts Russia inherited from the Soviet Union. In the early 1990s many of these officials shared this view, stressing in their comments that independent Russia was left with an unbearable burden of debts, which had been accumulated as a result of the reckless borrowing practices of the Soviet leadership. Russian leaders, nevertheless, had insisted that they would honour their country's debt obligations, but would like to see this debt reassessed (written off, restructured or postponed) by their foreign creditors. Throughout the 1990s this tactic has brought continuous success to the Russian government, with large parts of the Soviet debt restructured, postponed or even written off.

Figure 7.2   Russia's debt trend and capital flight (in billion current US dollars)

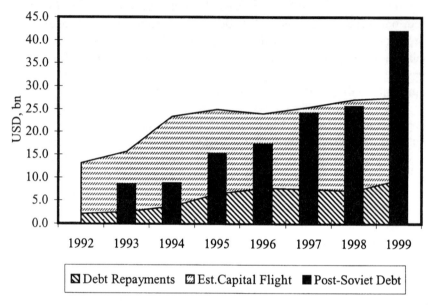

The available data also contradicts official Russian statements about large debt repayments. In Figure 7.2, I have put together the dynamics of Russian payments of principal and interest on the national public debt (including its Soviet part),[12] the total volume of Russia's post-Soviet debt[13] and estimated volumes of capital flight from Russia.[14] According to Russian official sources, de facto annual debt repayments made by Russia during the 1990s were between US$2.1 billion and US$9.5 billion, which was at least two times lower than the conservatively estimated volumes of capital flight during the corresponding years. In other words, these figures openly contradict the common view that a larger part of the money that Russia was earning was spent on repayments of accumulated debts. The same graph also shows that between 1992 and 1999 there was a steady and rapid growth in Russia's own (post-Soviet) debt: this debt grew from zero in January 1992 to US$42 billion eight years later.

Increase in Russia's public borrowing did not, however, have any impact on the debt repayment trend. During the larger part of the 1990s Russia maintained an extremely poor debt repayment record. In fact, between 1991 and 1994 Soviet and Russian governments were only repaying between 11% and 19% of their annual scheduled debt payments (Figure 7.3).[15] The rest of the debt payments during these years were either rescheduled (postponed) or were not paid in time and were carried over to the next year. It was not until 1995, following the expansion of internal borrowing through issues of state bonds, that the Russian government increased its payments to a respectable level of 35-55% of the total payments due.

Figure 7.3   Russia's foreign debt repayment record (payments made as % of due in the year stated)

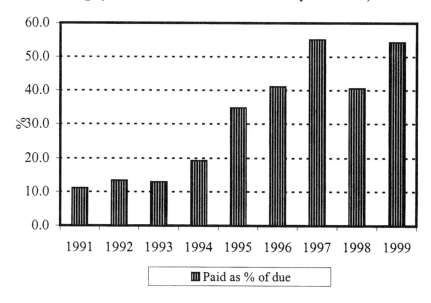

Most of the money that Russia paid to service its foreign debt during the 1990s was actually payment on newly acquired post-Soviet Russian debt. At the same time payments of principal and accumulated interest on the inherited Soviet debt were often significantly delayed. Throughout the last decade Russian officials have held numerous rounds of talks with their country's foreign creditors in the London and Paris clubs, most of which were held on the issue of Soviet debt. These negotiations have resulted in the signing of a number of technical rescheduling agreements, as well as in the writing off of parts of the Soviet debt. However, between the mid-1990s, when Russia accepted responsibility for all debts dating back to the Soviet era, and the end of the decade, this debt has been relatively stable at around the US$100 billion mark (Figure 7.4).[16] Thus, available data does not show any sign of large repayments being made by Russia towards reducing the principal part of this debt. The same graph also shows a rather rapid increase in the total amount of Soviet debt between 1992 and 1995, which was a reflection of the gradual process of acceptance of Soviet debt obligations by Russia as a result of debt talks held with other ex-Soviet states in 1992-94. Failure to make timely repayments on the existing debt also led to the rapid accumulation of interest on the Soviet debt during the same period of the early 1990s.

Figure 7.4   Russian foreign debt trends (in billion current US dollars)

In the mid-1990s there was clearly a shift in the official Russian attitude towards debt repayments, as indicated in Figures 7.3 and 7.4. This change, however, had more to do with the growing pressure on Russia by its creditors than a sudden unilateral change of Russian view on the problem. In order to secure a continuing flow of foreign aid and credits, which were seen by the Russian government as an easy and fast way of matching Russia's huge social expenditure and increased repayments on public debt with rapidly diminishing budgetary revenues, Russia in late 1994 was forced to settle the problem of the Soviet debt and to start making repayments on this debt, as well as in early 1995 to make attempts aimed at keeping its money supply under control. In addition to that, it should be noted that a growing portion of the public debt which was accumulated by the Russian government after the disintegration of the Soviet Union, began to mature in 1995-96.

Thus, the Russian government found itself in a tight corner, where its record of repayments of earlier accumulated debt, and its financial performance, finally became directly linked to the prospect of receiving of any significant credits in the future. The strategy that was chosen by the Yeltsin government in the mid-1990s was actually based on the principle of a radical increase of Russia's public debt obligations, through both internal (state bonds) and external (IMF, etc.) borrowing. Much of the newly acquired funds were channelled into stabilisation of the Russian financial market (mainly towards the maintenance of an artificially high exchange rate for the national currency); this was also accompanied by renewed government attempts to bring more budgetary discipline into state expenditure.

In the course of three years, starting from mid-1995, this 'new' economic policy allowed the Russian government to significantly bring down the rate of inflation,[17] increase the stability of the national currency[18] and improve its debt repayment record.[19] This, however, was done at the expense of a rapid expansion of Russian state borrowing. Between 1994 and 1996 the total amount of foreign credits disbursed to Russia increased from US$5 billion to US$14.4 billion, or by almost three times (CIA, 1996, Table 128, 1997, Table 125, and 1999a, Table 77). During the same period internal public debt on T-bills and state bonds increased by more than nine times, from US$4.9 billion to US$46.2 billion (Tikhomirov, 1999b, p.176).

Large increases in foreign borrowing in the mid-1990s were also accompanied by significant growth in revenues from foreign trade.[20] The positive trade balance and an increased flow of foreign credits ensured a rather substantial inflow of foreign money into Russia. However, if we take into consideration the issue of capital flight from Russia, what happened in net terms during this period was that Russia was actually losing more money than it was earning or receiving from abroad! In Figure 7.5 I have put together a simplified version of Russia's current account balance, which compares its major foreign cash inflows (trade balance and credits) with outflows (debt repayments and estimated volumes of capital flight). An analysis of the trends presented in this graph reveals that in 1994 and 1997 the combined volume of money that was exported by Russians abroad through import payments, debt repayments and various channels of capital flight was actually higher than the amount Russia was receiving through major currency inflow channels. At the same time, in the first year of Russian reform (1992), and then again in 1996 and in the period that followed the Russian financial crisis of August 1998, the country managed to maintain a rather high positive net foreign currency balance (between US$6 billion and US$10 billion a year).

Figure 7.5   Russia's main foreign currency inflows and outflows (in billion current US dollars)

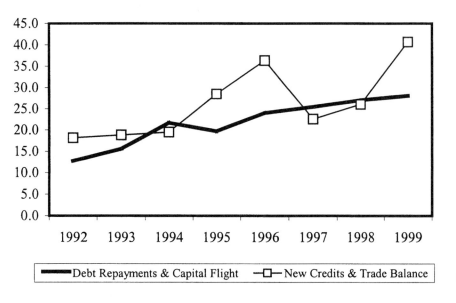

As Table 7.1 demonstrates, the fact that Russia managed to secure a large positive net currency balance during these years had no impact on its investment trends. In fact, during 1992, 1996 and 1998 capital investment in real terms continued to fall. This leads us to conclude that the component of the money that Russia received from credits and foreign trade and that was not exported out of the country was invested into areas that were not directly linked to the real economy.

In mid-1992 growing pressures from the Russian parliament, and the rapid increase in social instability resulted in the collapse of attempts by the Gaidar government to control money supply. This was followed by a huge and rather wasteful increase in social and other government expenditure in 1992-93. The outbreak of the first Chechen War in late 1994 and the Russian presidential campaign of 1996 were the two other developments that put a heavy burden on Russia's state budget. In the late 1990s the new round of presidential elections was again accompanied by a new military campaign in Chechnya with both developments once again requiring significant increases in state spending. In other words, during the 1990s Russia was continuously wasting large volumes of money that it either earned from revenues from trade or received from foreign creditors, on political and military campaigns, instead of channelling this money into the restructuring and modernisation of its economy.

Although the figures on capital flight, presented in Figures 7.2 and 7.5, are estimates, and therefore should be treated as rather raw assessments only, it is nevertheless surprising that during the 1990s the capital outflow trend did not show any significant fluctuations and from the mid-1990s remained at a steady rate of around US$17-20 billion per year.[21] This development requires some explanation. Despite a brief, three-year period of rather artificial economic stability in Russia during the mid-1990s, the majority of Russian investors and capital-holders never had much confidence in Russia's economic performance. Therefore, regardless of what the economic situation in the country was, or which government was in charge, the larger part of Russian capital that could be exported was exported, immediately. It is true that some of this money later returned in the guise of foreign investment; mostly as investment into the Russian bond market or in the purchase of shares in some large state-owned companies that were undergoing privatisation (see Tikhomirov, 2000b, pp.98, 144).

Capital flight poses a very serious problem for Russia. Although Russian officials often try to play down its importance and effect, the flight of capital has had a direct and strongly negative impact upon Russia's investment trend. Under different circumstances and in a different economic environment it is this capital that could, and should, have been invested in the modernisation and restructuring of the Russian economy. Instead it was exported out of the country and in the majority of cases was invested in Western developed economies. In this regard it is important to stress that the real causes of capital flight lie inside Russia, in aspects of its political and economic development. The volumes and trends in capital exports from Russia are just a consequence of what was happening within Russia, of the way its economic and political development has been handled. They are quite clearly a vote of no confidence by local businessmen in their country's future.

Another conclusion that could be drawn from the analysis presented above is that attitudes of foreign creditors to Russia, particularly during the first half of the 1990s, were probably motivated more by political factors rather than pure economic reasons. Data from the US Central Intelligence Agency shows that during the last decade it was in 1992, 1996 and 1998 that Russia managed to secure its largest foreign credits (CIA, 1996, Table 128, 1997, Table 125, and 1999a, Table 77).[22] In 1992 the Russian reform process, still at its very early stage, had nevertheless clearly demonstrated its inconsistent and wasteful character. Despite the failure of Russia to repay its former debts and to implement a clear economic policy, foreign nations and creditors gave significant financial backing to Yeltsin's reform attempts, mostly for the political motive of ensuring the irreversible character of anti-communist changes in their former Cold War enemy. In 1996, when four years had passed since the start of the reform but there were still no signs of any significant improvement in Russia's overall economic or social performance, the Russian leadership had managed to double its foreign financial support on an annual basis, with most of this money spent on Yeltsin's re-election to presidency. But the largest volume of credits that Russia managed to receive on an annual basis during the 1990s (almost US$20 billion) came in the seven and a half months that preceded the August 1998 financial collapse. At this time large amounts of foreign money were spent on trying to conceal the rapidly developing crisis on Russian financial markets, but to no avail.

Despite their unsatisfactory economic performance and exceptionally poor foreign debt repayment record, Russian leaders during the 1990s have become used to relying upon the 'easy money' that was readily available from the West and that on many occasions allowed them to evade tackling the country's real problems and pursuing fundamental reforms. This dependence on 'easy money' can be clearly seen in Figure 7.5. During the last decade, with the exception of two years, Russia was receiving significantly more money through credit and trade channels than it was paying back in debt repayments or was losing through capital flight. If we take into consideration the fact that between 1995 and 1998 the Russian government was also borrowing large amounts of money on the internal market, then the combined net financial gain from all sources of borrowing and foreign trade would be even higher. A rapid increase in Russia's internal public borrowing through issues of GKO-OFZ bills eventually resulted in the collapse of the 'bond pyramid' (see Gobbin and Merlevede, 2000; Malleret et al., 1999; Tikhomirov, 1999a). But the most important outcome of this borrowing expansion was that it had very little impact on Russia's struggling economy; the additional funding attracted was largely wasted on keeping alive the same unreformed and inefficient Soviet-type economic system in Russia.

The collapse of the Soviet centralised system of economic management in the early 1990s was followed by privatisation of the majority of state assets in Russia. Consequently, by the mid- to late 1990s Russian government institutions were no longer responsible for pursuing or managing an active investment policy. The result was a significant drop in state investment into the economy.[23] However, this emerging investment gap was not filled by a significant growth in private investment, mostly because of a general lack of interest on the part of the majority of local and foreign investors. Therefore, in order to continue production and develop their enterprises, many Russian companies had to generate investment from their own company funds and were often forced to seek commercial crediting. However, very low levels of capitalisation in the Russian banking sector and the boom in other, more profitable, investment areas (i.e. the short-term loan market in 1992-95 and the state bond market in 1995-98) meant that in most cases private funds available for investment into the real economy were scarce.

Thus, in the course of the 1990s investment crisis in Russia became significantly more acute. This lack of investment made already severe problems related to efficiency, modernisation and the profitability of Russian companies even more critical. In addition to this, due to the constant political and economic instability even local managers of the better-off Russian enterprises were not prepared to invest a larger part of their company earnings into longer-term development projects. For example, if we compare the investment trend with export earnings in one of the most profitable of Russia's industries, its oil sector, what becomes clear is that during the 1990s the investment tendency in the Russian oil industry was not following its export revenue trend (Figure 7.6). Under normal circumstances one might expect that an increase in export earnings should actually boost incentives for a further increase in production and, hence, for a consequent growth in investment. But in Russia's oil sector the reality in the mid-1990s was quite the opposite. The official Russian statistical data shows that while in 1994-96 oil export revenues grew by almost 70%, capital investment in the oil industry fell by almost 20%.[24] In the late 1990s a set of measures that the Russian government undertook to decrease the volume of capital exports from Russia started to bring some results. In 1999, following the rise in world oil prices, revenues from Russian oil exports increased by 1.45 times (on an annual basis). Although this rise was less than the one experienced during 1994-96, this time there was a direct impact from increased export earnings on the capital investment trend: during 1999 investment in the Russian oil industry grew by 1.2 times.

Figure 7.6   Indices of main trends in oil industry, 1992-1999 (in %, 1992=100)

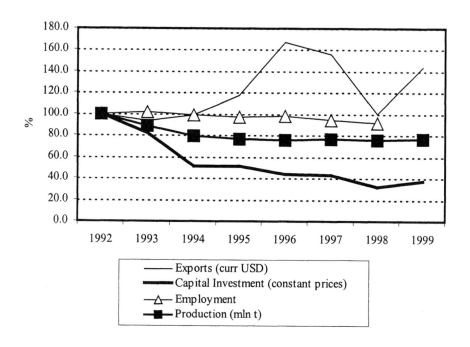

The above figures demonstrate that company managers in Russia were not always interested in enterprise development, even in such a profitable industry as the oil industry. This was particularly the case during the first years of reform, when political uncertainties and the existing gaps in

Russia's legal framework allowed a relatively small group of business people, bureaucrats and ex-Soviet directors to channel a significant portion of industry profits into their own private bank accounts. The other amazing development, as presented on Figure 7.6, is the one that indicates that in the Russian oil industry, as in all other major sectors of the national economy, employment levels were not directly linked to output. This meant that during the larger part of the 1990s the average productivity of labour in the Russian economy was constantly going down (also see Tikhomirov, 2000a, pp.207-36). For instance, while in 1992-98 overall production in the oil industry fell by 24%, employment in this industry decreased by only 9%.

In my view it would be wrong to place all the blame for Russia's poor economic performance solely on the Russian reformist leadership, despite the fact that, as most recent data from Russia suggests, the state continues to play a very important role there. But ineffective and irresponsible Russian industrial managers should also share responsibility for the acute economic crisis in the country. On many occasions in the recent past these managers have continually refused to invest money into their company's development, even if their companies were making substantial profits. Instead, regardless of their company's performance they have maintained high levels of employment and kept demanding state support. It will be hard to expect any breakthrough in the reform of the Russian economy if this Soviet-type industrial mentality is not changed.[25]

To conclude, I would like to argue that overall the results of the Russian reforms of the 1990s are highly questionable. The data presented above shows that in many core areas of the economy and management no reforms in fact took place at all (i.e. industrial relations, restructuring of the economy, modernisation of capital stock, closing down of loss-making enterprises, etc.). Due to the fact that the 'Soviet' content of the Russian economic system remained largely unchanged (despite some façade changes like privatisation), many enterprises continued to be highly dependent on outside (state) subsidies. Even when these companies recorded significant revenue inflows, as in the case of the oil industry, these additional earnings were not immediately transformed into funding for investment projects. Many company managers preferred to wait for funding to arrive from outside investors or they continued to lobby state authorities for more support. However, having lost its total control over the national economy, the Russian government in the 1990s had fewer possibilities to subsidise its economy than was the case in the past. Therefore, in order to at least partially respond to mounting pressures, Russian leaders were forced to increasingly rely on various forms of borrowing, particularly because tax collection for the Russian budget was continually diminishing.[26]

The larger part of money that Russia borrowed during the 1990s was spent on keeping the old and inefficient economy afloat, but not on its restructuring and modernisation.[27] Credits have helped to slow down the pace of economic collapse in Russia, but did little to change the prevailing economic trend. By the end of the decade investment in the real economy had fallen to about a quarter of what it was in the early 1990s. At the same time the bulk of money that the Russian government borrowed during the last decade was either spent on repaying earlier accumulated debts (mostly post-Soviet debts), or on subsidising the slightly modified 'Soviet economy'.

The so-called 'reforms' were also accompanied by an unprecedented liberalisation of financial, economic and trade activities in Russia. This has led to a further weakening of the revenue base of the Russian federal budget and created endless possibilities for smuggling of large volumes of money out of the country. In turn, the flight of capital has even further exacerbated the Russian investment trend.

At the time of writing, despite a number of public announcements that were made by the Putin government and that contained promises of new radical approaches to Russia's economic reform, the new Russian president and his cabinet have largely been pursuing an economic policy that could best be characterised as an exact replica of the policy pursued by all recent Russian governments. This policy was first formulated by the Primakov government in the 3 to 4 months that followed the August 1998 crisis.[28] It was based on two major principles: the continuation of attempts aimed at securing new foreign credits to Russia and the restructuring (postponing) of debt payments that were due, and pursuing timid but consistent actions aimed at reinstating state control in some key areas of the economy and finance. Since Vladimir Putin became Russia's Prime Minister in mid-1999 he has extended this policy further, to include a third new principle: increased state support for the military-industrial complex and the army and security forces in general.[29] Although this new direction in state policy can be seen as a logical result of Putin's decision to enforce a military solution to the Chechen crisis, state support to the military has quickly exceeded the immediate needs of the recent Chechen campaign.

In mid-2000 the economic platform of Putin's government was still being made.[30] It was still unclear whether the government would finally make public a full-fledged document outlining its economic policy, or it would continue its operations on an *ad hoc* basis, without such a document. However, for at least a year since Vladimir Putin became premier, he has been quite consistent in at least one principle of policy. He prefers to keep a continuous veil of secrecy around the issue of his future policies; this has allowed him to retain a considerable freedom of political choice.[31]

The current situation on world commodity markets, which is favourable to Russia and other major energy and mineral exporters,[32] has resulted in a significant increase of Russian export revenues in the late 1990s. In addition, progress was reached in early 2000 in negotiations with major foreign private creditors on the issue of restructuring part of Russia's sovereign debt.[33] This has meant that at least during its first months in office the new Russian government has been under no particular pressure to reassess its economic policy, giving President Putin a certain breathing space. He has attempted to use this space to pursue reform of the political system in the direction of a greater centralisation of executive power.

It is not yet clear whether Putin will eventually succeed in centralising and streamlining the Russian political system. Moreover, at the time of writing it is still not entirely clear that this is the overall goal of his policy. However, there are some developments that are beyond the control of the Russian government and that can to a great extent determine what policy choices Putin's administration will have in the future. On the one hand, in a scenario in which world energy prices continue to remain high, the likelihood of a new severe budgetary crisis in Russia will remain low. This means that Russia will be in a position to fulfil its repayment obligations on its public debt, which will significantly increase the chances of Russia's creditors softening their position on the issue of restructuring or even writing off a part of the remaining debt. Under this option Putin can continue pursuing an evolutionary reform approach, which is likely to be based on a rather contradictory combination of certain market-orientated liberal reforms supplemented by continuing attempts aimed at creating a more centralised state in Russia.

On the other hand, if current high levels of world energy and commodity prices fall to mid-1990s levels, and Russia's creditors continue to hold firm in debt negotiations, then President Putin will have far fewer options to choose from.[34] Putin might even be forced to consider a more revolutionary approach in his policies, which, given his background and the policies he has pursued so far, is unlikely to result in any breakthrough reforms. On the contrary, it is quite likely that Russia might start to slide further towards some sort of centralised or even possibly totalitarian model, both in political and economic terms.

It remains to be seen whether the appeals that the Russian government continues to make to local and foreign investors to increase their funding of the Russian economy will bear fruit.[35] At the time of writing, in September 2000, the majority of investors were still greatly discouraged by the continuing uncertainty as to what the economic priorities of the Putin government really are. The steady centralisation of state power in Russia, that is so reminiscent of its past, does not help to raise investors' confidence either. In general, the investment climate in contemporary Russia continues to remain very risky. Many potential investors have suspended their activities in Russia until such time as the Russian government will pay back the money they invested into Russian state bonds, repayments on which were frozen following the August 1998 financial collapse. That means that one can hardly expect a sudden change in non-state investment strategies towards Russia in the near future. This leaves the Russian government with only one realistic option: to rely on its own resources for the funding of the modernisation and restructuring needs of the national economy. Thus, we can expect that in the future the government will continue its efforts to increase the monetary base of the federal budget. This will be done through maintaining its control over financial flows, increasing tax discipline and pursuing a policy of controlled monetary expansion. It might also be accompanied by further attempts on the part of the state aimed at a partial or full reinstatement of government control over the national economy, including (partial) re-nationalisation of Russia's most profitable exporting industries (oil and gas, energy, metallurgy, etc.).

Notes

1   'Primakov Calls for More State Regulation of Economy', *Radio Free Europe/Radio Liberty Newsline (RFE/RL)*, vol.2, no.209, part I, 29 October, 1998; 'Primakov: Russia Building Socially-Oriented Market Economy', *Itar-TASS*, 27 October, 1998; *Komsomolskaya pravda*, 5 May, 1999.

2   For a recent discussion of economic policies of Putin's administration see World Bank newsletter *Transition*, vol.11, nos.3-4, May-July 2000, pp.19-28.

3   *RFE/RL*, vol.4, no.22, part I, 1 February, 2000; *Interfax*, 31 January, 2000; *RFE/RL Russian Federation Report*, vol.2, no.16, 26 April, 2000.

4   The first three decrees Putin issued after he was inaugurated as the new Russian President were dealt with the restructuring of Russia's system of government. Most important of these decrees was the subsumption of Russia's 89 administrative units into 7 federal districts. These decrees sparked series of political debates and were seen by some democratic opposition groups as a sign of emerging totalitarianism in Russia (see, for example, *Izvestia*, 14 May, 2000; *Kommersant*, 15 May, 2000; *RFE/RL*, vol.4, no.93, part I, 15 May, 2000). See also 'Russia's New Economic Program: Does 'Putinomics' Mean a Slimmed but Muscular State?', *Transition*, vol.11, nos.3-4, 2000, pp.25-6.

5   See May-June Russian newspapers on actions taken by the Prosecutor General's office against one of the largest private Russian media companies, Media Most. For example, *Segodnya*, 23 May, 2000; 'Relations between authorities, media still face problems', *Interfax*, 25 May, 2000; Dixon, 2000.

6   On 12 April 2000, two weeks after he was elected President, Vladimir Putin named well-known liberal economist Andrei Illarionov as his economics advisor. In mid-May he appointed other liberal economists as ministers of his new government. Mikhail Kasyanov became the New Prime Minister while Aleksei Kudrin was appointed as the new Finance Minister and German Gref as the new Minister of Economics and Trade ('Russia's Putin Names New Economic Advisor', *Reuters*, 12 April, 2000; *Izvestia*, 19 May, 2000).

7   On a year-to year basis the Russian GDP in 1999 grew by 1.5%, and during the first three months of 2000 it grew a further 8.4% (Goskomstat, 2000c and 2000e). Also see 'Kasyanov Sees Russian Economic Recovery in 3-4 Years', *Reuters*, 16 January, 2000; *Monitor*, vol.6, no.32, 15 February, 2000; *Interfax*, 23 February, 2000.

8   In May 2000 40.6% of the total number of enterprises and companies in all sectors of the Russian economy were making losses (Goskomstat, 2000e, p.155). See also my article on the second collapse of the Soviet economy (Tikhomirov, 2000a).

9   For more on Russian capital investment trends see Tikhomirov, 1998, pp.221-55.

10   For a detailed analysis see Tikhomirov, 2000b, pp.47-108.

11   Data on capital investment trends used in Figure 7.1 are own calculations based on sources to Table 7.1. Data on Russian trade balance was sourced from Goskomstat, 1999, p.564, and 2000d, p.80. Data on Russian borrowing (total credits disbursed to Russia) was taken from CIA, 1996, 1997 and 1999a, and from Russian official statements (*Itar-TASS*, 19 July, 1999, and *Interfax* as quoted in *RFE/RL*, vol.4, no.2, part 1, 4 January, 2000).

12   Debt accumulated by Russia after 1991 was calculated as a residual of total debt obligations less accepted Soviet debt. Sources used included statements on public debt made by Russian officials as cited in *RFE/RL*, no.48, 11 March, 1992, no.1, 4 January 1993, no.17, 27 January 1993, and no.192, 10 October 1994; *Russian Information Agency Report (RIA)*, 9 December, 1994, 27 January, 1995, and 8 February, 1995; *Reuters*, 22 November, 1994; *Interfax Business Report*, no.76(1246), 19 April, 1996 and no.163 (1583), 28 August, 1997; *St.Peterburgskie vedomosti*, 22 January, 1993; *Delovoi mir*, 5 January, 1995; *Open Media Research Institute (OMRI) News*, 19 January, 1995; *Russia Notes*, 8 July, 1998; *Interfax-FIA*, 25 December, 1998; *Obshchaya gazeta*, 23 December, 1999.

13   For sources see footnote 12 above.

14   Own estimates. For methodology used in estimating volumes of capital flight and some assessments see Tikhomirov, 1997, pp.591-615.

15   Data on Russia's due and *de facto* debt repayments was calculated and sourced from statements made by Russian officials and ministries, the Russian Central Bank, as well as from estimates made by the IMF and World Bank. See *Finansovye izvestia*, 27 January – 2 February, 1994, pp.1-2; *RFE/RL*, no.37, 24 February, 1992, and 17 December, 1992; 'Russia: Debt Rescheduling', *Oxford Analytica East Europe Daily Brief (OAEEDB)*, 4 October, 1993; Fischer, 1998; *Nezavisimaya gazeta*, 23 February, 1995, pp.1-2; *Interfax Business Report*, no.115(1033), 16 June, 1995; *RIA*, 8 February, 1995; *Economica Weekly Press Summary*, vol.2, no.18, 13 – 19 May, 1995; *Interfax Business Report*, no.117(1035), 20 June, 1995; Russian Central Bank, 1998, p.196, and 1999, pp.187-8; 'IMF Approves Augmentation of Russia's Extended Arrangement and Credit under CCFF; Activates GAB', *IMF Press Release*, no.98/31, 20 July, 1998; IMF, 1999, p.62; *Russia Notes*, 11 November, 1998, and 27 April, 1999; *RFE/RL*, vol.4, no.2, 4 January, 2000; *Monitor*, vol.5, no.199, 27 October, 1999.

16   For sources of data used in Figure 7.4 see footnotes 12 and 15 above.

17   The consumer price index fell from 315% in 1994 to 231% in 1995, 122% in 1996 and 111% in 1997 (Goskomstat, 1999, p.547).

18   During 1994 the Russian national currency, the rouble, depreciated against the US dollar by 2.9 times. In 1995 the tempo of depreciation had fallen more than twice, to 1.3 times and in 1996 to 1.2 times (calculated from Statkom, 1996, p.95, and 1997, p.127).

19   In 1992-93 the share of *de facto* debt repayments in the total amount due was around 13%. In 1997 Russia repaid over 55% of due payments on its public debt (Figure 7.3).

20   Between 1994 and 1996 the overall Russian trade balance increased from US$17 billion to US$19.8 billion (Goskomstat, 1999, p.564).

21   Own estimates (see also footnote 14 above). These estimates correspond to assessments made by the Institute of Economics of the Russian Academy of Sciences (*RIA*, 21 February, 1997), the Russian Federal Service for Currency and Export Control (*RIA*, 23 September, 1997); the Russian Central Bank (*Interfax*, 29 December, 1998); Moody's Investor Services (*The New Republic*, 18 January, 1999), the Russian Ministry of Economics (*Russia Notes*, 7 June, 1999), an international credit rating agency Fitch IBCA (*The Financial Times*, 21 August, 1999), and the Washington-based Institute for International Finance (Robert Lyle, 'Russia: Institute Estimates That $2 Billion a Month Leaves Country', in *RFE/RL*, vol.3, no.188, 27 September, 1999).

22   According to this data the total volume of credits disbursed to Russia in 1992 was US$10.3 billion, in 1996 – US$14.4 billion and in 1998 – US$19.7 billion.

23   According to official Russian statistics, in 1985 the share of expenditure on the national economy in the Russian consolidated budget (federal and regional budgets together) was 54.5%. In 1992 this share fell to 34.5% and by 1995 it was only 28% (Goskomstat, 1999, p.491).

24   Data used in Figure 7.6 was sourced and calculated from Goskomstat, 1996, p.75, 78, 161; Goskomstat, 1998, p.75, 76, 159; Statkom, 2000, p.112; Goskomstat, 2000d, pp.87-8, 116-9; Goskomstat, 1999, p.532, 570.

25   For more on the political behaviour of Russian industrial managers see Fortescue, 1998b, pp.1-9.

26   On tax collection problems and tax non-payments to the budget see Tikhomirov, 2000, pp.64-9.
27   For some recent overviews of the Russian structural crisis see Dyker, 2000; Polonsky and Aivazian, 2000; Schroeder, 1998.
28   An excellent overview of Russian economic policy choices and Primakov's government early policies is contained in Hanson, 1999, pp.1141-66.
29   See, for example Golts, 2000; *RFE/RL*, vol.4, no.58, part I, 22 March, 2000.
30   In late June 2000 a team of economists and advisers to the Russian government, led by German Gref, the Minister of Economic Development and Trade, produced a draft economic policy, which contained a set of measures to be implemented during the next 18 months. These measures included the streamlining of Russian economic and tax legislation, the reduction or elimination of various economic privileges and subsidies, starting bankruptcy procedures against loss-making companies, etc. However, the general undertone of the programme was increased state control over the economy. For a discussion of the programme see Russian newspapers between 23 June and 3 July 2000; Jack, 2000; 'Russia's New Economic Program: Does 'Putinomics' Mean a Slimmed but Muscular State?', *Transition* (World Bank), vol.11, nos.3-4, May-July 2000, pp.25-6.
31   According to Putin's colleagues and many observers secrecy has been a constant theme of his career. See Matloff, 2000; Bovt and Kolesnikov, 2000; Medvedev, 2000.
32   The current surge in world oil prices was expected as early as 1996. See 'New Oil Price Shock Seen Looming as Early as 2000', *Wind Energy Weekly*, vol.15, no.684, 12 February, 1996; Considine and Larson, 1996. For an overview of the situation on world oil markets see EIA, 2000.
33   In February 2000, on the eve of Russian presidential elections, the London Club of private bankers agreed to reschedule almost US$32 billion of debt payments that Moscow had defaulted on following the August 1998 crisis. In addition, about 35% of the debt Russia owed the London Club was forgiven (Sikri, 2000). However, soon after Putin assumed the presidency the problem of huge foreign debt repayments started to emerge as one of the biggest obstacles to Russia's future economic development. In July 2000 the need to achieve a restructuring of foreign public debt was even named as one of the main goals of the Russia's new foreign policy doctrine. The new 'Foreign Policy Concept of the Russian Federation' stated as one of government's tasks in the international economic area 'to bring the servicing of Russian foreign debt into compliance with the country's real possibilities' (*Rossiiskaya gazeta*, 11 July, 2000). However, at the G-7 summit meeting in Japan Putin's request to cancel part of Russia's debt repayments was met with no enthusiasm by Western leaders. Only Germany agreed to reschedule until 2016 US$3.8 billion of Soviet-era debt, but at the same time the German Chancellor Schröder categorically rejected any possibility of debt forgiveness ('No Question of Cancelling Russia's Debt: France', *AFP*, 8 July, 2000; *RFE/RL*, vol.4, no.140, 24 July, 2000).
34   According to latest official reports from Russia, in 2003 the country might face a chain of disasters, if no preventive measures are taken in what time is left. These disasters are associated with the large foreign debt repayments that fall due that year (US$17 billion), Russia's eroding infrastructure, and an aging population (see Shukshin, 2000). In the recent past similar predictions turned out to be quite accurate. For instance, in late 1996 the then Russian Deputy Finance Minister, Oleg Vyugin, warned

that Russia was heading toward a debt crisis by the end of 1998 ('Russian Debt Crisis Possible by End of 1998 – Deputy Minister', *Reuters*, 18 December, 1996).
35   'Candidate Putin Woos Foreign Investors', *RFE/RL*, vol.4, no. 52, part I, 14 March, 2000; Tennenbaum, 2000.

References

Bovt, G. and Kolesnikov, A. (2000), 'Tainaya demokratiya', *Izvestia*, 9 February.
CIA (1996), *Handbook of International Economic Statistics. 1996*, U.S. Central Intelligence Agency, Directorate of Intelligence, Washington, D.C.
CIA (1997), *Handbook of International Economic Statistics. 1997*, U.S. Central Intelligence Agency, Directorate of Intelligence, Washington, D.C.
CIA (1999a), *Handbook of International Economic Statistics. 1999*, U.S. Central Intelligence Agency, Directorate of Intelligence, Washington, D.C.
Considine, T.J. and Larson, D.F. (1996), *Uncertainty and the Price for Crude Oil Reserves*, Policy Research Working Paper 1655, The World Bank, Washington, D.C., September.
Dixon, R. (2000), 'Pushing the Boundaries of a Free Press', *Los Angeles Times*, 1 June.
Dyker, D.A. (2000), 'The Structural Origins of the Russian Economic Crisis', *Post-Communist Economies*, vol.12, no.1, March, pp.5-24.
EIA (2000), *Short-Term Energy Outlook, September 2000*, Energy Information Administration, Washington, D.C., 6 September.
Fischer, S. (1998), *The Russian Economy at the Start of 1998*. Speech at the 1998 U.S.-Russian Investment Symposium, at Harvard University, on January 9 1998. IMF, Washington, D.C. http://www.imf.org/external/np/speeches/1998/010998.htm.
Fortescue, S. (1998b), 'Privatisation, Corporate Governance and Enterprise Performance in Russia', *Russian and Euro-Asian Bulletin*, vol.7, no.5, pp.1-9.
Gobbin, N. and Merlevede, B. (2000), 'The Russian Crisis: a Debt Perspective', *Post-Communist Economies*, vol.12, no.2, 2000, pp.141-63.
Golts, A. (2000), 'The Arming of Russia's Economy', *The Russia Journal*, 7-13 February.
Goskomstat (1992), *Narodnoe khozyaistvo Rossiiskoi Federatsii. 1992*, Goskomstat Rossii, Moscow.
Goskomstat (1993), *Sotsial'no-ekonomicheskoe polozhenie Rossii, yanvar'-noyabr' 1993 g.*, Goskomstat Rossii, Moscow.
Goskomstat (1994), *Rossiiskii statisticheskii ezhegodnik. 1994*, Goskomstat Rossii, Moscow.
Goskomstat (1995), *Rossiiskii statisticheskii ezhegodnik. 1995*, Goskomstat Rossii, Moscow.
Goskomstat (1996), *Promyshlennost' Rossii. 1996*, Goskomstat Rossii, Moscow.
Goskomstat (1998), *Promyshlennost' Rossii. 1998*, Goskomstat Rossii, Moscow.
Goskomstat (1999), *Rossiiskii statisticheskii ezhegodnik. 1999*, Goskomstat Rossii, Moscow.
Goskomstat (2000c), *Sotsial'no-ekonomicheskoe polozhenie Rossii. 1999 god*, Goskomstat Rossii, Moscow.
Goskomstat (2000d), *Sotsial'no-ekonomicheskoe polozhenie Rossii, yanvar' 2000 goda*, Goskomstat Rossii, Moscow.

Goskomstat (2000e), *Sotsial'no-ekonomicheskoe polozhenie Rossii, yanvar'-iyun 2000 goda,* Goskomstat Rossii, Moscow.

Hanson, P. (1999), 'The Russian Economic Crisis and the Future of Russian Economic Reform', *Europe-Asia Studies,* vol.51, no.7, November, pp.1141-66.

IMF (1999), *World Economic Outlook. October 1999,* IMF, Washington, D.C.

Jack, A. (2000), 'Russian Reform Plan Strikes Liberals as Too Good to Last', *The Financial Times,* 4 July.

Malleret, T., Orlova, N. and Romanov, V. (1999), 'What Loaded and Triggered the Russian Crisis?', *Post-Soviet Affairs,* vol.15, no.2, April-June, pp.107-29.

Matlack, C. (1998), 'What Disasters Lie Ahead in Moscow?', *Business Week,* 19 October.

Matloff, J. (2000), 'Putin Who? Russia's Presidential Enigma', *Christian Science Monitor,* 28 January.

Medvedev, R. (2000), 'Byla li u Putina maska?', *Rossiiskaya gazeta,* 5 April.

Peach, G. and Bivens, M. (1998), 'Primakov's Six weeks Magically Confused', *The Moscow Times,* 24 October.

Polonsky, G. and Aivazian, Z. (2000), 'Restructuring Russian Industry: Can It Really Be Done?', *Post-Communist Economies,* vol.12, no.2, June, pp.229-40.

Russian Central Bank (1998), *Godovoi otchyot Tsentral'nogo banka Rossiiskoi Federatsii, 1997,* Tsentral'nyi bank Rossii, Moscow.

Russian Central Bank (1999), *Godovoi otchyot Tsentral'nogo banka Rossiiskoi Federatsii, 1998,* Tsentral'nyi bank Rossii, Moscow.

Schroeder, G. (1998), 'Dimensions of Russia's Industrial Transformation, 1992 to 1998: An Overview', *Post-Soviet Geography and Economics,* vol.39, no.5, May, pp.243-70.

Shukshin, A. (2000), 'Russia Sets Out to Tackle "2003 Problem"', *Reuters,* 13 September.

Sikri, A. (2000), 'Debt Deal Prompts Fresh Investor Interest in Russia', *Reuters,* 11 February.

Statkom (1996), *Finansy i tseny stran Sodruzhestva Nezavisimykh Gosudarstv v 1991-1995 gg. i pervom polugodii 1996 g.,* Statkom SNG, Moscow.

Statkom (1997), *Finansy i tseny stran Sodruzhestva Nezavisimykh Gosudarstv v 1995-1996 gg. i pervom polugodii 1997 g.,* Statkom SNG, Moscow.

Statkom (2000), *Sodruzhestvo Nezavisimykh Gosudarstv v 1999 godu,* Statkom SNG, Moscow.

Tennenbaum, J. (2000), '"National Liberals" Try to Kidnap Russia's Economic Policy', *Executive Intelligence Review,* vol.27, no.15, 7 April.

Tikhomirov, V. (1997), 'Capital Flight from Post-Soviet Russia', *Europe-Asia Studies,* vol.49, no.4, June, p.591-615.

Tikhomirov, V. (1998), 'Investment Crisis in Post-Soviet Russia' in H.Shibata and T.Ihori (eds), *Welfare State, Public Investment and Growth,* Springer-Verlag, Tokyo, p.221-55.

Tikhomirov, V. (1999a), 'State Finances and the Effectiveness of the Russian Reform' in V.Tikhomirov (ed.), *Anatomy of the 1998 Russian Crisis,* CERC, Melbourne, pp.164-203.

Tikhomirov, V. (ed.) (1999b), *Anatomy of the 1998 Russian Crisis.* CERC, Melbourne.

Tikhomirov, V. (2000a), 'The Second Collapse of the Soviet Economy: Myths and Realities of the Russian Reform', *Europe-Asia Studies,* vol.52, no.2, pp.207-36.

Tikhomirov, V. (2000b), *The Political Economy of Post-Soviet Russia,* Macmillan Press, London, St.Martin's Press, New York.

TsSU (1984), USSR Central Statistical Department, *Narodnoe khozyaistvo SSSR v 1983 g.*, Finansy i statistika, Moscow.

TsSU (1985), USSR Central Statistical Department, *Narodnoe khozyaistvo SSSR v 1984 g.*, Finansy i statistika, Moscow.

USSR Goskomstat (1987), *Narodnoe khozyaistvo SSSR za 70 let*, Finansy i statistika, Moscow.

USSR Goskomstat (1988), *Kapital'noe stroitel'stvo SSSR. Statisticheskii sbornik*, Finansy i statistika, Moscow.

USSR Goskomstat (1989), *Narodnoe khozyaistvo SSSR v 1988 g.*, Finansy i statistika, Moscow.

USSR Goskomstat (1990a), *Narodnoe khozyaistvo SSSR v 1989 g.*, Finansy i statistika, Moscow.

USSR Goskomstat (1991), *Narodnoe khozyaistvo SSSR v 1990 g.*, Finansy i statistika, Moscow.

8 Vegetative Adaptation, Oil Prices and the Current Economic Situation in Russia

GENNADI KAZAKEVITCH

Introduction

The experience of the countries of the former Soviet bloc has shown that the transition from centralised planning to a market economy is a difficult and time-consuming process. It includes a gradual introduction of elements of the market mechanism while vestiges of the old economic system continue to function. The economy of the transitional period thus has properties of both systems, and no individual theory can fully explain the results of such a mixed situation.

Certain general conclusions can be drawn about the content of transitional processes in all post-communist countries. Upon coming to power, the new governments proclaim the same reform goals, abolish centralised planning and price/wage controls to one degree or another, and, depending on the chosen strategy, are more or less successful in overcoming the substantial imbalance in the money and commodity supplies inherited from the old regimes. Some countries, notably Poland and Hungary, came closer to attaining economic stabilisation and sustainable growth. However, the macroeconomic and financial situation of other countries, including Russia, has been much more complex.

The price that Russian society was forced to pay for the initial stages of reforms, even if they appeared to be successful, was a significant reduction in the volume of production, transformation of hidden inflation into open inflation, and a rapid rise in prices and nominal income. As well, there has been the emergence of stark unemployment and hidden unemployment, along with the surfacing of the hidden structural and frictional components that existed in the past. The seeming stabilisation and beginning of growth in real terms of the most recent past has not yet proven itself to be a long-term, sustainable tendency.

Many researchers and commentators believe that post-communist recession is the result of incorrect economic policy, not objective causes. Others refer to the experience of China, where reforms have been accompanied by economic growth. However, regardless of the cause, the stage of reforms that followed the initial attempts at macro-financial stabilisation – structural reorganisation, microeconomic deregulation, demonopolisation and privatisation of large and medium-size enterprises – unfolded against the background of a recession that has appeared to be prolonged and difficult.

The goal of this chapter is a theoretical explanation for the slowdown of reform during the privatisation stage and an attempt to provide a general forecast of further developments, based on both theoretical considerations and historic analogies. We examine the macroeconomic consequences of the abolition of centralised planning and the introduction of privatisation, and an attempt is made to show that reduced production and high inflation during the initial stage of reforms was inevitable.

In the short term, the economic behaviour of the state apparatus and the management of state enterprises, work collectives, and trade unions *objectively* involved further reduced production. No substantial improvement should have been expected. If privatisation included the transfer of ownership of an enterprise to a work collective, the benefits bestowed upon it in the process of acquiring stocks or other methods of de facto formalisation of elements of worker self-management in new forms of ownership would be in accordance with the criterion of 'maximum profit per enterprise worker'.

In the long term, restoration of the volume of production and further economic growth are possible, but only if the concept and methods of privatisation lead to formation of stimuli for maximisation of the absolute profit volume under competitive conditions. The sooner 'proper' privatisation and subsequent structural reorganisation of the economy are carried out, the faster the transition from recession to growth and the higher the growth rate will be. However, reduced gross national product (GNP) and galloping inflation lead to a significant lowering of living standards and to an inevitable rise in unemployment as a direct and short-term consequence of privatisation. This impedes reforms. To explain this phenomenon, the present paper proposes using a modification of Kornai's concept of 'vegetative adaptation', according to which even the most radical government cannot choose a reform strategy freely. The 'normal' upper limit of unemployment and the lower limit of real per capita income that are acceptable to society are the constraints.

On the other hand, international financial bodies, such as the IMF, pressure the Russian government for further, more rapid, reforms and make further aid subject to tough fiscal and reform policies. This situation will be considered here in conjunction with the other source of revenue – oil dollars. Based on retrospective analysis and the hypothesis of 'vegetative adaptation', an attempt at foreseeing further tendencies of the Russian economic reform will be made.

The Initial Reform Period: Comparative Factors

The deep recession that occurred in all former socialist countries during the initial stage of reforms has usually been explained as follows:

- decrease in demand for defence industry products;
- the breakup of economic ties between partners in the former CMEA (Council for Mutual Economic Assistance) and between former Soviet republics;
- technological backwardness and the worn-out condition of equipment at enterprises in the branches of heavy industry that lose their competitiveness under the new conditions; and
- the disintegration of work collectives of large enterprises whose personnel, in the face of galloping inflation and the advent of new possibilities for earnings, seek more effective application of their efforts and skills.

Each factor could in itself cause a reduced production volume. However, they can be regarded as subjective factors that at least theoretically could be avoided. We will try to answer the question of whether there exists a general objective and inevitable component of 'post-communist recession'.

Any macroeconomic theory must be based on certain microeconomic prerequisites. In the given instance, they must be theoretical ideas about the functional goals of the socialist enterprise before and after the beginning of reforms.

The idea of the ambiguity of the goals of a socialist enterprise is well known in the Western literature (Gregory and Stuart, 1990). On the one hand, in accordance with the concept of operating on a self-supporting basis *(khozraschet)* it was assumed that an enterprise should maximise profits. At the same time, since the investment process and the depreciation fund were centralised, enterprise management had to view at least current costs as a factor in maximising the objective function. As a result of gradual liberalisation of the investment process and decentralisation of depreciation funds, capital expenditures also became an optimisation factor. Like any firm maximising profits under the conditions of stable prices, such an enterprise will in the short term (i.e., as long as the volume of fixed capital remains stable) strive for the scale of production that is optimal for it and that is associated with equality of marginal costs and price. As a result of the abolition of directive planning, if it is assumed that the price remains stable, the volume of production at every enterprise should decline from the planned less profitable or loss making level to the lower level, which is optimal in the short term. At the same time, as a socialist enterprise functioning within the framework of directive centralised planning, it is forced to produce at a level higher than is optimal and thus is either less profitable or altogether unprofitable.

These two absolutely incompatible criteria have had different values during different periods of history. If we recall the times directly preceding the disintegration of the communist system, they can be interpreted as gradual disappearance of *stimuli* to fulfil the plan and intensification of the profit maximisation criterion. This *ceteris paribus* meant that the lowering of the production volume from the level dictated by the planned optimal level was inevitable. In precisely the same way, it is obvious that it was impossible to avoid the rapid rise in prices just as soon as (and even before) the price formation process was liberalised.

Thus, in an economy where the state sector was still dominant, there arose a new situation that can be characterised by the following properties:

- the demand for the products of large state enterprises continues to diminish;
- trade unions and work collectives bring pressure to bear on the government and on enterprise management, demanding the most complete indexing of income possible;
- prices continue to rise rapidly. As a result of galloping inflation, the nominal interest rate and the expected return on investment prove to be less than the actual inflation rate, which leads to a substantial lowering in the propensity of domestic investors to invest and a dampening of the investment climate in the nation as a whole from the standpoint of foreign entrepreneurs, especially in the case of projects that cannot be expected to yield a return within a short time period;

- managers of state enterprises, even if they are not advocates of privatisation, understand its inevitability. It is thus difficult to expect them so make fundamental investment decisions beyond the limits of state financing and/or the necessity to at least partially compensate for worn-out equipment;
- as a result, making ends meet becomes the objective function of enterprise rather than profit maximisation. In the best case (for the enterprise), by raising the prices of its products and thus promoting inflation, it can cover the growing costs of wages and raw materials, supplies, energy, and equipment.

The impact of declining production volume on employment differs from country to country, even though it has been more or less inelastic in the majority of cases, with the exception of Poland. Until now, the level of unemployment in Russia has not matched the reduction in GDP since 1990, when all the fundamentals of the Russian economy started to dramatically deteriorate. This means that employment has been to a certain degree artificially supported by the government under pressure from the populist lobby.

We now consider the situation in the Russian economy that directly preceded mass privatisation and that occurred at its very beginning. The majority of enterprises functioned at that time according to the criterion of making ends meet, along with artificially supported employment. Within the state-owned sector there was a total absence of the propensity to invest, along with only partial replacement of worn-out equipment. The enterprise was then, at best, only capable of maintaining the balance between income and costs. In such a situation, price was the only parameter that could ensure balance. However, if and where prices were not entirely liberated, and the state's obligations to protect employment were quite strong, the only way that employment and wages could be secured was to subsidise enterprises that could not make ends meet on their own. This leads to further disintegration of the economy.

In Kazakevitch (1994 and 1995), it was theoretically proven, that under the above-listed conditions, an enterprise has an incentive to decrease the volume of output as prices rise. The prevailing economic conditions caused further inflation, which inevitably entailed a further lowering of the volume of production. Therefore, the longer radical microeconomic reform measures were delayed, the more powerful were demands for strict anti-inflationary measures. These were not then caused by the high-handedness of the International Monetary Fund or monetarist romanticism, but as a necessary condition for emerging from the post-communist recession. At the same time, the situation could not be improved substantially by monetarist methods alone. It is for this very reason that privatisation is understood as the other key direction of the reforms.

Conditions of Privatisation and Short-term Macroeconomic Consequences

Abolition of directive planning also means that the absolutely inelastic aggregated supply, which is a characteristic of the command economy, becomes more or less elastic. This means that an increase in price is generally an incentive for the industry to increase its output. However, this is theoretically true only if a competitive market environment is created where managerial decisions are made on behalf of owners with the objective of maximising profit. These decisions should be determined only by a mechanism of market forces.

There are kinds of market, however, where an increase in price causes a decrease in output. Such a market was found, for example, in the 'market socialism' in Yugoslavia, where state enterprises were collectively managed by hired workers. The work collective of each enterprise was to have paid the state rent for the use of fixed capital and, according to the key concept in the analysis of the Illyrian economy, functioned according to the criterion of 'maximum net income per worker' (Ward, 1958). It was exactly such a character of the objective function that led to a situation where in the short term (in neo-classical terms, this corresponds to a fixed volume of fixed capital), the microeconomic supply function was decreased, and, as a result of rising prices of enterprise products, the volume of output and the size of the workforce should theoretically have decreased. In the long term, additional capital investment can lead to a higher level of optimal production volume, to an increase in employment, and to distribution of a new volume of net income among the increased number of members of the work collective.

The following question arises: are enterprises other than state-owned ones possible in an Illyrian economy but with an analogous optimality criterion?

We now consider a small or average former state enterprise that as a result of privatisation is transformed into either a limited partnership or a closed corporation exclusively owned by its workforce. We will also look at an open corporation whose work collective holds the controlling block of stocks in its hands, or, by any means, is capable of considerably affecting managerial decisions. Generally speaking, in both instances no one prevents enterprise management from making decisions about investment and hiring additional personnel in the free labour market and so it does not act like the classic Yugoslav enterprise, i.e., not according to the criterion of maximum net income per worker, but rather according to the criterion of maximum profit. However, at the initial stage of privatisation, with its galloping inflation and uncertainty about return on investment, it does not, at least in the short term, allow hope for increased employment by hiring outside workers. Members of the work collective can above all be expected to pay heed to their corporate interest, which inevitably leads to the optimality criterion of a Yugoslav-type enterprise and to a decreased production volume and rising prices. If we assume that such syndicalist-type enterprises comprise the majority in the privatised sector, then such privatisation cannot in principle solve the problem of emergence from recession. In Russia, at least, some of the newly privatised enterprises were acting more like Illyrian-type companies, and therefore, were not capable of acting to remedy the post-communist recession.

On the contrary, if as a result of privatisation decisions are made in isolation from the work collective and the enterprise functions according to the laws of the market by maximising its absolute profit volume, its supply function will grow with rising prices, which, in the absence of investment, even in the short term should theoretically lead to increased production against the background of continuing inflation. Therefore, if the adopted privatisation schemes lead to the formation of such enterprises in a certain proportion of the economy, then a certain degree of improvement could be expected of such privatisation in the short term. However, as is well known, in the absence of capital investment, the law of diminishing marginal labour productivity operates and limits the potential for economic growth due to just the one factor. Thus, the beginning of a return to economic growth should be reinforced by the certainty that there will be a return on investment, which in turn could be attained only by an adequate monetary and tax policy. However, such an investment climate was not created in Russia at the earlier stages of privatisation.

Therefore neither of two above-mentioned privatisation outcomes could initially contribute significantly to pulling Russia out of its post-communist recession.

Another question is whether normal privatisation leading to maximisation of profit should necessarily increase the demand for factors of production including labour. The answer is no, not always. It depends on whether movement begins in the direction of equilibrium in the markets before mass privatisation commences. As a result of the elimination of directive planning and the subsequent reduction in production one would expect reduction in factor usage. That is, a corresponding decrease in employment and only partial, if any, replacement of depreciated physical capital. As was mentioned earlier, this was not the case at the initial stage of the Russian post-communist transformation, where a policy to support employment was pursued prior to mass privatisation. This is why factor clearance, in general, and a decrease in employment, in particular, were inevitable during the initial stage of privatisation. This was one of the reasons for the decrease in effective demand and the continuing shrinkage of the Russian economy even after mass privatisation had been mostly completed.

The Concept of Vegetative Adaptation and the Dynamics of Reforms

The concept of vegetative adaptation was originally developed by J.Kornai (Kornai, 1980, 1982; Kornai and Martos, 1981) with reference to centrally planned economies. The idea of vegetative adaptation is that the key factor of both market and macro-economic policy decision-making in communist countries was a single scalar signal.

Such a signal is of non-market character, in general, and non-price, in particular. Furthermore, a decision made at a particular time (t) was made based on the value of the signal related to only the previous period of time (t-1). For example, if such a signal is the stock of a particular product, then the stock exceeding a particular critical level causes a decision to reduce production. On the contrary, the deficiency in stock below a critical level causes the amount of production to be increased.

Another such signal is the level of shortage. The nature of this signal, with respect to the command economy, was studied by Kornai (1980 and 1982). Assuming that the level of shortages in the economy could be measured and aggregated, Kornai suggested that each centrally planned economy at any period of time could be characterised with a level of shortage that could be considered as 'normal'. The objective of the centrally planned system was economic and political survival. At the normal level of shortages, there was no threat to the decision-makers' survival, and therefore, no substantial managerial decision was necessary. If the actual level of shortages exceeded the normal one, an investment decision was required for increase in production.

During the early stage of the transition, economic policy decisions coexist that are appropriate to both the old command and the new market systems. Moreover, this policy-making is run by the generation of politicians that grew up, were educated, and gained at least some of their experience, during the Soviet time. Therefore, it is appropriate to ask the following questions: Is a kind of vegetative adaptation inherent in the post-communist economic policy decision-making process? If yes, then can it be described with a scalar endogenous variable? And finally, can the theory of 'vegetative adaptation' help in the explanation of the economic fundamentals of transitional economies in general, and the reason for the slowing down of the reforms themselves, in particular? [1]

Let us assume the situation when the early period of reforms has been completed:

- the legislative base of the new system has been established based on private ownership;
- the directive planning institutions and practices have been abolished;
- prices and wages have been liberalised; and
- the financial system has been normalised, at least to the extent that there is no danger of an immediate collapse.

Therefore, there is at least some investor confidence for participation in either privatisation or in new investment projects. At the same time, as is well known from the experience of both Russia and other post-communist countries, at that stage of transition part of the economy, including employment, was (and still is) artificially supported.

Consider the next stage of reform, the one that includes further deregulation and systematic privatisation. From the macroeconomic perspective, there are three components of the economy: the government, the aggregate entrepreneur and the aggregate population (household).

The government, via its structures and the managers of the government owned business entities, is involved in two major kinds of activities at the microeconomic level: privatisation, and running businesses that are not yet privatised or are not considered for privatisation at all.

One would expect that no matter if an enterprise is assigned for privatisation or not, there would be at least some incentive for productivity improvement. Even if the enterprise were scheduled for privatisation, this would increase its market value.[2] If an enterprise is to be retained by the government, the government authorities, as well as the management of the enterprise, should be interested in investment and structural and organisational adjustment to the new conditions of the market economy. However, due to the generally poor financial situation, a lack of investor confidence, and the extremely large scale of the privatisation campaign, the government cannot in fact, look after either kind of enterprise. Instead, it can be assumed that during the transitional period only one microeconomic policy decision the government makes will be visible at the macro level. This is the intensity (speed) of privatisation at any given period of time.

The aggregate entrepreneur accumulates the entire amount of financial resources available in the economy, at a particular period of time for investment, and makes a decision on the allocation of investment between domestic and foreign assets. As far as domestic investment is concerned, decisions are made by the aggregate entrepreneur on:

- which privatised assets to invest in;
- how much to invest in them;
- how much to invest in the improvement of privatised assets; and
- how much to spend on their improvement; and
- how much to invest in new capital assets.

The aggregate population (household) sells labour, accumulates aggregate income, pays taxes, forms the consumer demand and, in the capacity of the aggregate entrepreneur, makes investment decisions.

Assume that a certain enterprise in the economy is to be privatised. The goal of privatisation from the standpoint of the idea of economic reform is an increase in effectiveness based on the initiatives of investment in the new enterprises whose behaviour is determined by market stimuli. If we generalise the measures that owners and managers can take to attain their goals in real (physical) rather than monetary-financial terms, this will mean reconstruction and technical retooling of enterprises, as well as more rational use of labour, raw materials, and energy.

In macroeconomic terms, the first of these measures inevitably entails a further temporary reduction of employment, which is partially offset by the additional demand for labour to participate in the reconstruction process. It is essential to recall that, since the production volume at state enterprises has substantially dropped without a corresponding reduction in production capacities during the stage of reform that preceded privatisation, the optimisation of production factors at a lower level of demand for products must inevitably lead to a decrease in the volume of resources used. This is in itself a factor in lowering aggregated demand and consequently employment during the initial stage of mass privatisation. The second of these measures is also a direct cause of further reduced employment and hence of aggregated final demand.

Thus, privatisation of every enterprise, at least during the time required for its reconstruction, reduces aggregated production still more, even though it promises restoration and growth after a certain period of time.

Under these conditions, the government seeks a compromise between two strategies:

- acceleration of the privatisation process in order to return to economic growth as soon as possible, but at the price of further lowering of the standard of living while enterprises are undergoing reconstruction by their new owners, and
- deceleration of privatisation in order to avert losses and negative, even if only temporary, social consequences.

The challenge of finding the mechanism for attaining this compromise is at the junction of economic and political-scientific analysis.

A post-communist government comes to power as the result of more or less democratic elections, promising the population to build a market-type economy potentially capable of raising living standards. Such a government offers a reform programme that promises to restore the national economy and to improve the quality of life during a certain period of time if people are willing to work stubbornly and to reconcile themselves to the difficulties of the transition period. However, the political aim of this, and of any other, government is to retain power and defeat alternative political forces at election time. Therefore, before venturing into this compromise, we must also be mindful of the other side: the reaction of the population to the economic situation.

Figure 8.1   Vegetative adaptation in the post-communist era

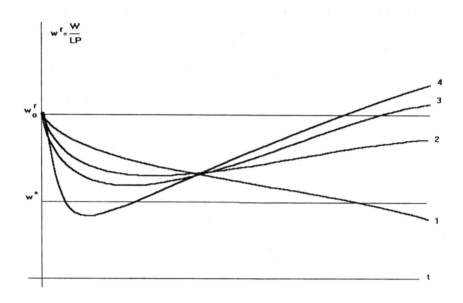

W - aggregate nominal income
P - price index
L - population
$W^r = W/(PL)$ - real income per capita
W^r_0 - real income per capita in the beginning of the reform
W^* - the critical level of real income per capita

We assume that this reaction is based on some macroeconomic indicator that reflects the standard of living, for example, real per capita income. We also assume that there is a certain critical normal level of the indicator, by analogy with the normal level of shortage in Kornai's model of a socialist economy. While being in principle quantifiable, this critical level cannot be directly calculated for the purpose of making decisions at every moment in time. However, the government does receive information about approaching the dangerous critical level indirectly via a multitude of feedback signals.

The hypothesis of vegetative adaptation[3] for a post-communist government discussed here consists of the fact that, if the de facto level of per capita real income is lower than the critical level, the government will evaluate the situation as unstable and dangerous, and as a result will slow down the reform process. This will be expressed in the form of the volume of state fixed capital that is privatised per unit of time or in the intensity of other reform measures.

This concept is graphically presented in Figure 8.1. The four curves reflect different reform strategies in terms of the outcome of the reform that is measured dynamics of real per capita income (W^r). All variants begin at the same level of this indicator (W^r_0) and entail its reduction during the initial stage of reforms. The first curve corresponds to a strategy either without general privatisation or in those forms of it that do not create stimuli for maximising profit volume. Variants 2 and 3 are more or less moderate strategies that nevertheless lead to maximisation of profit as the goal of functioning enterprises. At the same time, the more rapid reforms are, the lower the level of real income will fall during its initial stage, but the higher the value of this indicator will be in the future. The fourth curve corresponds to the most rapid reform and to peak long-term results, but also leads to a decline in real income below the critical level during the initial stage.

So, which of the curves 1-4 describes the process of economic reforms in Russia during the period of Yeltsin's presidency? Consider the trends in the Russian economy during the recent decade. Figure 8.2 represents the fundamental economic indicators, Figure 8.3 – the situation in the agricultural sector, traditionally one of the most vulnerable sectors.[4] Both figures show the declining stage of the basic economic indicators directly affecting living standards.

The fact that a considerable part of the Russian economy has already undergone microeconomic reforms does not allow the assumption that the country's economic situation corresponds to the declining segment of curves 3 or 4. Russia is not going through an intensive reform process of the kind that may soon be followed by dramatic growth. More realistically, we are observing a moderate recovery stage after a period of rather cautious and inconsistent reforms during the Yeltsin era, this is better described with curve 2. This means that the Russian leadership has basically avoided a decline of living standards below the critical level.

However, the price paid for such a 'gradualist' approach is both an inability to return to the higher pre-reform level of fundamental indicators as well as a lack of investor confidence. The latter result, in particular, means insufficient *aggregate entrepreneur's* confidence. This is the reason for potential domestic investors tending to use any possible opportunity not to repatriate export revenue back to the country and/or to invest abroad. In addition, this worsens the situation of traditional drastic tax avoidance by the *population (households)* and their increasing propensity to keep savings in a liquid form and/or in secure deposits and/or to invest abroad. All of the above contributes to the explanation of the chronic *Government* interest in international financial assistance in general, and IMF tranches in particular.

Figure 8.2   Macroeconomic and oil industry performance indicators (indices, 1990 = 100)

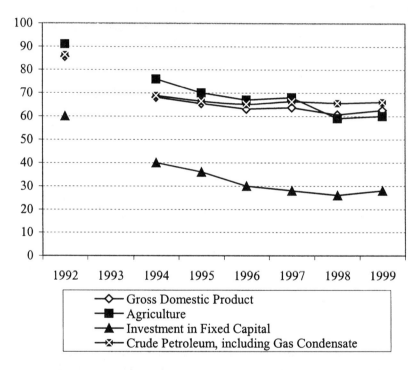

Meanwhile, a fundamental principal that international financial organisations have applied to the post-communist countries has been that of 'assistance for reform'. Any request for further tranches leads to a scrupulous analysis of what has been wrong with the microeconomic situation and macroeconomic governance of the Russian economy. The most likely outcome of such an analysis would be, and normally was, a request for further, more radical reforms in the microeconomic sphere and for improvement of controllability of the microeconomic and fiscal situation, based on best practices adopted in developed industrialised nations.

Figure 8.3   Russian domestic food production per capita (indices, 1990 = 100)

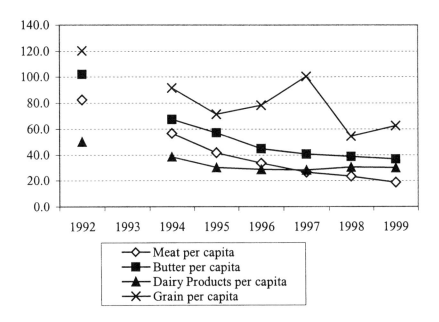

However the more compliant the government is with such conditions for obtaining further assistance, the tougher the financial policies that must be adopted, and the more radical the expected changes in the microeconomic sphere. Therefore, the population becomes more vulnerable, and that may cause de-stabilisation of the political situation. Based on the principle of vegetative adaptation, the government is facing certain limits on how much further they can go with reforms. Meanwhile, the stability of the political situation is one of the factors considered by both domestic and foreign investors when deciding on the level of investment activity. If the political situation worsens their confidence decreases and they tend to reallocate their funds. Part of the Russian problem is also the diversion of export revenue from its repatriation to the country. This further diminishes the ability of the authorities to cope with financial problems and causes requests for further international assistance, creating a vicious circle (see Figure 8.4). Requests for further assistance cause further conditions by the IMF before issuing tranches.

Figure 8.4   Investor confidence and IMF's expectations

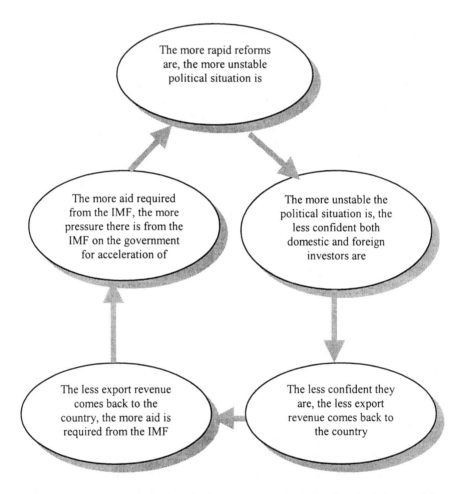

Can the Government break this vicious circle? The decision-making alternatives (Figure 8.5) depend on which of the following opportunities the Government has.

Figure 8.5   Possible strategy-making decisions for a Russian government facing financial hardship

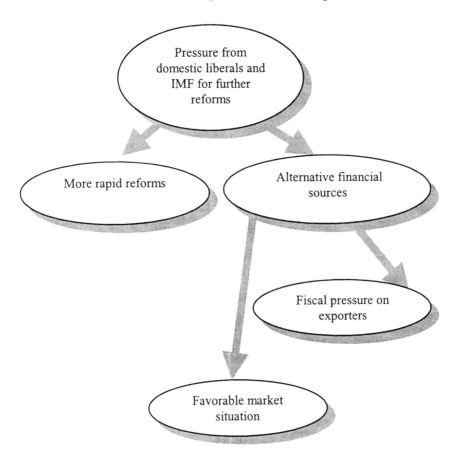

Of course, the continuation of reforms is possible within certain limits. However, it could also be politically dangerous if not suicidal. An alternative would be to find financial sources that are not subject to unpopular conditions imposed from outside. There are two obvious sources. The Government could consider reversing the reforms in the area of international trade and finance. Restrictions, tough licensing mechanisms or other kinds of pressure could be placed on exporters. Foreign currency accounts could be frozen or compulsory conversion of export revenue requested. Some of these kinds of measures are just hypothetical or among those desired by certain opposition political forces. Some are part of the recent history of reforms.

Such measures, however, may be extremely unpopular among Western trading partners and may cause the suspension of any further assistance. Therefore, in the current political environment, they are better partially or completely avoided if there any other financial opportunities available. Traditionally, throughout the recent history of the USSR and post-Soviet Russia, such an opportunity was an increase in the prices of the major commodities exported by Russia – oil and gas.

Let us have a look at the dynamics of US prices for crude oil – a consistent long-term indicator of world trends (Figure 8.6).

Figure 8.6   Oil prices: long-term trend, 1920-2000

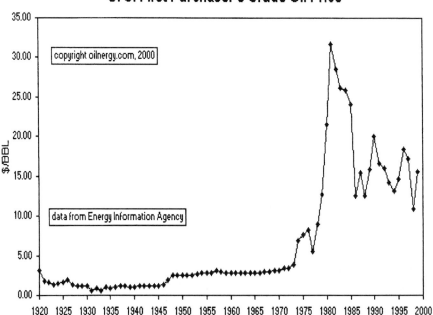

Source: Oilnergy (2000).

The poor performance of the Soviet Economy in the 1970s and early 1980s was compensated for by dramatic increase in the inflow of oil dollars due to the increase of prices during that period. Despite the overall decrease in the productivity of major industries, the Soviet Union was able to increasingly import food products as well as to fund the early stages of the Afghan war. On the other hand, Andropov and Gorbachev's calls for reform coincide with the slide of oil prices in the late 1980s.

Oil prices were rather volatile throughout the 1990s. This was of course compensated for by the readiness of the West to contribute to the success of the reforms. However, the financial crisis of August 1998 corresponds to the lowest oil prices of the 1990s.

Figure 8.7   Oil prices: the last 12 months trend, July 1999 – July 2000

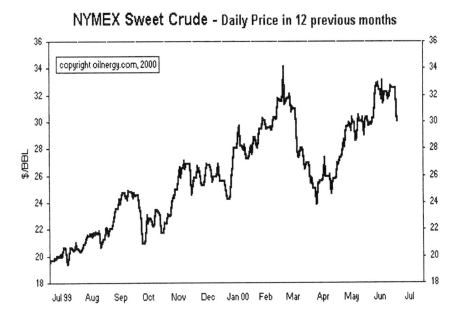

Source: Oilenergy (2000).

During the past two years (1999-2000) the situation of domestic manufacturing has dramatically improved, as imported goods have been less affordable since August 1998. At the same time the inflow of oil dollars steadily increased (Figure 8.7), including during the period since Putin became Prime Minister. This helped improve the Russian economic situation, has funded the Second Chechen War, and has contributed to Putin's popularity and elevation to the post of President. It has also made

Russia capable of developing economic polices that are less dependant on IMF requirements and more in tune with rising nationalist ambitions.

Figure 8.8   Oil prices: the current year trend, April–October 2000

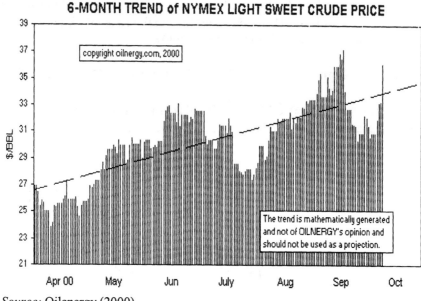

Source: Oilenergy (2000).

A conclusion about future developments in Russian economic policy may perhaps be linked with oil price trends as well. If prices continue to increase (Figure 8.8), then one would expect Russia to have a better economic situation, less reform, and more nationalist and militarist decision-making. If, on the other hand, prices for oil stabilise or go down, a more rigorous and risky reform process should be expected.

Notes

1   From the theoretical perspective, this question was considered in Kazakevitch (1994 and 1995).

2   This is what can be observed in the case of the deregulation of public utilities in developed countries, such as the electricity supply industry in UK in the 1980s or in the Australian State of Victoria in the 1990s.

3   This was initially considered in an analytical form in Kazakevitch (1994 and 1995).

4   Both figures are based on data from Statkom (2000).

References

Desai, M. and Estrin, S. (1992), *Some Simple Dynamics of Transition: From Command to Market Economy*, Discussion Paper No.85, Centre for Economic Performance, London School of Economics, London, July.

Gregory, R.S. (1990), *Soviet Economic Structure and Performance*, Forth Edition, Harper and Row, New York.

Kazakevitch, G. (1994 and 1995), 'Macroeconomic Issues of Privatisation in Russia and Eastern Europe', *Ekonomika i matematicheskie metody*, Moscow, no.3, 1994. Translation into English in *MATECON*, Spring 1995, vol.32 (3).

Kornai, J. (1980), *Economics of Shortage*, Vols. A and B, North-Holland, Amsterdam.

Kornai, J. (1982), *Growth, Shortage and Efficiency*, Basil Blackwell, Oxford.

Kornai, J. and Martos, B. (eds) (1981), *Non-Price Control*, North-Holland, Amsterdam.

Oilnergy (2000), *Oilnergy Website* (www.oilnergy.com, accessed on 16 October, 2000).

Statkom (2000), *Sodruzhestvo Nezavisimykh Gosudarstv v 1999 godu*, Statkom SNG, Moscow.

Ward, B. (1958), 'The Firm In Illyria: Market Syndicalism', *American Economic Review*, vol.48 (4), pp.566-89.

9 Russia Compared to Soviet and World Standards

GEOFFREY JUKES

For assessing the prospects of post-Yeltsin Russia, there is some point in examining Russia as Putin inherited it, and comparing it both to what Yeltsin inherited from the Soviet Union, and to high-income countries the Soviet Union aspired to compete with and Russia aspires to join. There are, of course, problems with any such comparisons. Countries do not always use identical definitions, data may be unreliable because of faulty collection methods, falsification, or the existence of a large 'black' economy, or may refer to different years. However, if attention is concentrated on data where Russia differs greatly from the countries with which it is compared, a large number of indicators are used, covering a wide range of fields, the impact on the overall picture of shortcomings in individual indicators is reduced. As far as possible those principles have been adopted in what follows. Groups of indicators have been tabulated under living standards, the economy, industry, agriculture, transport, construction, capital investment, energy efficiency, pollution, reserves, and international trade. In many cases numbers have been rounded to the nearest integer or one place of decimals, as use of figures to two or more places of decimals can convey an impression of greater precision than is actually the case. Some tables use Gross Domestic Product (GDP), others Gross National Product (GNP). However, no table mixes the two, and the differences found are far larger than the differences between GDP and GNP.

The principal sources used are statistical handbooks published by the Interstate Statistical Committee of the Commonwealth of Independent States (CIS) (Statkom, 1999 and 2000), World Bank (1998, 1999 and 2000) and the Russian State Statistical Committee, *Goskomstat* (1999a, 1999c, 2000a, 2000b, 2000e and 2000f). These publications are all compendiums of data collected from a variety of sources, and may therefore help to mitigate any charge of reliance on too few sources. Some other sources have been drawn upon for individual points.

The first group of tables dealt with living standards, as it is they that impact most obviously on the Russian public. Average life expectancy at birth in most industrialised countries in 1998 ranged from 74 years (USA) to 77 (Japan) for males, and from 80 (USA) to 84 (Japan) for females. The Soviet figures in 1990 were 64 for males and 74 for females. By 1994 they had fallen to 57.6 for men and below 71.2 for women. They improved somewhat thereafter, but in 1998, at 61 for males and 73 for females, were still below the Soviet level and well below the 1997 average (75 and 81) of the industrialised countries (Statkom, 1999, pp.44-5, World Bank, 2000, p.277).

The main reasons for the deterioration are declines in incomes, and in health and welfare services. But two other factors probably played a part. One is alcohol consumption. In absolute terms (equivalent litres of pure alcohol per head per annum) Russian consumption in 1997 (7.5 litres) was almost the same as in Australia (7.6) or the United Kingdom (7.8 in 1996), and well below those of France (11.5 litres) or Germany (9.9). But while in those countries most alcohol is consumed as beer or wine, a high proportion of Russian consumption was in spirits (14.8 litres, versus 6.3 in France, 5.5 in Germany, 3.4 in Australia, 3.5 in UK), and had increased considerably from 9.8 litres in 1990 (Statkom, 1999, pp.71-2).

The second factor was infant mortality. Deaths in first year per 1,000 live births in most industrialised countries in 1990 ranged from 4.6 in Japan, via 7.9 in UK and 8.2 in Australia, to 9.2 in the USA. The Soviet figure then was 17.4. By 1997 the industrialised countries had reduced theirs to a range from 3.8 in Japan to 7.2 in the USA (Australia 5.3, UK 5.9). But in Russia it fell only to 17.2 (Statkom, 1999, pp.38-9). It then improved slightly, to 16.5 in 1998 and 1999 (Goskomstat, 2000b, p.71).

Diet also worsened. In 1990 the average Russian consumed 75 kilos of meat (including poultry), 20 of fish, 386 of dairy products, 119 of bread, 106 of potatoes, and 297 eggs. By 1996 consumption of meat had fallen to 50 kilos, of fish to 9 kilos, of dairy products to 229 kilos, and of eggs to 210. But bread consumption (118 kilos) was almost unchanged, while that of potatoes had risen by almost 20% to 130 kilos. Consumption of other vegetables, of sugar, butter and vegetable oils also fell significantly (Statkom, 1999, pp.69-70; Goskomstat, 1999c, p.115). In summary, there was a shift towards cheaper carbohydrates, a classic response to reduced purchasing power but not necessarily conducive to health. A household consumption survey in 1997 found increased consumption of all foods in urban areas over 1996, but in rural areas a continued fall in all except fish and sugar-based products (Goskomstat, 1999c, p.115). A 1998 survey of household expenditures showed that since 1993 spending on food had risen from 43.5% of average household income to 51.4% (Goskomstat, 1999c, p.113). In 1999 it rose further, to 52% (Goskomstat, 2000b, p.107).

The range of cash incomes in the Soviet Union was not very wide, as most of the elite's privileges were in fringe benefits such as cars, superior housing and medical care, special shops, parcels of luxury foods, or trips abroad. This situation has changed radically. Surveys of income distribution are not made annually, so comparisons cannot be based on the same year. But in Russia in 1996 the 10% of lowest incomes had 1.7% of total incomes, about the same as in the USA in 1997 (1.8%). The highest 10% had 38.7% of total incomes in Russia, versus 30.5% in the USA, the industrialised country with the greatest gap between rich and poor. On the Gini index, which measures inequality of income distribution on a scale of 0 (all on same income) to 100 (maximum inequality), the USA (1997) came out at 40.8 and Russia (1998) at 48.7, Australia (1994) at 35.2, UK (1991) at 36.1 and Sweden (1992) at 25.0 (World Bank, 2000, pp.282-3.).

Income inequality has increased in most industrialised countries since the Gini surveys were made. It is officially claimed that by June 2000 the figure for Russia dropped to 40 (Goskomstat, 2000e, p.187), and that between the first quarter of 1999 and that of 2000 the top 10%'s share of total earnings dropped to 33.4%, while that of the poorest 10% increased from 2.7% (Goskomstat, 2000f, p.198). Nevertheless, of 132 countries listed by the World Bank (2000, pp.282-3), only 20, mostly in Latin America and sub-Saharan Africa, showed a larger gap between rich and poor than Russia.

Real disposable income in the post-Soviet years has fluctuated, but with a general downward trend. In 1998 average real income was only 50.4% of what it was in 1991 (Goskomstat, 1999c, p.101). Data on the population living below the poverty line are sometimes rubbery, because definitions differ between countries, poverty in a rich country can equal relative wealth in a poor one, and within a country, an income insufficient for urban living may be adequate for a rural area. Also the tables in the World Bank 1999 Development Report provide data on poverty for only 69 of the 132 countries surveyed, and for widely differing years. Of the other 68 countries providing data, 29 claimed a lower percentage below the poverty line than Russia (World Bank, 1999, pp.236-7). Russia in 1994 assessed 30.9% of its population as living below the poverty line, and 22.4% as having less than the minimum necessary for survival. By 1998 the latter figure had risen to 23.8%, and in 1999 it escalated to 29.9%, or almost 44 million people (Goskomstat, 2000b, p.98).

Russian labour market statistics showed a decline in the 'economically active' from 72 million in 1992 to 63.6 million in 1998, peaking at 74 million in November 1999, thereafter declining slightly to 73.6 million by May 2000 (Goskomstat, 2000f, p.207). Unemployment rose from 3.9 million (4.7% of the labour force) in 1992 to a peak of 10.4 million in

February 1999, declining thereafter to 8.5 million (11.5%) by May 2000 (Goskomstat, 2000f, pp.206-7). Numbers of registered unemployed per vacancy rose from 3 in 1990 to 11 in 1996, but by the second quarter of 2000 were down to 1.4 (Goskomstat, 2000f, p.211). Nevertheless, an unemployment rate of 11.5% remains a serious problem, especially for a country that until 1991 officially had no unemployment, and therefore no system for handling it. The number of unemployed registered with the state employment service peaked at 2.51 million in 1996, even at that only 37.2% of that year's 6.7 million unemployed. By the end of 1999 unemployment had risen to 8.1 million, but the number registered had halved, to 1.26 million (15.7%).[1] Numbers of registered unemployed per notified job vacancy peaked at 11 in 1996, were 6.6 in January 1999, but fell steadily thereafter to 1.4 in May 2000. This was due both to an increase in vacancies (from 329,000 in January 1999 to 868,000 in May 2000), and to the fall in registered unemployed, mentioned above (Goskomstat, 2000b, p.84, and 2000f, pp.210-1). Women were more inclined than men to register. In 1998, for example, they were 46.1% of all unemployed, but 64.6% of those registered.[2]

Nor was the number of unemployed the only bad news. At the end of 1999 the age group 15-24 was 15.2% of the population, but 23.3% of the unemployed, indicating a serious youth unemployment problem. The average age of the unemployed was 35, and 87% were under the age of 50, rendering devices such as early retirement of very limited utility (Goskomstat, 2000b, pp.84-5).

Categorisation of the labour force by reference to sectors of the economy showed that employment in industry fell from 30% of all employment in 1991 to 22.2% in 1999, while industrial production fell to 50% of 1991. Employment in agriculture had actually risen slightly as a proportion, from 13.2 to 13.4% and in transport fell only from 7.7 to 6.3% (Goskomstat, 2000b, p.79), even though agricultural production shrank by over one-third and both goods and passengers transported by over two-thirds. In short, labour productivity, low in Soviet times, has declined further, and underemployment and concealed unemployment are even higher than they were then.

From 1992 to the end of 1999 state/municipal employment was more than halved, from 49.7 to 23.9 million, while private sector employment more than doubled, from 13.2 to 29.3 million. Joint ventures with foreign firms provided only 195,000 jobs in 1992 (0.3% of jobs). This increased more than six-fold, to 1.26 million in 1999, a respectable rate of growth, but from that low base still providing only 2% of jobs (Goskomstat, 1999c, p.80, and 2000b, p.77).

Data on crime (including attempted crime) levels showed that total reported crimes declined by 7%, from 2.76 million in 1992 to 2.58 million in 1998, but then rose to 3 million in 1999. The number arrested also rose, and so did the numbers of more serious crimes. From 1992 murders (including attempted murders) went up from 23,000 to 31,100 in 1999, robbery with violence from 30,400 to 41,100, and drug-associated crimes increased over sevenfold, from 29,800 to 216,000. Attacks causing grievous bodily harm but not involving theft rose from 53,900 in 1992 to a peak of 67,700 in 1994, then declined to 45,200 in 1998, but rose again to 47,700 in 1999. Rape, including attempted rape, fell from 13,700 to 8,300 cases. This seems a very low figure for a population of 146 million with high and rising levels of other violent crimes, but it is likely that in Russia, as in many other countries, most rapes go unreported. The most common form of crime, theft without violence, fell substantially, from 1.8 million in 1992 to 1.26 million in 1998, but rose to 1.55 million in 1999. Although the number of cars almost doubled between 1992 and 1999, traffic offences fell from 90,100 to 53,700. Bribery of traffic police may help to explain this, especially as the least bribable traffic offences, those involving a death, fell only from 17,500 to 15,100 (Goskomstat, 1999c, p.145, and 2000b, p.112).

A fall in crime accompanied by an increase in detained criminals can be ascribed to more efficient policing, or viewed as paradoxical. That the latter may be nearer the truth is suggested by the data on gender and age of defendants. From 1992 to 1999 criminals apprehended increased by 49%, from 1.149 to 1.717 million. Males apprehended increased by 43%, from 1.018 million to 1.456 million, women by no less than 99%, from 131,000 to 261,000. For both sexes the increase over 1998 was substantial, 15% for males and 19.7% for females. The only age group in which crime fell from 1992 to 1999 (by only 2.8%) was ages 14 to 17 years, and the 1999 figures were 14% higher than those of 1998 (Goskomstat, 2000b, p.112). Among those aged 18-24 the 1992-99 increase was 83%, 25-29 52%, and among over-30s 51%. The numbers with no steady income at the time of the offence rocketed by 324%, from 294,000 to 954,000 (Goskomstat, 2000b, p.113). Only 37,200 (12.7%) of these defendants in 1992 and 93,700 (10.2%) in 1999 were registered as unemployed at the time they offended.

Table 9.1   Russia's main macroeconomic indicators, 1999

1999 as % of 1998

GDP	103.2
Industry	108.0
Agriculture	102.4
Capital Investment	104.5
Retail Trade	92.0

Source: Statkom, 2000, p.95.

Data in Table 9.1 suggested that Russia's economy may have bottomed out, the reduction in retail trade being a transitory effect of the economic crisis of August 1998. More recent data suggest that retail trade ceased declining in March 1999, began to rise in the fourth quarter of 1999, and in January-May 2000 was running at 107.6% of the same period of 1999, i.e. had almost (99.3%) re-attained its 1998 pre-crisis level (Goskomstat, 2000f, p.66). However, the volume indices of Gross Domestic Product (GDP) showed that in mid-1998 it stood at only 57.6% of the 1991 level (Statkom, 1999, p.97), and rose modestly in 1999 to 62.5% of 1991 (Statkom, 2000, p.13). The first quarter of the year is normally the least productive, and 2000's was no exception; output was only 90.9% of the preceding quarter. But it was 108.4% of the first quarter of 1999 (Goskomstat, 2000f, pp.9-10), indicating that recovery is continuing.

World Bank (2000) figures for Gross National Product (GNP) in 1999 (in billion US Dollars) showed Russia's GNP, at 333 billion, less than Australia's (381 billion), 8.2% of Japan's (4079 billion) and 4% of the USA's (8351 billion). At US$2,270 per head,[3] Russia ranked 98th of the 132 countries listed. When corrected for Purchasing Power Parity (PPP), to allow for differences in internal costs, Russia's GNP per head rose to $6,339, and its ranking to 80th, well behind some South-East Asian 'tigers' (e.g. Singapore, 7th, Malaysia, 72nd), but slightly ahead of Thailand, 90th) (World Bank, 2000, pp.274-5).

The role of the various branches of the economy is expressed by the value each adds as a percentage of the total GDP. In Russia in 1999 agriculture contributed 7%, Industry/manufacturing 34%, and Services 58%. The corresponding figures for Australia (1998) were 3, 40 and 71%, for the UK (1998) 2,31 and 67%, and for the USA (1999) 2, 26 and 72%. In the high-income countries the contribution of Services averaged 64%, and by 1998 some ex-Communist economies had reached this level (e.g. Poland 63%, Estonia 66%). Russia's indicators most resembled Thailand's (13, 40 and 49%), and its Services' contribution of 49.4% at May 2000, while a considerable advance on 1990's 35%, suggest Russia's Services sector is still relatively underdeveloped (Goskomstat, 2000f, p.10; World Bank, 1999, pp.252-3, 2000, pp.296-7).

Russia's development was not helped by the steady depreciation of its currency. In Soviet times, when the rouble was not convertible, various devices were employed to keep it artificially higher than the US dollar for long periods. After it became convertible, it plummeted, and by December 1997 had sunk to 5,960 to $1. A new rouble, equal to 1000 old ones, was introduced on 1 January 1998, at 6 to $1. By February 2000 it had dropped to 28.875,[4] but thereafter staged a modest recovery, and in July 2000 stood at 27.5.

Industrial Production

This has declined steadily, and in 1998 officially stood at only 46% of the 1990 level (Statkom, 1999, p.120). Electricity generated had fallen to 78% of its 1990 level, from 7,297 Kilowatt-Hours per head then to 5,663 in 1997, and dropped a further 2% in 1998. The fall mostly reflected reduced industrial demand (Statkom, 1999, p.124; Goskomstat, 1999c, p.175). That it has not fallen nearly as much as industrial production reflects several factors. One is that a factory's power requirements do not necessarily fall in direct proportion to falls in production. Another is that domestic and municipal demand is relatively inelastic. A third factor is production for the 'black economy', the exact dimensions of which cannot be precisely calculated. Oil production was down from 516 million tonnes to 306 million, only 59% of 1990. Natural gas production stood up better, mainly because of demand in Central and Western Europe; it fell only from 641 to 571 million cubic metres, 89% of 1990. Coal production, down from 395 million tonnes to 245 million, stood at only 62% of its 1990 level in 1998 (Statkom, 1999, pp.132, 134, 136). In December 1997 the World Bank approved a second loan of $800 million to further restructuring and privatisation in Russia's coal industry, and to improve the social 'safety net' for miners and their families most affected by restructuring (World Bank, 1998, p.43).

Production of iron and steel, plastics, chemicals, cement, mineral fertilisers, tyres, timber, paper, cardboard, textiles and footwear fell greatly, in some cases catastrophically. Car production fell only from 1.1 million in 1990 to 956,000 in 1999 (Statkom, 1999, p.148; Goskomstat, 2000b, p.116). By contrast, production of more economically useful trucks fell from 616,000 in 1991 to 134,000 in 1996, and rose only to 175,000 in 1999 (Goskomstat, 2000b, p.116). That is perhaps more a tribute to market freedom than a response to economic needs. An enormous fall in tractor production, from 214,000 in 1990 to 8,300 in 1998, and 13,100 in 1999 is one of the factors in the fall in agricultural production discussed below (Goskomstat, 2000b, p.117). Reduced consumer purchasing power was reflected in falls in production of television sets to only 7% and of refrigerators to only 31% of their 1990 levels (Statkom, 1999, pp.150, 152).

Agriculture

Production by volume in 1999 was only 57.3% of 1990, but labour employed in agriculture fell by only 10.2%, from 9.9 million in 1990 to 8.9 million in 1999 (Goskomstat, 2000b, pp.78, 199). This meant a considerable fall in productivity per worker from already low Soviet levels. Figures for value added per person employed in agriculture (calculated in 1995 US Dollars) were not available for the Soviet period, but will have been at least 30% higher in 1979-81 than in 1996-1998, or about $3,300 in 1979-81, which compared badly with Australia (20,880), or European producers such as France (14,956) or Denmark (21,321). By 1996-98 the Australian figure had increased by 48% to $30,904, in the two European countries more than doubled (to $36,889 and 46,621 respectively), but in Russia it had sunk to $2,476, in round figures one-twelfth of the Australian or one-eighteenth of the Danish level (World Bank, 1999, pp.244-5, 2000, pp.288-9).

Low and declining productivity per farm worker has been paralleled by low and declining productivity per hectare, and by a fall of 25% in the sown area, from 108.7 million hectares in 1992 to 77.6 million in 1999 (Goskomstat, 2000b, p.200). Crop yields naturally vary considerably from year to year, so in many countries yields per hectare in 1998-9 were below those of 1990. But a feature across a range of crops in Russia is that yields per hectare, low in Soviet times, were lower still in 1999. An important factor in this decline is inability to afford fertilisers. From 1993 to 1999 total sales of organic fertilisers to farms fell from 241 million to 69 million tonnes, and of mineral fertilisers (converted to 100% nutrients) from 4.3 million to 1.1 million tonnes (Goskomstat, 2000b, p.206). Because of climatic similarities, comparisons with Canada are especially relevant here. Russia averaged 1.85 tonnes of cereals or pulses per hectare in 1990, Canada 2.62. In 1997 Russia averaged 1.65 tonnes, Canada 2.47, USA 4.71 and UK 6.57 tonnes. In 1990 Russian potato growers averaged 9.9 tonnes per hectare, Canadians 23.8. In 1997 the Russian yield increased slightly, to 11.1 tonnes; but the Canadian, at 26.4 tonnes, was almost 2.5 times as much, while in less severe climates, yields averaged 31.3 tonnes in Australia, 40.8 in UK, 39.4 in the USA, and 46.5 in Denmark (Statkom, 1999, pp.198-9, 210-1). In 1999 the Russian yield fell again, to 10.2 tonnes per hectare.[5]

It was a similar story with sugar beet. Russia in 1990 averaged 22.1 tonnes per hectare, but dropped to 14.8 in 1997. Canadian yields in those years were 38.8 and 46.8 tonnes, UK 40.7 and 48, US 44.8 and 45.9, Japanese 55.5 and 54.3, French 66.8 and 70.9 (Statkom, 1999, pp.214-5). In 1999 the Russian yield improved, but only to 17.6 tonnes per hectare.[6]

Livestock and dairy farming also told a tale of decline. From 1990 to June 2000 the number of cattle in Russia dropped by 48.5% (from 58.8 to 30.3 million), of pigs by 53% (40 to 18.7 million), sheep and goats by 72% (61.3 to 17.1 million), and of poultry by 43% (from 654 to 372 million) (Statkom, 1999, p.221-28).[7] Dairy products dropped from 55.7 to 34.1 million tonnes, a fall of 39%, and declined again, to 33.2 million tonnes, in 1998 (Statkom, 1999, p.231). This was partly due to a drop in the yield of kilos (sic) per cow per annum. In 1990 a Canadian cow yielded on average 5,463 kilos, not quite twice the Russian average (2,781 kilos). But by 1997 the average Canadian yield was 6,225 kilos, whereas the Russian had fallen to 2,142 kilos. Average yields in a wide range of countries in 1997 were from 4,547 kilos in Australia to 5,713 kilos in UK, 7,690 in the USA and 8,444 in Israel (Statkom, 1999, pp.237-8). In 1998 yield per cow increased in Russia to 2,233 kilos, but the number of cows fell, from 15.9 to 14.5 million (Goskomstat, 1999c, p.218). By mid-2000 the number of cows had fallen even further, to 13.3 million (Goskomstat, 2000e, p.61).

Another factor contributing to the decline is the low and falling level of agricultural mechanisation. Figures for the number of tractors per thousand agricultural workers are available for Russia in 1994-6, but not for the Soviet period. However, there was 1 tractor per 92 hectares of arable land in 1992, versus 1 per 130 hectares in 1999 (Goskomstat, 2000b, p.205). After allowing for the reduced post-Soviet agricultural labour force and sown area, in 1990 there were at least 130 tractors per 1000 agricultural workers, falling to 122 in 1997, and 106 in 1998. International comparisons can be made for 1994-6. They show an average for high-income countries of 877 tractors per 1000, ranging as high as 1,452 in the USA and 1,683 in Canada. In 1999 alone the number of tractors in Russia dropped by 9% (Goskomstat, 1999c, pp.78, 210, and 2000b, p.204; World Bank, 1999, pp.244-5).

Reduction in agricultural machinery was not confined to tractors. For example, from December 1992 to December 1999 the number of ploughs dropped from 460 to 253 thousand, and of combine harvesters from 540 to 295 thousand.

Russian agriculture, under-mechanised in Soviet times, has clearly suffered a progressive and accelerating process of 'demechanisation' since. Russian agriculture is caught in a vicious circle of declining incomes reducing ability to buy machinery, fertilisers and pesticides, leading to lower yields and further decline in incomes.

Transport

Both passenger and freight transport showed very large declines. Freight moved by all transport modes (rail, road, inland waterways, sea, oil pipelines) fell by two-thirds, from 6,313 million tonnes in 1990 to 2,088 million in 1997.[8] When gas pipelines are included the 1997 figure was 2,571 million tonnes, but fell to 2349 million in 1998. A modest recovery then began, to 2,428 million in 1999 (Goskomstat, 2000b, p.230). The recovery was sustained into 2000; results for the first half of the year showed an overall increase of 5.6% over the first half of 1999 (Goskomstat, 2000e, p.65). If natural gas output is deducted, to make the mid-2000 figure directly comparable with 1990, freight transport, after eighteen months of recovery, was still only 33% of the 1990 level.

Passenger journeys fell by only 21%, from 31,860 to 25,291 million. But travel by rail and air - the principal modes for long journeys because of the inadequate road network and low numbers of private cars - fell much further. Journeys by rail fell by 1998 to only 47% of 1990, from 3,143 to 1,471 million. In 1999 the basis of calculation was modified;[9] on the new basis the 1998 figure was 1,208 million, and the 1999 total of 1,338 million indicated a rise of almost 11%. In the first half of 2000, rail transits (in passenger-kilometres rather than numbers of journeys) were 26.3% above the first half of 1999, though even this increase brought transits to only 52% of the 1990 level.[10]

Journeys by air in 1999 totalled 22 million, only 24% of the 91 million of 1990 (Statkom, 1999, pp.270-2; Goskomstat, 2000b, p.232). For both freight and passengers, the reductions in rail and air movements reflect not only reduced economic activity and incomes, but charges greatly increased from the very low Soviet levels.

A bizarre indicator of Russia's transport problems is that to generate one million dollars' worth of GDP at Purchasing Power Parity in 1998 Russia had to carry over five times as many ton/kilometres of goods by rail as the United States (1.042 million versus 213,000). The figures for the world's six largest countries cover a very wide range, the lowest being Brazil (31,663 in 1998) and Australia (76,786 in 1990), in both cases because of large rail-borne mineral exports over fairly short distances to ports. China (304,775) and Canada (440,137) occupied an intermediate position in 1998 (World Bank, 2000, pp.308-9). Russia's unfavourable figures reflect its distances, heavy dependence on railways, and poor road network. But the main factor is its inheritance of the gigantomaniac Soviet practice of building very large plants and power stations to serve several Republics. Any economies of scale compared to building more but smaller plants closer to regional source of supply and demand are offset by the need to transport raw materials (often of low value per tonne), fuel and components over large distances, and by long journeys to deliver finished products. In the Soviet period unrealistically low transport charges concealed the true costs.

The ratio of private cars to commercial vehicles (trucks and buses) also showed Russia's situation to differ widely from the generality. In 1990 there were 8.7 million cars there, about 1 per 17 of population, compared to an average of about one car per 2-3 persons in high-income countries. By the end of 1996 the number of cars in Russia had almost doubled, to 16.6 million, despite the shrinkage in the economy (Statkom, 1999, pp.259-61). Stranger still was Russia's very high ratio of cars to trucks and buses, 18 to 1 in 1990, 50 to 1 in 1996, compared to an average around 4 to 1 in high-income countries, and 7 to 1 in the ex-Communist countries of Central and Eastern Europe. The data are not always strictly comparable, because some countries, including Russia, count small goods vehicles (vans and utilities) as cars, whereas others rank them with trucks. However, to bring Russia's 1996 ratio down to the 4 to 1 of high-income countries would require at least one 'car' in five to be a van or utility, much higher than random observations of road traffic suggest to be the case.

High-Tech Industries and Information Technologies

High Technology exports are defined as 'products with high R & D intensity' (World Bank, 2000, p.329). The percentage of a country's exports definable as High Technology provides a rough indication of whether it ranks overall as an 'old' or 'new' economy. Among high-income countries high technology exports as a percentage of manufactured exports ranged in 1998 from 14% (Germany) to 59% (Singapore), with Australia at 11%, Canada at 15%, France at 23%, Japan at 26%, UK at 28%, USA at 33% and Russia 12% (World Bank, 2000, pp.266-7).

In personal computers per thousand of population in 1997, the high-income countries averaged 311, the leaders being USA (459), Singapore (458) and Switzerland (422). The next group comprised Australia, Norway, Denmark, Sweden and Finland, clustered in the range 412-350, then Canada, the Netherlands, New Zealand, Germany, UK, Ireland, Belgium and Hong Kong in the range 320-250, Japan (237), Israel (217) and France (208). The figure for Russia was 41, slightly above the average (34) for Latin America and the Caribbean. At that level almost all computers would be in offices, not homes or schools. Thus few Russian children can gain the 'hands on' exposure to computers now taken for granted by their coevals in many other countries, and this will affect the 'marketability' of the next generation of Russian labour.

A picture of the extent of computerisation in Russia's economy can be gained by juxtaposing data extracted from two tables in *Russia in Figures in 2000* (Goskomstat, 2000b). These give the figures for the end of 1998 of the numbers of 'enterprises' (firms), and the numbers having 'computing equipment' (Table 9.2).

The generally low levels of computerisation, and their concentration in administration are worthy of note. So, also, are the figures for total stock of computers and rate of growth of their use. The total stock of computers in enterprises at the end of 1998 is given as 2,054,497, of which 260,152 (12.7%) had been obtained during that year, and of the 95,580 'enterprises' which had computers, 37,601 (not necessarily all first-time users) had acquired a computer during the year. With computers available in 13.4% of educational 'enterprises', education looks better provided for than most other sectors, but its total of computers (306,300) is only 33 per 'enterprise' with computers, 4.4 per 'enterprise' over the sector as a whole, and, for the 21.97 million under education (Goskomstat, 2000b, p.116), one computer per 72 students. Even if all the computers are available to students, this is a very low figure for a generation whose contemporaries in most industrialised countries have an even chance of access to one at home, in addition to what may be provided at school or university.

Table 9.2   Computerisation in the Russian economy, 1999 (thousand)

	Total number of firms	Firms with computers
All Economy	2901.2	95.6
Industry	352.4	14.1
Agriculture	332.0	4.2
Construction	298.0	6.3
Transport	67.4	4.4
Communications	12.1	1.5
Finance, credit, insurance, etc.*	52.4	3.7
IT and Services **	7.6	1.1
Education	69.6	9.3
Administration	61.0	16.9

* Including issuing of pensions.
** It may be wondered what kind of computer information and servicing is available if, as the data indicate, only one firm in seven in that field actually has any computers.

Source: Goskomstat, 2000b, pp.156, 275.

On the World Bank figure of 40.6 computers per 1000 population, Russia's computer 'stock' should be 5.97 million rather than the 2.1 million cited above, which, of course, does not include computers in homes. Even if the higher figure is correct, a 'stock' of under 6 million for a population of 147 million is very small compared to most other industrialised countries. Using the World Bank figures cited above, the total 'stocks' of computers in 1998-99 were (in millions): USA 125, Japan 30.1, Germany 25, UK 15.5, France 11.2, Canada 10.2, Australia 7.8, the Netherlands 5, Sweden 3.3, Switzerland 3 and Singapore 1.5 (World Bank, 2000, pp.274-5, 310-1).

Low as it was, Russia's 40.6 computers per thousand population in 1998 nevertheless constituted an increase of two-thirds over 1996 (24). However, from such a low base a one-third increase per annum would have to be sustained until 2004 to pass the level reached by UK in 1997, and until 2006 to pass the US level of that year. This rate of increase will become harder to sustain as the base grows, if only because as yet Russia is not part of the world-wide system for mass-production of computers, peripherals and components for them. In the short term, therefore, the speed of computerisation of Russia will depend on its ability to import, which is constrained by its relatively low economic level and competition from the import requirements of other sectors in urgent need of modernisation. In the longer term, successful establishment of indigenous hardware and software production will depend on ability to compete with other low-wage economies, for example China and India, which are already well established within the worldwide system for producing them.

This low availability of personal computers naturally affected Internet access. In January 2000 the high-income countries averaged 777 Internet hosts per 10,000 population, the highest being the USA (1,940) followed by Finland (1,218). Russia had only 14.7, below the average level (18.9) for developing countries in Latin America and the Caribbean (World Bank, 2000, pp.310-1). Although Russia's very low figure represented 267% growth compared to mid-1997 (5.5), this was well below the average growth rate of Internet use in the high-income countries, in which it almost quadrupled in the same period, from 203 to 777 (World Bank, 1998, p.227, and 2000, pp.310-1). With exchange of information via the Internet (and its increasing use for commerce) a key feature of globalisation, Russia's comparatively low growth-rate in Internet access appears yet another short to medium-term disadvantage.

The high-income countries averaged 567 mainline and 265 mobile telephones per thousand of population, the highest for mainlines being Sweden (674) and for mobiles Finland (572). Russia, with 197 mainline and 5 mobile telephones per thousand, ranked just above the average (176) of 'upper middle income' countries for mainline phones, but at the 'low-income' countries' average (5) for mobiles.[11]

A potentially more promising situation exists in research and development, where Russia over the period 1987-97 had 3,587 scientists and engineers engaged in R&D per million of population. Out of 72 countries that provided data on this, Russia's was the fifth highest proportion, exceeded only by Japan (4,909), Sweden (3,826), the USA (3,676) and Norway (3,664) (World Bank, 2000, pp.310-1). Russia's R&D, like the rest of its economy, is short of funds, but the three countries most receptive of immigrants from Russia, Germany, Israel and the USA (Goskomstat, 2000b, p.73), all have high levels of research and development. Some well-qualified citizens of Russia can therefore escape current hardships by joining a 'brain drain', and some of them may return to Russia after accumulating enough capital and experience to start their own businesses. The overwhelming majority, however, are likely to be lost to Russia, together with their skills. In 1999 52,832 persons emigrated from Russia to Germany, and 7 from Germany to Russia. The corresponding figures for Israel were 36,317 and 12, and for the USA 11,078 and 4 (Goskomstat, 2000b, pp.72-3).

Firms wholly or partly foreign-owned provided only 1,260,000 jobs (2% of jobs) in Russia in 1999. But their growth from 739,000 jobs (1.1%) in 1997 represented 521,000 additional jobs (Goskomstat, 2000b, p.77), confirming anecdotal evidence that a growing number of Western firms are opening subsidiaries in Russia, if only because to do so is cheaper and easier than importing Russian scientists or engineers.

Overall, however, Russia can only be regarded as poorly equipped for the post-industrial, information-based age. The Soviet state's desire to control the flow of information to the public undoubtedly contributed to its slowness in developing personal computers up to 1991, and economic decline since has further impeded development in the IT field.

In general education Russia had 1,508 pupils per 10,000 of population in 1997, up from 1,404 in 1990, a reasonably high figure considering its low birth rate, and providing primary education to 92% of the relevant age group (Statkom, 1999, p.83; World Bank, 2000, pp.284-5). However, at 221 per 10,000 of population, the proportion of students in tertiary education was lower than in any industrialised countries except Norway (181) and Japan (207).[12] The CIS survey contained data for the 12 CIS members and 45 non-CIS countries. Of the CIS members, only Georgia (235) had proportionally more students in higher education, and only Belarus and Ukraine (220 each) about as many as Russia. But of the 45 non-CIS countries, 14 high-income countries plus Bulgaria (282) and the Philippines (236) had a higher proportion than Russia at various years in the 1990s, ranging from 242 in France to 333 in the USA and 346 in Australia. The Russian increase from 190 in 1990 to 221 in 1997 was smaller than in several high-income countries (e.g. Australia, from 284 to 346, Italy 250 to 293, Sweden 225 to 324, Spain 291 to 343). It should also be noted that the figures for some countries such as Switzerland (125) and the United Kingdom (75 in 1990, no later figure) and Ireland (147) are remarkably low, suggesting that they define tertiary education more narrowly than others in the table (Statkom, 1999, pp.85-6). In particular, the low figures for Norway and UK are in total conflict with a recent

OECD survey, detailed below, which showed them as having the highest proportion of graduates and graduands in the 28 OECD countries.

So Russia appears to be increasing provision of higher education at a lower rate, and to a lower proportion of students, than most high-income countries, and also spending a lower proportion of GNP than most of them on education. The World Bank (2000, p.285) estimated public expenditure on education in Russia in 1997 at 3.5% of GNP, the same as in 1980, but low compared to the average not only of the high-income countries (5.6% in 1980, 5.4% in 1997), but also of the middle-income group (4% in 1980, 5% in 1997) (pp.284-5). Even at Purchasing Power Parity Russia's 1999 GNP per head of $6,339 was only about one-quarter of the high-income countries' average of $24,430 (World Bank, 2000, pp.274-5). A recent OECD survey noted that in 23 of the 28 OECD countries numbers in tertiary education increased by over 20% between 1990 and 1997, and in eight of them it increased by over 50%. By 1998 they averaged 230 graduates or graduands per 1000 population, the highest being Norway (383), UK (352) and USA (329).[13] In Russia the increase from 1989 to 1994 was of the order of 16%, from 130 per thousand over the age of 14 in 1989 to 151 in 1994. No later figures were cited, but from 1993-4 to 1998-9 the number of higher education students increased from 2.6 to 3.6 million, a rise of 38% (Goskomstat, 1999, pp.121-2, 128). If 70% of these complete their degrees,[14] the number of graduates per 1000 will rise to about 170 by 2004. However, in age group 25-49 it will average about 220,[15] close to the OECD average.

OECD countries were spending on average 4.8% of their GDP on education in 1997-8, the mean annual expenditure per student being $5,200 in secondary and $8,300 in higher education.[16] No comparable figures were cited for Russia, but 3.5% of a 1998 GDP of $333 billion equals 11.7 billion. Divided by 22 million students (Goskomstat, 1999, p.123), that approximates $532 per student. This figure is not strictly comparable with the OECD data, which do not include primary education, nor is there any inevitable correlation between the amount of money spent and the quality of education received. Nevertheless, it is reasonable to assume that disciplines requiring expensive infrastructure, such as physics, engineering or computer studies, are more easily catered for in countries which can spend several thousand dollars per student per annum than in one that can spend only several hundred. Options for reforming vocational ('middle specialised') education (the level reached by around 30% of the population aged between 20 and 49) were being studied by the World Bank. Its report made a general criticism of existing programs in the ex-Communist countries as 'not designed to produce workers with profiles that labour markets increasingly demand' (World Bank, 1998, p.44).

Energy Efficiency

This is measured by calculating GNP per head (expressed in US Dollars at Purchasing Power Parity) generated per unit of energy used, the unit being the equivalent of one kilo of oil. In 1990 the figure for Russia was $1.70, compared to a range in the high-income countries from $2.60 in Canada, via $2.90 in USA, $3.20 in Australia, $4.40 in UK and $5.40 in Japan, to $6.20 in Switzerland and $8.70 in Hong Kong (World Bank, 2000, pp.292-3).

Soviet supply of energy resources at unrealistically low prices encouraged profligate use of energy in the USSR and its Warsaw Pact allies. In 1990 they were all at the low end of the countries providing data, ranging from $1.30 (Ukraine) to $3.30 (Hungary). In 1996 data were available for 110 countries, and the high-income countries' average had risen to $5. Averages were not provided for 1997, but in that year Canada had improved to $3, the USA to $3.60, Australia to $4, UK to $5.30, Japan to $6, Switzerland to $6.90, and Hong Kong to $10.60. Russia had improved only from $1.60 in 1990 to $1.70. The Eastern Europeans, though still ranking low, had improved, to range from $1.90 in Bulgaria to $4 in Hungary. In 1997, of 105 countries providing data, 97 ranked as more and 7 as less energy-efficient than Russia (World Bank, 2000, pp.292-3). As in agriculture, comparison of Russia with Canada is the most relevant, because of high winter heating requirements. Canada was 63% more energy-efficient than Russia in 1990, and 76% more in 1996. Low energy-efficiency remains a bar to Russia's industrial competitiveness, as well as making its environmental pollution high in relation to output.

Environmental Pollution

World Bank data here are for 1996, when Russia accounted for 7% of world carbon dioxide emissions, third highest after the USA (23.4%) and China (14.9%). This amounted to 10.7 tonnes per head of population, 11th highest in the world, after Singapore (21.6 tonnes), USA (20), Australia (16.7), Saudi Arabia (15.8), Norway (15.3), Canada (13.7), Finland (11.5), the Czech Republic (11.2), Estonia (11.2) and Kazakhstan (10.9) (World

Bank, 2000, pp.292-3; Goskomstat, 1999a, pp.262-8). So in per capita terms Russia was not among the worst offenders. However, the Soviet heritage of large factories and power stations, obsolete machinery, profligate use of energy, and inadequate infrastructure for vehicle maintenance renders the environment in many cities less than salubrious. [17]

Nor is air pollution confined to carbon dioxide. By 1998 emissions of other contaminants (e.g. sulphur compounds) from stationary plants fell to 55% of the 1990 level (Goskomstat, 2000a, p.266). But as industrial production in 1998 was only 49% of 1990, contaminant emission per unit produced actually increased. Contaminants removed at plants were 115.9 million tonnes in 1990, 59 million in 1998, i.e. had fallen to 50.4% of the 1990 level (Goskomstat, 2000a, pp.266-78, and 2000b, p.176).

Finance

In 1994 the budget deficit was about 10.5% of the GDP. This was reduced to 2.5% in 1995, but rose again in the next two years, to 5.8% in 1998, then was cut to less than 2% in 1999 (Goskomstat, 2000b, p.288). That year's budget envisaged revenues of 473.7 billion roubles, and expenditures of 575.1 billion, a deficit of 101.4 billion. In fact revenues exceeded expectations by 29.1% and expenditures by only 15.6%, so the deficit (53 billion) was only a little over half that expected. As in Soviet times, the highest source of revenue (221 billion, 53.8% above expectation) was the turnover tax (VAT, GST), followed by taxes on external trade (86.3 billion, 94.5%) and profits tax (81 billion, 220% of expectation). Income tax yielded only 79.9% of expectation, but at 25.2 billion expected and 19.9 billion received, it remained a very minor revenue source.

On the expenditure side the largest single item (166.8 billion expected, 162.6 actual) was servicing of the state debt, the second largest defence (93.7 expected, 116.1 actual) (Goskomstat, 2000b, p.289).

That the income from profit tax was 120% and of turnover tax 53.8% above expectation tends to suggest improved collection methods and perhaps success in bringing some black economy activities under control. But to keep this in proportion, estimates of money illegally leaving Russia each year are in the range of 330-660 billion roubles, or 54-108% of 1999's actual budget revenue.

Debt servicing was 6.8% of the GDP and 26.6% of budget expenditure, defence 4.8% and 19% respectively.

Foreign Direct Investment, External Debt and Aid

In 1997 Russia attracted $6.2 billion in FDI. This compared poorly with the $44.2 billion attracted to China, 93.4 billion to the USA, 37 billion to the United Kingdom, or to, for example, Brazil (19.7 billion), Mexico (12.5), Sweden (9.9), the Netherlands (9.0), Australia (8.7), or Singapore (8.6) (World Bank, 1999, pp.270-1). In 1998 FDI in Russia increased to $11.77 billion (Goskomstat, 1999c, p.347).[18] The top six investing countries in that year were Germany (24.2% of the total), USA (19%), UK (13.5%) France (13.1%), Cyprus (7.8%), and the Netherlands (7.5%). Japan was conspicuously absent from the list of major investors, and is likely to remain so until the territorial dispute over the Southern Kuril Islands, seized by the USSR in 1945, is resolved, and a peace treaty signed.

That some FDI is in fact Russian 'mafia' money returned after laundering is suggested by the prominence of Cyprus in 1998, and reinforced by the list of major investing countries in 1999. Total FDI in that year dropped to $9.56 billion, with the USA (2,921 million, 30.6%) overtaking Germany (1,695 million, 17.7%). Cyprus (923 million, 9.7%) had risen to third place, and fourth was a 'new entrant' to the top ten, Gibraltar (780 million, 8.2%), UK (734 million, 7.7%) dropping to fifth place (Goskomstat, 2000b, p.327). Both Cyprus and Gibraltar provide offshore banking facilities; Cyprus is also a very popular destination for *nouveau riche* Russians, and so is Spain, from where access to Gibraltar is nowadays easy.[19] The FDI reaching Russia from these two places in 1999 equalled $1,225 per Cypriot and $28,527 per Gibraltarian; the bulk of it must have been foreign money in transit, and it appears likely that much of it originated from Russia's black economy.

Russia's relatively low attractiveness for FDI, compared to other countries, reflects several factors. They include uncertainties in law relating to investment and taxation, the lack of clear distinctions between powers of the three levels of government (central, regional and local), infrastructure/communications problems, bureaucratic slowness and arbitrariness, and perception of corruption as widespread. In longer perspective it can also perhaps be seen as reflecting Gorbachev's error in instituting political decentralisation before legislating for strict demarcation of central/regional/local responsibilities and powers. This omission resulted in 43 of the 89 sub-national entities declaring themselves sovereign, and withholding transfer of locally collected taxes to Moscow, and/or threatening secession if their demands were not met, in order to extract concessions from the government (World Bank, 1999, p.123). The situation has improved somewhat since new rules were introduced in 1994, major steps were subsequently taken to increase tax collections, and tax administration and budget management are being improved with World Bank support (World Bank, 1998, p.40). However, centre/region/local and parliament/government tensions continue to cause problems for potential investors.

Russia's external debt more than trebled, from $60 billion in 1990 to 184 billion in 1998. This was 62% of the GDP; of 103 countries for which data were supplied, 37 showed a higher, 1 the same, and 64 a lower proportion. They included all the Asian 'tigers' except Hong Kong and Singapore (no data supplied for either), external debt as a proportion of GDP ranging from 43% (South Korea) to 169% (Indonesia) (World Bank, 2000, pp.314-5).

Assessment of risk and creditworthiness was provided to the World Bank by two US firms. Both use a scale of 0 to 100, the highest figures representing highest safety for investment and highest credit-worthiness as at March 2000. Risk ratings were provided for 115 countries, of which 103 were rated as 'less risky' for investment than Russia. Credit-worthiness ratings were provided for 120 countries, 85 of which were rated better than Russia. Some of the ratings seemed surprising, rating Russia below several countries that have an ongoing civil war or other conflicts proportionally far more destabilising than Russia's war in Chechnya. But without knowing what criteria are used in the assessments, the figures can only be taken at face value (World Bank, 2000, pp.306-7).

The extent to which businesses can borrow for expansion depends heavily on the Interest Rate Spread, i.e. the difference between the interest rates banks pay on deposits and the higher rates they charge on loans. The Interest Rate Spread in 1999 averaged, for example, 2.9 percentage points in Australia, 1.5 in Canada, 1.4 in South Korea, 2 in Japan, 2.7 in UK, 3.7 in France and 6.4 in Germany. Data were provided for 98 countries. Russia's spread, 26 percentage points, was fourth largest, exceeded only by Belarus, Ukraine and Uruguay. Given this very high cost of borrowing, it is no surprise that domestic credit provided by Russia's banking sector in 1998 was only 35% of GDP, compared to an average 92.5% for the lower-middle income countries to which Russia belongs, and 139% for the high-income countries (World Bank, 2000, pp.304-5). Apart from their depressive effects on private sector development, Russia's high interest rates on short-term debt were noted as becoming a major burden on public finances (World Bank, 1998, p.39).

Military Expenditure (as percentage of GNP, 1992 onwards)

The World Bank tables show Russia spending 8% of its GNP on defence in 1992 and 11.4 % in 1995, among 132 countries surveyed second only to Kuwait (11.6%) in the latter year (World Bank, 1999, pp.262-3 and 2000, p.307). This appears unlikely in the current state of Russia's armed forces. Their manpower was halved from 3.4 million in 1990 to 1.7 million in 1995, large numbers of warships, aircraft, tanks and other equipment were scrapped and few replaced. Pay is sometimes months in arrears, and thousands of married officers are housed inadequately or not at all, for lack of funds. A Russian analysis published in 1998 gives a post-Soviet peak of 5.6% in 1994, with subsequent expenditures less than 4% in 1995, 3.5% in 1996, 2.7% in 1997 and under 3% in 1998 (Zyuganov, 1998, p.17).[20] These figures are much more consistent with the known state of Russia's armed forces. In 1999, as noted above, defence spending rose to 4.8% of GDP.

Putin has declared his intention to increase defence spending, and within a few weeks of election as President secured ratification by the Duma of the START-2 nuclear arms reduction treaty (which Yeltsin had sought unsuccessfully ever since he signed the Treaty with the USA in 1992). The consequent reductions of US and Russian nuclear weapons will help Russia to retain strategic nuclear parity at relatively low cost.

The USA is seeking to revise the 1972 Anti-Ballistic Missile Treaty (ABM). It claims that it wishes only to protect itself against small-scale nuclear missile attack by a 'rogue' state such as Iraq or North Korea. However, the first reported installations envisaged for the scheme are radar in Northern Norway close to Russia's border, and emplacements for 100 anti-ballistic missiles on an island in the US-owned Aleutians nearest to the Russian Far East. If the USA goes ahead without Russia's agreement, Russia may riposte by accelerating introduction of a new land-based Intercontinental Ballistic Missile system and/or a new class of missile-firing submarine. However, as excessive military expenditure was among the factors leading to stagnation and then to decline in the Soviet economy, Putin is likely to concentrate Russia's negotiating effort on curtailing US deployments rather than on matching or countering increased ones.

His task may have been eased by President Clinton's decision in September 2000 to leave a decision on the ABM question to the next President. But it is likely to be made more difficult by a difference of opinion between his Minister of Defence, Marshal Igor Sergeyev, and the Chief of General Staff, General Anatoly Kvashnin, which erupted into the media in July 2000. Kvashnin advocates merging the Strategic Missile

Forces with the Air Force, and giving priority to improving Russia's general purpose forces, particularly the Army, to enable it to control small conflicts and undertake peace-keeping duties such as it already has in Kosovo, Tajikistan and Transcaucasus. Sergeyev apparently opposes this, on the grounds that the nuclear forces are the basis of Russia's status as a great power. The continued unrest around Russia's periphery (Chechnya, Abkhazia, Ossetia, along the borders with Afghanistan of the Central Asian republics which, although independent still, except for Uzbekistan, rely on Russia's Border Guards to protect their frontiers) is likely to incline Putin towards Kvashnin's viewpoint. So will progress on START-2 and START-3, in particular by reducing the American nuclear inventory and thereby enabling Russia to maintain nuclear deterrence at a lower and less expensive level, hence to spend more of its limited defence budget (about one-eighth of 1990's) on its conventional forces.

The *Kursk* submarine tragedy may also help Kvashnin's case. Although not a strategic missile submarine, the *Kursk* was a nuclear-powered sea-denial weapon for war against major maritime powers. It was of no use for small border wars or peacekeeping, and several army brigades can be equipped for the cost of replacing it. But the mere fact that nine years into a much-advertised 'reform' process, Russia's two top military men are in such basic disagreement over future development of the armed forces tends to reflect lack of political leadership on this issue during the Yeltsin years.

Official Development Assistance

In 1998 aid received by Russia equalled $7 per head of population, or 0.4% of its GNP. Of 109 countries listed as receiving aid, 21 received less per head, and 22 received amounts lower in relation to their GDP. The two other Slav Republics of the former USSR, Belarus and Ukraine, received about $3 per head respectively. By contrast most non-Slav ex-Soviet Republics received more per head, ranging from $6 in Uzbekistan to $62 in Estonia. The same applied to the USSR's former Warsaw Pact allies, aid ranging from $23 per head to Poland to $43 for the Czech Republic (World Bank, 2000, pp.324-5). The World Bank (1998, p.39) defined the fiscal situation in Russia as 'fragile', and noted that high interest rates on short-term debt became a major burden on public finances in the latter part of the fiscal year. It added that as important ingredients in restoring growth 'structural reforms aimed at sustained and predictable reductions in fiscal deficits' were necessary 'to restore market confidence and reduce interest rates'. A second Structural Adjustment Loan of $800 million was approved in December 1997, its stated purpose being to facilitate 'more transparent, open and competitive case-by-case privatization', with particular reference to accelerating privatisation of medium and large enterprises (World Bank, 1998, pp.39, 41, 44).

Gross International Reserves (to nearest billion US Dollars)

In 1999 Russia's foreign currency reserves stood at just under 8.5 billion dollars, a drop of over 29% on their 1998 level, and a modest sum compared to Australia (21 billion), Canada (28), Switzerland (36), Singapore (77), Hong Kong (96), China (158) or Japan (287 billion). In US dollars per head of population Russia's reserves, at 58 dollars, looked even more modest compared to China's 132, Canada's 903, Australia's1105, Japan's 2260, Hong Kong's 19,200 or Singapore's 24,062 (World Bank, 2000, pp.278-9). The level of reserves is probably not crucial barring a need (and willingness) to defend the exchange value of the rouble. Russia's relatively low reserves would not be adequate for that contingency, but it does not appear very likely; the rouble, after dropping severely in August 1998, has fluctuated very little since. The smallness of the reserves must also be viewed in the context of illegal flights of capital abroad, estimated to total between 100 and 200 billion dollars since 1992, and to continue at up to 2 billion dollars a month.

International Trade

Russia's merchandise exports in 1998 totalled $74.2 billion, and imports $59.1 billion. This turnover of $133.3 billion was not much greater than Australia's (120.5 billion), and much below those of Singapore (211.5), Hong Kong (361.6), China (324), or Canada (420.7), the Netherlands (388.4) and Belgium-Luxembourg (345.6), let alone Japan (668.4), UK (588), Germany (1013.5) or USA (1625.1) (World Bank, 2000, pp.312-3). Data or estimates of merchandise exports were given for 130 countries; Russia ranked 18th. Import data or estimates were given for 109 countries. Russia ranked 21st.

World Bank (1999) data for imports and exports of commercial services were also for 1998 (pp.312-3). They showed Russia as exporting

$12.9 billion-worth of such services, and importing 16.1 billion. These figures were roughly comparable to Thailand, Malaysia or Denmark, slightly below Australia or Sweden, well below South Korea, Singapore or Hong Kong, and far behind the leading exporters of services, USA (240 billion exports, 165.8 billion imports), UK (99.1/78.2) and France (84.6/65.4). Of 99 countries providing data on their exports and imports of services, Russia ranked 25th for exports and 16th for imports.

Figures for manufactured goods as a percentage of imports or exports are for 1998. 23% of Russia's exports and 46% of its imports were manufactures, whereas the high-income countries' averages were 81% and 74% respectively (Australia 27% and 80%, Canada 62% and 80%, UK 83% and 81%, USA 80% and 78%, Japan 95% and 54%) (World Bank, 1999, pp.268-9).

Table 9.3   Russian socio-economic development trends, 1991-1999

	1999 as % of 1998	1999 as % of 1991
Gross domestic product	103.2	62.5
Industrial production	108.1	54.6
Agricultural production	102.0	64.0
Capital investment	101.0	29.1
Goods transported *	107.0	28.8
Retail trade turnover	92.1	69.4
Paid services	102.4	27.9
Consumer price index **	136.5	...
Real disposable incomes	77.5	...
Exports (at current prices)	97.0	...
Imports (at current prices)	67.0	...

*   Excluding pipelines.
** December 1999 compared to December 1998.

Source: Statkom, 2000, pp.7-13.

Russia therefore remained a minor player in world trade, an 'old' economy, exporting mostly raw materials, importing mainly manufactures and food, and showing a falling trend in both exports and imports (Table 9.3).[21] Pursuit of self-sufficiency for much of the Soviet period, and concentration of trade within the former Soviet bloc, combined to marginalise the USSR to world trade. Russia's former allies and other ex-Soviet Republics are actively diversifying their trade away from Russia faster than Russia can find new trading partners or increase trade with existing ones; so the situation has not since changed to Russia's advantage. Compared to the other members of CIS, however, Russia is still less dependent on its trade with them than they are on trade with Russia. In January-November 1999 only 14% of Russia's exports went to other CIS countries, and only 27% of its imports came from them. Among the other CIS members, even the most active diversifiers (Azerbaijan, Armenia, Turkmenistan, Ukraine and Uzbekistan) in 1999 sent 24 to 28% of their exports to other CIS countries, and received from 24 to 58% of their imports from them (Statkom, 2000, pp.32-3).

Conclusion

Few of the indicators give ground for excessive optimism about Russia's short-term prospects. Although most suggest an improvement in 1999 sustained to mid-2000, they are still a long way below those of the Soviet Union's final year. Russia remains in a depression far deeper and more prolonged than the Great Depression of the 1930s.[22] Both industry and agriculture are handicapped by productivity in general below, sometimes far below even unimpressive Soviet levels. Industry is additionally handicapped by continued wasteful use of energy, and agriculture by inadequate mechanisation and lack of fertilisers and pesticides. Services, while much expanded since the Soviet period, still contribute much less to GNP than in high-income countries. The banking sector's ability to help finance, e.g. private-sector expansion, is limited by very high interest rates. Foreign Direct Investment is low by international standards, and so is foreign aid in per capita terms.

A caveat needs to be made here. In Soviet times most incentives were to inflate production statistics where possible, because promotions and bonuses were linked to meeting or surpassing targets set under Five-Year and annual plans. The reverse is now the case. Firms are motivated to understate their labour force, output and profits, to minimise their payments of payroll, turnover and profits taxes, and to make barter deals where no taxable cash changes hands. The precise extent of tax evasion is not known, but two pointers suggest it is widespread. The first is that major electricity consumers, industry and rail transport, were in 1999 officially running at only 50% and 28.8% of the 1990 level, but electricity consumption has declined far less, to a lowest point (1998 and 1999) 76% of the 1990 level (Goskomstat, 2000b, p.176). Granted that domestic demand is relatively inelastic, and that even a closed plant consumes some power, electricity supply running at over three-quarters of the 1990 level is hard to reconcile with industry running at half and rail transport at scarcely above a quarter of that level.

The second pointer to concealment of income is that in January-May 2000 only 59.6% of all businesses claimed to be making a profit (Goskomstat, 2000e, pp.155-6). But in April 2000 27,643 new businesses were registered, while only 6,280 were liquidated (Goskomstat, 2000f, p.108). Granted, one month's figures are of limited validity, and over one-third of businesses registered with EGRPO (the Unified State Register of Enterprises and Organisations) are believed inactive (Goskomstat, 2000e, p.119). Nevertheless, if 40% of businesses were loss-makers, would business confidence be high enough for new registrations to outnumber liquidations by over four to one?

In virtually every respect except political freedoms Putin has inherited Russia in far worse a state than Yeltsin did. Apart from some of its natural resources Russia's principal comparative advantage at present is its possession of an educated urban labour force available to work for payment far below international standards. However, this could easily become a wasting asset because of its low level of computer literacy relative to the rest of the industrialised world. Personal computers are available to few in Russia, mostly imported, and expensive relative to incomes.[23] Russia's current inability to provide them to schools and universities on the scale of high-income (and some middle-income) countries means that relatively few of the current labour force, and not many more of those now in education, can acquire the computer-literacy seen as indispensable elsewhere. Remedying this particular deficiency may be the most useful thing Putin could do to assure Russia's longer-term future.

Notes

1   After deducting students and pensioners from the published totals. See Goskomstat, 2000b, p.84.
2   The figure of 8.876 million unemployed includes 686,000 students and pensioners, and I have subtracted these (Goskomstat, 1999c, p.87).
3   All financial indicators presented in this chapter are in US dollars, unless stated otherwise.
4   *Russian and Euro-Asian Bulletin*, vol.9, no.2, March-April 2000, p.16.
5   *Agrafood East Europe*, October 1999, p.6.

6   Ibid.
7   Goskomstat (2000b, p.200) gives much lower figures: in 1999 Russia had only 17.5 million cattle, 10 million pigs, and 4.8 million sheep and goats, but on p.211 Goskomstat gives figures for 1 January 2000 which are consistent with those cited in a more recent source (Goskomstat, 2000f).
8   Sourced from Statkom (1999, pp.262-9). Goskomstat (1999c, p.243) gives a higher total, 2,571 million, for 1997. The difference arises because Goskomstat data includes gas pipelines, whereas Statkom's do not. Goskomstat (1999c) gives a fall in total transport to 2338 million tonnes in 1998.
9   To remove journeys made by railway employees (Goskomstat, 2000b, p.232).
10   Goskomstat, 2000e, p.69. Data adjusted to take account of the 1999 change in methods of calculation.
11   World Bank (1999, p.227) defines 'low-income' countries as those with Gross National Product below $760 per head, 'lower-middle' as $760-3,030, 'upper-middle' as in range $3,031-9,560, and 'high-income' above $9,560, all in 1998.
12   Many Norwegians undertake tertiary education elsewhere in Scandinavia or in English-speaking countries. Many Japanese also go abroad, particularly for post-graduate studies and to English-speaking countries. Within the European Union 'migration' of students to other EU countries is now a widespread phenomenon. While Russians, for financial and other reasons, overwhelmingly have to be educated in Russia.
13   *The Guardian Weekly*, 25-31 May, 2000, p.23.
14   Completion rates vary greatly between countries. In the OECD survey mentioned above they ranged from over 80% in Japan and UK to 35% in Italy.
15   Own estimates based on Goskomstat, 1999, pp.122, 128, and USSR Goskomstat, 1990, pp.128, 131.
16   *The Guardian Weekly*, 25-31 May, 2000, p.23.
17   A list of 49 towns and cities with especially high levels of atmospheric pollution can be found in Goskomstat, 2000b, pp.62-3.
18   World Bank 2000, p.315, gives FDI in Russia in 1998 as only $2,764 billion. This is undoubtedly an error.
19   A count of 500 travel agents' advertisements, taken at random from Moscow press in July 2000, showed Turkey (146) the most popular destination, Spain (101) second, Cyprus (99) third.
20   Another study (Yanovskiy, 1999, p.30) gives far higher figures, ranging from 11% in 1990 to 6.4% in 1995, via a peak of 16.7% in 1992. But as these figures give the 1995 GDP as only 23.5% of 1990, versus the generally accepted 46%, they cannot be taken as reliable.
21   For example, from December 1997 to April 2000 exports surpassed the December 1997 level in only one month (December 1999). By September 1998 imports had fallen to less than 40% of the December 1997 level, and thereafter reached 50% of that level in only one month (also December 1999) (Goskomstat, 2000f, p.89).
22   In the USA industrial production fell by 1932 to 63.4% of the 1929 level. By 1936 the 1929 level of GNP had been re-attained in the USA and surpassed in Germany and Japan, so the worst of the depression was over within seven years. By contrast, Russia's industrial production went on declining over 8 years, and in 1998 stood at only 46% of the 1990 level (Galbraith, 1994, pp.87, 114-23).
23   In most high-income countries a medium-range computer costs from two to four weeks' worth of the average wage. In Russia in 1998 51.3% of the employed earned

less than 800 roubles a month (Goskomstat, 1999c, p.110). At year's end in 1998 a computer costing the equivalent of $500 or 10,325 roubles (Goskomstat, 1999c, p.411) would have taken 13 months' worth of an 800-rouble salary, and up to 5 months for the 7.5% of the labour force earning over 2,000 roubles a month. By March 2000 the further decline of the rouble had taken the computer's cost to 14,000 roubles, equivalent to 18 and 7 months' wages respectively. At such ratios of cost to wages availability of PCs to businesses and schools is bound to remain low, and clearly out of the question for the vast majority of households.

References

Galbraith, J.K. (1994), *The World Economy Since the Wars: a Personal View*, Sinclair-Stevenson, London.

Goskomstat (1999a), *Regiony Rossii 1998, Volume 2*, Goskomstat Rossii, Moscow.

Goskomstat (1999c), *Rossiya v tsifrakh. 1999*, Goskomstat Rossii, Moscow.

Goskomstat (2000a), *Regiony Rossii 1999, Volume 2*, Goskomstat Rossii, Moscow.

Goskomstat (2000b), *Rossiya v tsifrakh. 2000*, Goskomstat Rossii, Moscow.

Goskomstat (2000e), *Sotsial'no-ekonomicheskoe polozhenie Rossii, yanvar'-iyun' 2000 goda*, Goskomstat Rossii, Moscow.

Goskomstat (2000f), *Sotsial'no-ekonomicheskoe polozhenie Rossii, yanvar'-mai 2000 goda*, Goskomstat Rossii, Moscow.

Statkom (1999), *SNG i strany mira*, Statkom SNG, Moscow.

Statkom (2000), *Sodruzhestvo Nezavisimykh Gosudarstv v 1999 godu*, Statkom SNG, Moscow.USSR Goskomstat (1990), The USSR in Figures for 1989, Finansy i statistika, Moscow.

World Bank (1998), *Knowledge for Development. World Bank Annual Report 1998*, World Bank, Washington D.C.

World Bank (1999), *Entering the Twenty-First Century. World Development Report 1999-2000*, Oxford University Press for World Bank, New York.

World Bank (2000), *Attacking Poverty. World Development Report 2000-2001*, Oxford University Press for the World Bank, New York.

Yanovskiy, R.G. (ed.) (1999), *Armiya Rossii: sostoyaniye i perspektivy*, ISPI RAN, Moscow.

Zyuganov, G.A. (ed.) (1998), *Voyennaya reforma. Vooruzhennyye sily Rossiyskoi Federatsii*, AO RAU-Universitet, Moscow.

10 Russian Military Power at the Turn of the Millennium

ALEXEY MURAVIEV

The history of Russia is directly linked to the question of military power and wars. Military questions have traditionally occupied a special place in Russia's domestic and foreign policy over the centuries. Since 1240, the Russian state has been involved in more than 300 wars and armed conflicts, thus spending approximately 570 years fighting. In the 20th Century alone, national human losses to wars almost reached 50 million. The theme of this chapter is the future of Russian military power in the 21st Century. Russia's military future has a bearing on world security, in particular in the Asia-Pacific region. Regardless of the dramatic changes inside the country over the past ten years, the Russian Federation remains a world military power, and a nuclear superpower. Moreover, the events of 1999 and 2000, especially the march of the Russian paratroopers to the capital of Kosovo, Pristina, and the second military campaign against rebels in Chechnya, have shown that military power remains an effective instrument for the Russian leadership in either achieving foreign policy goals, or to protect the national interests of the state.

This chapter outlines changes in Russia's geo-strategic environment in the 1990s, and assesses the capabilities of the country's armed forces. Special attention is given to the analysis of the ongoing military reform, the new Military Doctrine, and the role the new Russian President Vladimir Putin is playing in determining the future of the Russian military.

Changes in Russia's Geo-Strategic Environment West of the Ural Mountains in the 1990s

Following the collapse of the Soviet Union, Russia's security environment changed dramatically, especially west of the Ural Mountains. Russia's European side has encountered the abandonment of alliance relationships by the Central and East European countries and the independence of former republics of the USSR, both of which resulted in a dramatic reduction in the span of Russia's geographical reach. The impact on the military stature of the new Russian Federation was immediate and profound. Russia retained only 8 of the 16 Soviet military districts. The Russian military lost the majority of the USSR's most capable military units, the so-called 'first strategic echelon', which had been stationed in the newly independent states. In particular, 13 field armies and corps, 4 tank armies, 2 missile armies, 3 armies of the anti-missile defence, 5 air armies; various-purpose military units and establishments; enormous stockpiles of armaments, ammunition and other reserves fell under the control of new independent states (Zolotarev, 1998). Russia was left with troops of the so-called 'second operational echelon'. In the three years after 1991, Russia had to absorb a redeployment of military forces from the former Warsaw Pact states and former Soviet republics involving 29 infantry, tank and airborne divisions, 51 missile, artillery and surface-to-air missile (SAM) brigades, 66 fixed wing and helicopter regiments and more than 300,000 personnel (accompanied by 900,000 family members) (Georgiev, 1999). Russian military power has pulled back some 1,500 km from the centre of Europe: from Eastern Germany and Czechoslovakia to Smolensk and Kursk in European Russia. The Leningrad, Moscow, and the North Caucasus Military Districts (MDs) have turned from the deep rear into the advanced defence lines of Russia in the west and southwest. In other words, the strategic environment of Russia's Western strategic direction has changed fundamentally, requiring the formulation of a new strategic approach, which stands in contrast to the Far Eastern region, which, from a strategic viewpoint, mainly consists of relationships with the United States, China, and Japan, and is not expected to undergo any fundamental transformation in its environment.

Russia's Geo-Strategic Position in Siberia and the Far East

From a security perspective, Siberia and the Far East have seen little geo-political change, besides Mongolia's departure from Russia's sphere of influence. Far Eastern Russia's basic military stature as a secondary front has not changed from the Soviet period. Russia's main strategic concerns continue to be directed towards the West and the South. Furthermore, with the improvement in relations with China, with which Russia shares an extensive border, the strategic military status of the Far East has declined relative to other strategic directions. Since the Russian forces in the Far East receive relatively low priority as an area requiring emergency or rapid response capabilities, the Far East is being treated as a defensive zone within the overall strategic layout for the Russian military.

Military power in Russia's east, long the basis of the Soviet claim to regional influence, has drastically declined in recent years. In 1992, Russia completed the withdrawal of its 100,000-strong contingent from Mongolia. While part of the decline was by design – in accord with the border troop reduction agreement of April 1997 between China, Kazakhstan, Kyrgyzstan, Russia and Tajikistan - and part can also be justified by a reduced perception of threat in the region, much of the reduction in Russian military power east of the Urals has been driven by the funding crisis. By 1999, the grouping of Russian forces east of the Urals had been reduced by 200,000 personnel: from 43 divisions (390,000 personnel) in 1989 to 15 divisions (190,000 personnel) by 1998. Approximately 200 different military units and formations have been disbanded. Nearly 600 tactical missiles, formerly deployed in the Asian part of Russia, have been destroyed.[1] Russian naval forces in the Pacific have also been significantly reduced. Since 1990, the total number of submarines fell by over 75%, while the overall number of surface combatants fell by 47%.[2] More than 20 submarines, and approximately 30 surface warships, of the Russian Pacific Fleet have been taken out of service in recent years.[3] Yet the Pacific Fleet is still regarded as the second largest of Russia's four fleets in terms of strength and combat potential.

On the other hand, Russian military forces in Siberia and the Far East continue to receive modern military equipment (those removed from the West in compliance with the Conventional Forces in Europe (CFE) Treaty reductions) east of the Urals, as well as the deployment of new weapons systems. This has resulted in an accumulation of advanced high-performance weaponry (such as T-90S main battle tanks (MBTs), BMP-3 infantry fighting vehicles (IFVs) and *Oscar II* class nuclear-powered attack submarines) in the country's eastern regions, and has qualitatively enhanced the equipment managed by the Russian forces in Asia. What these trends show is that, along with troop reductions, the Far Eastern region is being equipped with the latest weapons, although limited in number. In other words, as troop reduction progresses in the Russian Far East so too does the limited deployment of new equipment and the transfer of weapons to rear positions as dictated by the CFE Treaty. Therefore a certain level of modern force capability is being built in the region.

Russia's New Security Concept and Military Doctrine

Russia's 1993 Military Doctrine and 1997 National Security Concept represented an uncomfortable mix of Soviet tradition with new circumstances. They took for granted Russia's role as a great power and its need for global reach, both in terms of nuclear and power-projection forces. However, they also showed some awareness of Russia's diminished resources and the new challenge posed by crime, insurgency and separatism. Russia's military-political leadership still sees the United States and its allies as a threat. While old-style Soviet thinking has much to do with this, the West cannot be absolved of all of the responsibility. NATO's eastward expansion; high-handed actions in Kosovo that circumvented international law, the United Nations and the Organisation for Security and Co-operation in Europe's (OSCE) attacks on Russia's friends; and interference in what Russia regards as its rightful sphere of influence in the Caucasus and Central Asia have all combined to give the impression that the West is determined to remodel the world according to its wishes, no matter what Russia wants.

The Improved National Security Concept, which was approved by President Vladimir Putin on 10 January 2000, is in principle a new document. Among other threats the 2000 National Security Concept identifies:

- Russia's economic weakness and instability, including an increase in crime;
- Strengthening of military-political alliances, especially NATO's eastward expansion;
- The use of force by NATO outside its zone of responsibility [an obvious reference to NATO's campaign against Yugoslavia];
- Proliferation of weapons of mass destruction;
- The weakening of integration processes within the CIS;
- International terrorism (Russian Government, 2000a, p.6).

The 2000 National Security Concept underlines the point that under specific circumstances, a Russian military presence may be required in 'certain strategic regions of the world' (Russian Government, 2000a, p.7).

The new 2000 Military Doctrine, approved on 21st April 2000, is an immediate response to an increasingly pessimistic Russian view of current trends. Compared with the 1993 Doctrine, the 2000 version takes a more realistic and assertive view of the world, and Russia's geo-strategic and military-political position in it:

> [The] doctrine's omission of the distinction between dangers and threats and the positive prefatory comment may reflect a Russian perception that NATO and some other states harbour hostile intentions towards the Russian Federation (Dick, 2000, p.15).

The new Military Doctrine declares the safeguarding of Russia's military security the most important area of the state's activity. In many ways, this is a more 'Soviet' document than ever, downplaying the threat from low-intensity conflicts and putting increased emphasis on the need to maintain advanced and sizeable strategic nuclear forces, which are viewed as an effective deterrent factor. It also enshrines an even wider range of circumstances in which Russia should resort to the use of nuclear weapons:

> The Russian Federation reserves the right to use nuclear weapons in response to the use of nuclear and other types of weapons of mass destruction against it and (or) its allies, as well as in response to large-scale aggression using conventional weapons in situations critical to the national security of the Russian Federation (Russian Government, 2000c, p.4).

While acknowledging Russia's weakened potential, the 2000 Military Doctrine sets as Russia's main priorities its restoration as an influential centre of power with global interests. This was reflected in particular in paragraphs about the necessity of safeguarding Russia's national interests in the World Ocean, and the possibility of deploying groups of forces in 'strategically important regions outside the territory of the Russian Federation'. The Doctrine also calls for the 'implementation of servicemen's rights and freedoms and the safeguarding of their social protection and appropriate social status and living standard' (Russian Government, 2000c, pp.4-5). This signals that the state is finally turning its focus onto the social hardships the Russian military currently face.

Military Reform under Yeltsin

Following the establishment of a Russian Ministry of Defence (MoD) in May 1992 a three-stage plan was put forward to reduce, reform, and restructure the armed forces by the end of the 1990s. However, General Pavel Grachev, Russia's first Defence Minister (1992-96), lacked professional judgement. He was more concerned about his relationship with President Boris Yeltsin (Supreme Commander-in-Chief) than the welfare of the armed forces. Reform was basically replaced with the mechanical reduction of the numerical strength of the Russian military and the re-deployment of military units and equipment from the foreign states and territories of former Soviet republics. The Russian military blamed the government for its numerous problems: systematic delays with cash allowances, poor living conditions, inadequate combat training, the failing prestige of military service, and conflicts with local authorities. Moreover, one by-product of the MoD's poor political standing has been the rise of parallel armies - military and paramilitary formations controlled by various internal security agencies. The Russian media also reported extensive corruption within the MoD. According to reports, a 'military-financial mafia' was manipulating money in the military budget by delaying the transfer of huge sums to troops in the field. The first campaign in Chechnya (1994-96) seriously drained servicemen's resources as well. Russian failure in the First Chechen War provoked General Grachev's replacement with a professional military theoretician, Colonel-General Igor Rodionov (1996-97). However, he was sacked in less than a year for not being willing to compromise on the matter of the military reform.

President Yeltsin made it clear in mid-1997 that military reform would be restrained by available economic resources. This decision was confirmed in the 1997 National Security Concept. Following Yeltsin's decision, concrete steps were taken to reform the armed forces within a severely retrenched defence budget under the strong leadership of new Defence Minister, Marshal Igor Sergeyev. In accordance with the reform programme, the strength of the armed forces was reduced to 1.2 million personnel by 1999. As part of the organisational reform aimed at increasing efficiency and cutting military personnel, the Strategic Missile Forces, Military-Space Forces (MSF) and the Missile-Space Defence (MSD) were integrated into a single fighting service, the Strategic Missile Forces. The Air Defence Forces merged with the Air Force. The integration allegedly allowed the elimination of duplicate structures, unified combat training, rear services etc., thus reducing the overall cost of maintenance of each fighting service.

Also, the Directorate of the Commander-in-Chief of the Land Forces was abolished and the Main Directorate of the Ground Forces and the Main

Directorate of Combat Training of the Armed Forces were established. Each MD was assigned the status of an operational-strategic command for the corresponding strategic direction (*strategicheskoe napravlenie*) and given operational command of all military and paramilitary forces in its borders (Russian Government, 1997, p.5). Commanders of each MD have become virtually autonomous in their districts with regard to peacetime training, operational plans, and the mobilisation of resources.

According to the decision, passed in late 1997, some MDs were merged and the total number of military districts was reduced from 8 to the following 6: Moscow, Leningrad, Trans-Caucasus, Trans-Volga-Urals, Siberia, and Far East. By 2000, this structural reorganisation was complete.

As part of the overall reform of the Russian Armed Forces, combined-arms special operational strategic groups were formed in Russia's remote and isolated regions. The main reason behind these military-administrative reorganisations was to increase control and management on par with the reduction of costs. In December 1997, troops of the former 11th Guards Army, deployed in the Kaliningrad Special District (*Kaliningradskiy osobyi raion*), were re-subordinated to the command of the Baltic Fleet. A similar group was formed on the Kamchatka and Chukotka peninsulas by the end of May 1998. The main idea behind this reorganisation was to ensure the combat stability of the nuclear-powered ballistic missile submarines' (SSBN) force, based in Rybachiy, near Petropavlovsk-Kamchatski, and to improve the management and control of troops in one of Russia's most remote regions. The Kamchatka Group is under the command of the Commander of the Kamchatksaya Flotilla, and is subordinated to the Russian Pacific Fleet HQ in Vladivostok.

Composition of the Russian Armed Forces and Their Capabilities

In early 2000 the Armed Forces of the Russian Federation consisted of four fighting services, the Strategic Missile Forces (SMF), the Air Forces (AF), the Navy, and the Ground Forces (GF). In addition the MoD had about 200,000 personnel, including centrally controlled units for electronic warfare, logistic support and training, and intelligence. The total estimated strength of the armed forces in late 1999 was 1,004,100 active personnel.

Strategic Missile Forces (SMF)

In early 2000, Russia's SMF consisted of 4 missile armies made up of 19 divisions, and they were equipped with some 771 intercontinental ballistic missiles (ICBMs). These ranged from the RS-20 (SS-18 *Satan*) to the newly introduced RS-12M-2 *Topol-M* (SS-27). The estimated strength of the SMF personnel was about 100,000, approximately half of whom were conscripts. After the integration, the SMF now incorporate up to 20 radar sites. These include the long-range, early-warning, Moscow anti-ballistic missile (ABM) system, known as A-135 (100 ABMs), 3 space-launch centres (consmodromes) in Baikonur (Kazakhstan), Plesetsk (Russia's North) and Svobodny-18 (Far East), and an orbital group that consists of nearly 130 satellites. According to the SMF Commander, Colonel-General Vladimir Yakovlev, integration of the MSF and the MSD has allowed Russia's strategic defence to increase its combat efficiency by up to 15-20% (Grigoriev, 2000). The SMF continues to remain Russia's main deterrent force: it is responsible for 90% of the combat tasks of Russia's nuclear Triad in any retaliatory counter-force strike (*otvetno-vstrechny udar*), and up to 60% of them in a counter-value strike (*otvetny udar*) (Baichurin, 1999).

In 1999, the SMF was the only fighting service that was fully provided with appropriate logistic support. In 1999, the SMF conducted 5 ICBM launches, including 2 of the new RS-12M-2, as well as 25 space launches. In particular, 4 new military satellites were launched into orbit (Baichurin, 1999). Another regiment of *Topol-Ms* (10 missiles) was also deployed, bringing the number of RS-12M-2s up to 20. In 2000, the SMF Command expects to deploy another 20-30 new *Topols*, and to bring to operational status the early-warning radar station *Volga* in Baranovichi (Belarus) (Sokut, 1999c).

With the ratification of the START-2 Treaty by both houses of the Russian Parliament (Duma and the Federation Council), Russia's strategic deterrent forces will undergo some significant reductions: from the approximately 6,600 nuclear warheads Russia had in the early 1999 down to 3,000-3,500 by 31 December 2007. However, Russian parliamentarians made several amendments to the Treaty. In particular, Russian heavy ICBMs (RS-20) are to be scrapped in 2007, not 2003;[4] R&D and procurement of nuclear weapons will continue to receive stable and guaranteed funding; Russia's state nuclear test range on the Novaya Zemlya archipelago will be preserved in operational condition. In addition it was stated that Russia reserves the right to withdraw from the Treaty if the United States does not honour other strategic reduction treaties.

Chemical and Biological Weapons (CW and BW)

In addition to its nuclear weapons, the Soviet arsenal possessed substantial stockpiles of other weapons of mass destruction: chemical and biological combat agents. In November 1997, President Yeltsin signed the bill of the Federal Assembly that ratified the Chemical Weapons Convention, which prohibits the development, production, stockpiling, and use of chemical weapons. According to the Convention's provisions, Russia is supposed to destroy its CW stockpile by 2007. Today, the Russian CW arsenal (about 40,000 tons), which is almost half of the overall world stockpile of CW, is distributed among seven storage facilities: Gorny, Kambarka, Kizner, Leonidovka, Maradykovsky, Pochep, and Shchuch'ye. Most of these are located in European Russia.[5] Russia is planning to destroy its stockpile of 1940s-50s CWs (7,500 tons) by April 2002. Later on Russia will destroy all of its CW shells and warheads (more than 32,000 tons). However, due to lack of funding, it will be 2013 before Russia will be able to complete the total destruction of its CWs.[6]

As far as BW program is concerned, Russia strongly denies the existence of an offensive BW program, as well as reports that it stockpiles combat biological agents. According to Russian officials, R&D into BWs stopped in 1992. According to Lieutenant-General Valentin Evstigneev, Chief of the Biological Defence Directorate of the Russian MoD, current Russian military biological research is undertaken for purely defensive purposes and focuses on the development of vaccines against viruses and combat biological agents, such as anthrax.[7] Still, the 1995 report by the US Defence Intelligence Agency suggested that Russia has continued to pursue its BWs program, which involved at least 20 facilities and 6,500 to 25,000 working and research personnel.[8]

Ground Forces (GF)

Once the largest fighting service of the Soviet military machine the GF consist of nearly 300,000 personnel, more than half conscripts, with the rest serving under contract. The level of staffing of the officer corps of the GF was about 86% in early 1999, with a shortage of approximately 8,000 low-ranking officers.[9] According to *The Military Balance*, Russia's GF consists of 5 field armies and 6 army corps, made up of 37 divisions (including 6 tank divisions) and 38 brigades. Russia's elite troops, airborne and special forces (*Spetsnaz*) are an integral part of the GF. The Airborne Troops (nearly 40,000 personnel) consist of 4 airborne divisions and 1 airborne brigade. The military *Spetsnaz* consists of 7 brigades (5 operational) located in each MD. GF are equipped with some 15,500 MBTs, 26,300 armoured vehicles (ACVs), 15,700 artillery pieces, 316 tactical missile (SSM) launchers, and 2,300 combat assault and transport helicopters. Army wartime reserves comprise 11,000 MBTs and 13,000 pieces of artillery (IISS, 1999, pp.112-3).[10] Only 25-30% of their armaments and equipment can be considered as modern and advanced, among them: reconnaissance equipment – 7 % and; combat helicopters – 2 %.[11]

One of the most visible achievements of the ongoing military reform was the creation of so-called units of constant combat readiness - UCCR (able to commence combat operations on 24 hours notice). In 1999, Russia's GF had 7 UCCRs: 3 divisions, and 4 brigades on 24-hour stand-by alert. These military formations are fully equipped (100%) and 80% - manned. Russia's Airborne Troops are also considered to be forces of constant combat readiness (CCR) and in 1999 had 10 CCR battalions.[12] Similar units were set up in other fighting services of the Russian Armed Forces. The government plans to increase the number of UCCRs as economic circumstances permit.

Apart from units and formations of CCR, GF in 1999 had 21 divisions and 10 brigades of the so-called cadre composition (100% equipped but only 10-15% manned). Their primary objective is the reinforcement of the UCCRs, as well as screening the state borders.[13] Since August 1999, there has been a clear rise in the intensity of combat training among units of the GF. The main reason for this was preparations for large-scale military operations in Chechnya. The Second Chechen War called for the mobilisation of all combat-ready troops in the GF (approximately 100,000 personnel).

Russia's military contingents abroad

There are also some significant forces deployed outside Russian territory. The largest contingent is the Transcaucasus Group of Forces (10,000 personnel in 1999), based in Georgia and Armenia. Some of Russia's forces deployed abroad are assigned to participate in peacekeeping and peacemaking operations on the periphery of the former USSR, as well as the former Yugoslav Federation. The most significant contingents are deployed in the Crimean Peninsula (Black Sea Fleet), Tajikistan (7,500-strong 201st Motor Rifle Division), and former Yugoslavia (approximately 5,000 personnel in Bosnia and Kosovo). Russia's peacekeeping formations are fully-manned (largely with contract soldiers) and well-equipped.[14] However, they are not regarded as part of the country's combat forces, since their tasks are not directly related to the defence of the state.

The next two to three years are expected to see a reduction of Russia's military presence in the near abroad. During the Istanbul summit of November 1999 Moscow committed itself to the withdrawal of its military forces from Moldova. Russia will have to pull out 2,500 troops, 120 MBTs, 1,000 APCs and 130 artillery pieces. The first echelons with equipment of the former 14th Army left Moldova in November 1999.[15]

Russia will also have to significantly reduce its military presence in Georgia. During the Moscow talks between Tbilisi and Moscow officials in April 2000 it was confirmed that Russia would close two of its military bases (in Vaziani and Gudauta) by 1 July 2001. The remaining Russian military contingent will be able to have only 153 MBTs, 241 ACVs and 140 pieces of artillery (Korbut, 2000). Moreover, there is an indication that Russia may completely withdraw its forces from Georgia in the next three years. This would mean that Russia would be able to maintain its military presence in the Transcaucasus only though its contingent stationed in Armenia.

Finally it should be noted that Russia has access to a few overseas facilities in Cuba (Cienfuegos), Syria (Tartus) and Vietnam (Cam Ranh Bay).

The integrated Air Force (AF)

Numbering just over 180,000 personnel, the integrated AF is equipped with some 1590 combat aircraft (excluding strategic bombers, transport and training planes), and 2,150 SAM launchers. The AF is organised into 4 Air Force/Air Defence (AF/AD) armies (HQ St.Petersburg, Rostov-on-Don, Chita, Khabarovsk), 2 AF/AD corps (HQ Samara, Yekaterinburg), and Moscow AF/AD District (Chernorechensky and Sokut, 2000). Nearly 12,000 AF personnel are involved in combat duty activities every day.[16] In 1999, the level of advanced armaments and equipment in the AF was: approximately 50% of all combat aircraft; 50% of all radio/radar/electronic equipment and; nearly 100% of all SAMs that could be considered modern and advanced.[17]

The strategic elements of the integrated AF are the 37th Air Army of the Supreme High Command (Long-Range Aviation, LRA), and the 61st Air Army of the Supreme High Command (Military-Transport Aviation, MTA). The 37th Army consists of 2 heavy-bomber divisions, the 22nd (Engels Air Base, Saratov region), and the 73rd (Ukrainka Air Base, Amur Province) and: 74 strategic bombers, plus 12 aircraft for testing and other activities.[18] As well, there are 4 regiments, equipped with over 120 Tu-22M-3 *Backfire-C* intermediate-range bombers, and there are 10 Tu-22M-2/-3 reconnaissance aircraft subordinated to the LRA Command. LRA has a training base for the Tu-95 aircraft at Dyagilevo, near Ryazan, and a testing centre in Zhukovskiy (Moscow region). The 61st Air Army consists of 2 divisions (4-5 regiments each) and the 610th Training Centre. MTA is equipped with 270 Il-76 *Candid* heavy-lifters and other aircraft, including the long-range An-124.[19]

After years of fruitless negotiations, Russia has been able to reach an agreement with Ukraine about the transfer of some strategic bombers left in Ukraine after the collapse of the USSR. By early-2000, the LRA had received 11 bombers (8 Tu-160 and 3 Tu-95 MS) and 575 Kh-55/55SM ALCMs. The bombers were transferred to the 22nd Heavy bomber Division (Kedrov, 2000). The addition of 11 advanced bombers plus 1 Tu-160, received from the industry, has significantly increased the striking capabilities of the LRA (Butowski, 2000b).

Despite fuel shortages, the 1999 level of combat training in the AF was quite high. All in all, AF units participated in more than 300 exercises, among them: *Vozdushny Most-99* [Air Bridge-99], *Zapad-99* [West-99], *Boyevoe Sotruzhestvo-99* [Combat Friendship-99], *Vostok-99* [East-99]. With the beginning of combat operations in Dagestan and Chechnya, the intensity of flight training increased significantly.[20] Nonetheless a lack of aviation fuel and other logistic support has meant that pilots have not received sufficient training. In 1999, the average flying hours were: fighter and tactical strike units – 16-24; tactical bomber units – 12-26; LRA – 20; MTA – 44-60 (Chernorechensky and Sokut, 2000).

The Navy

Along with 171,500 personnel, the Russian navy has at its disposal more than 70 various-purpose submarines (including 21 nuclear-powered and armed with ballistic missiles – SSBNs) and 147 surface combatants. These include the 67,500-ton *Admiral Kuznetsov* aircraft carrier, 4 *Ushakov* class nuclear-powered guided missile cruisers (CGNs) and 3 *Moskva* class guided-missile cruisers (CGs). The auxiliary fleet includes more than 430 auxiliaries and naval aviation has approximately 716 naval aircraft. The Navy is organised into four fleets: Northern, Pacific, Baltic and Black Sea, and one flotilla – Caspian. The Navy has access to overseas naval facilities in Tartus and Cam Ranh Bay. The Navy's current major objectives are:

- Strategic nuclear deterrence;
- Protection and defence of maritime approaches to Russia;
- Protection of the state's economic interests in the exclusive economic zone and the World Ocean;
- Demonstration of the flag and participation in peacemaking and humanitarian actions.[21]

Russia's power projection capabilities are centred on naval infantry units (1 division and 4 brigades), these remain one of Russia's most well-trained and highly-motivated combat formations.[22] Currently the Russian marine force is assigned defensive tasks. Although its amphibious capabilities are quite limited, thus preventing significant overseas troop deployments, Russian naval forces did show an impressive ability to quickly deploy contingent forces in 1999, when the major portion of Russian peacekeepers were transferred to Kosovo by sea.

By 1995, the number of combat squadrons and naval bases was reduced by half. All of Russia's divisions for coastal defence were disbanded. The Navy has lost 41% of its ships and 63% of naval aircraft. Russia's Northern Fleet is currently the most powerful naval entity, with more than 60% of all SSBNs concentrated in naval bases on the Kola Peninsula. The Navy remains the most conservative of all four arms of service, determined at all costs to maintain its traditions and identity. In 1999 each fleet staged a number of large-scale exercises. Naval strategic deterrent forces undertook unprecedented activity by conducting several launches of submarine-launched ballistic missiles (SLBMs), two of them performed by the Pacific Fleet *Delta III* class SSBNs (Kedrov, 1999). In 2000, the Navy was planning to deploy the *Kuznetsov* carrier battle group to the Mediterranean Sea. The *Kuznetsov* group will include among other ships *Ushakov* class CGN *Pyotr Velikiy*, *Moskva* class CG *Marshal Ustinov* and 5 nuclear-powered submarines. The Northern Fleet SSBNs was planning to conduct several launches of SLBMs.[23] Overall, the Russian Navy remains second most powerful naval force in the world.

Russia's naval policy 2000

On March 4 2000, President Putin approved 'Foundations of the Policy of the Russian Federation in the Field of Naval Activity Until 2010'. This document outlines the basic principals of Russia's maritime policy, and touches upon the main aspects of the preservation and future development of Russian naval power, as well as ways of using naval forces to protect Russia's national interests and security in areas of the World Ocean. It is clearly stated that only by relying on its naval potential will Russia be able to strengthen its security and defence, rebuild its economy and stimulate developments in social and economic spheres (Russian Government, 2000b, p.6). According to Naval Policy 2000, Russia's naval activity belongs in the 'category of the highest state priorities', and, as a consequence, Naval Policy 2000 emphasises that an increase of state support for the Navy remains one of the key priorities for the Russian Government (p.7).

To preserve Russia's status of being a great maritime power, the main emphasis will be given to:

- Construction of new-generation SSBNs and SLBMs; modernisation of operational SSBNs;
- Construction of multi-purpose submarines and surface combatants, including aircraft carriers, armed with high-precision weapons-systems;
- Acquisition of multi-purpose aircraft (ship- and shore-based), as well as new strike systems for coastal defence;
- UCCR to be equipped with advanced armaments and equipment;
- Unification of armaments and equipment;
- Modernisation of existing, and acquisition of new, reconnaissance, combat management, and navigation (including space-based) systems (Russian Government, 2000b, p.9).

In 1999, the Navy received 87% of its requested funds. However, more resources are now committed to maintaining operational condition, as well as acquiring ships, armaments and equipment: according to the latest data, the share of funding for these purposes increased from just 10% in 1997 to 40% in 1999 (Korbut, 1999). In 1999, the Navy commissioned the *Akula II* class SSN *Gepard*, the *Udaloy II* class DDG *Admiral Chabanenko*, the *Dergach* class missile corvette *Samum*, and a small amphibious craft.[24] The Navy estimates that in the 21st Century it needs to have a force of 12 SSBNs, 50 multi-purpose nuclear-powered and 35 conventional submarines and 70 major surface combatants. As a consequence, the naval share of the defence budget needs to rise to 25%. According to Chief of Naval Staff Admiral Viktor Kravchenko the naval share of the current defence budget does not exceed 12%.[25]

Paramilitary forces

There are six other forces, and some of them have received substantial political and financial support in the 1990s. Each military institution has its own administration and chain of command. For example, in 1999, the total strength of the army's strongest rival, the Internal Troops, was 203,000 personnel. They were organised into some 20 divisions, including 5 independent special-purpose divisions, 29 brigades (10 special-purpose brigades), and various units, among them elite *spetsnaz* detachments *Rus* and *Vitayz*. The forces are well equipped: 1700 ACVs, an artillery and an aviation wing, the latter comprising various types of aircraft from Il-76 *Candid* heavy-lifters to Mi-24 *Hind* combat assault helicopters. The combined strength of other paramilitary forces (Border Guards, Ministry of Emergencies and Civil Defence, Railway Troops, Federal Service of Special Construction, Federal Government Communications and Information Agency (FAPSI), and Federal Security Service (FSB)) is about 340,000 personnel (IISS, 1999, p.118; own estimates).

Defence industry

In the past ten years Russia's military production capabilities have seriously deteriorated. The state of the once mighty military-industrial complex (*voenno-promyshlenny kompleks, VPK*) has been severely affected by declining domestic procurement, as well as reductions of foreign arms sales in the early-1990s. By 1998 Russia's armaments production had dropped by 31.2%. By 2000, the overall debt to the VPK since 1992 had reached nearly 40 billion roubles.[26] Out of concern for the situation the Russian Government has sorted weapons-producing enterprises into those which are strategically important and those which are not. It is devoting a major effort to the rehabilitation of the former. In December 1997 the government adopted a programme of reconstruction and conversion of the VPK to run until 2005, and in April 1998, laws enabling the execution of the programme were enacted.

At present, the reconstruction of the VPK has become a top priority for the Kasyanov Government and President Putin. In 1999, Russia's military industry underwent significant reform of management control, this was the eleventh such reform since 1991. A special State Commission, responsible for the VPK, was established.[27] Ilya Klebanov, former Director of the St.Petersburg-based *Lomo* enterprise and Vice-Governor of St. Petersburg, was given the post of the First Vice-Premier and was placed in charge of the State Commission (Sokut, 1999a). Four federal agencies – for Russia's aerospace, shipbuilding, conventional armaments, and control systems – were established to control sectors of the VPK.[28] In 2000, a new Ministry of Industry, Science and Technology was established to implement more effective policy in regards to the state industrial policy, state defence order and military-technological cooperation with foreign states. The newly established ministry will be under the control of Aleksandr Dondukov, Chief Designer and Director of the Yakovlev Aircraft Construction Bureau (Sokut, 2000c). Russia's defence industry currently comprises more than 1690 enterprises (635 state-owned) and employs approximately 2 million workers. But only 120 enterprises are considered to be plants that are capable of fulfilling pilot projects within the framework of the state defence order (Pimenov, 1999). One task to which the Russian Government attaches particular importance is fostering companies capable of producing high-tech weapons systems. The government wants deeper integration within the VPK; it strongly favours the creation of large financial-industrial concerns, specialising in the production of high-tech armaments, such as combat aircraft, space systems or warships. In 1999, there were some signs of the recovery of Russia's defence industry. Production growth reached 130-140% (Sokut, 2000d), largely due to the increased state defence orders, and foreign arms sales. Since internal large-scale procurement will be almost impossible until 2005 because of budgetary stringency, the VPK is now being encouraged to export its products.

Although Russia attaches importance to arms exports as a source of foreign currency, these decreased sharply in 1997. However, by 2000 Russia's defence exports were on the rise again. In 1999, Russia earned

US\$3.393 billion.[29] According to Klebanov, the anticipated income from foreign arms sales in 2000 should be at least US\$4.3 billion. This figure is projected to reach US\$5 billion in 2001 with the overall aim being to make Russia the world's second biggest arms exporter by the year 2004.[30] Russia is aggressively promoting its armaments on the world market, even using its intelligence agencies (SVR and GRU) to do so. Asia remains one of Russia's main markets. India and China remain Russia's principal strategic partners in terms of military-technological cooperation.

Regardless of economic hardships and restraints in state funding, Russia's VPK continues to develop new advanced armaments. High technology R&D has already produced several advanced weapons systems, with other under development for the 21st Century. Among them:

- Continuous deployment of the silo-based RS 12M-2 *Topol-M* ICBM;
- Development and initiation of series production of new high-precision weapons systems, in particular the airborne cruise missiles Kh-555 and Kh-101;
- Development of the new tactical SSM *Iskander* (SS-X-26) with a range of 400 km;
- Trials of the new MBT T-95;
- Trials of fifth-generation combat aircraft by Russia's leading aircraft builders Sukhoi and MiG (S-37 *Berkut* and 'Object 1.44' respectively);
- Continuous construction of the new-generation SSBN *Yuri Dolgorukiy* and the *Severodvinsk* class SSN;
- Ongoing R&D of combat laser systems as well as radio-frequency particle beam weapons.[31]

Military Exercise Activity in 1999

In 1999, Russian military forces staged several large-scale manoeuvres, including a number of strategic command-and-staff exercises (CASE). In March Russian Airborne Troops and MTA conducted the large-scale exercise *Vozdushny Most-99* [Air Bridge-99] to test the employment of the 'rapid reaction force' in a regional conflict. The exercise involved the airdrop of 709 paratroopers and equipment from the 98th Airborne Division. In late March-early April Russian forces of the Far Eastern MD, together with the Pacific Fleet and various paramilitary forces, staged the largest CASE in 8 years, which involved more than 4,000 personnel.[32] However, the culmination of Russia's exercise activity in 1999 was the strategic CASE *Zapad-99* [West-99]. Held from the 21 to 26 June 1999, it was the largest display of military power in Russia's Western regions, as well as Belarus (Russia's principal ally), over the past decade. *Zapad-99* involved troops and forces of Russia's four MDs: Leningrad, Moscow, North-Caucasus, Trans-Volga-Urals. Forces and management structures of the Northern, Baltic and Black Sea fleets, the Caspian Flotilla and Russian airborne troops were also involved in these large-scale manoeuvres. Approximately 50,000 personnel were reportedly involved (Polkovnikov, 1999). GF conducted six tactical exercises, while the Navy staged nine, involving surface combatants (among them the cruisers *Pyotr Belikiy*, and *Marshal Ustinov*), support vessels, and several nuclear-powered submarines. However the most surprising part was the conclusion of the exercise, which involved combat aircraft of the 37th Air Army (Long-Range Aviation). Two of Russia's most advanced strategic bombers, the Tu-160 *Blackjack*, flew down the Norwegian coastline, while a pair of Tu-95MS *Bears* reached Iceland. Both pairs conducted simulated launches of the *Raduga* Kh-55/55SM ALCMs (Sokut, 1999b).

The Second Chechen War: a Preliminary Assessment

When compared with the same situation at the end of 1994 it is clear that the Russian army was more prepared to fight another military campaign in Chechnya in 1999. Critical analysis of military operations in Dagestan and Chechnya (August 1999 – May 2000) indicate principal differences between current campaign and that of 1994-96. Among them:

- At the beginning of the campaign Command of the Joint Group of Federal Forces (JGFF) managed to cut off all communications and power supplies in Chechnya, which has become a demoralising factor for the Chechen fighters;
- A desire to avoid direct contact with the enemy forces. Heavy reliance on strike aircraft (Su-24, Su-25) and assault helicopters (Mi-24) (80%), as well as artillery (15-17%);

- Better coordination between regular army units and paramilitary forces (internal troops, special militia units etc.);
- High morale of JGFF personnel;
- Closer contact with the local population;
- The military campaign in Chechnya receives firm support in Russia: from the political elite, the mass media and the majority of the population;
- Better information support for the federal forces operations in Chechnya.

The adoption of new tactics was driven not just by the re-evaluation of painful mistakes of the first unsuccessful campaign. Careful assessment was made of the tactics used by the United States and its European allies during recent military conflicts, in particular, against Yugoslav forces (Soloviev, 1999). Their emphasis on non-direct contact with the enemy was noted. By May 2000, the army had basically fulfilled its role of liquidating large rebel forces. Some of the Russian military units were pulled out of Chechnya. However, Russia is planning to maintain its permanent military presence in the rebellious republic: the 15,000-strong 42nd Guards Motor Rifle Division and the 46th Brigade of the Internal Troops will be permanently stationed in there. They will have to deal with numerous groups of rebels who have waged an uncompromising guerrilla war against federal forces.

Zapad-99 was intended to demonstrate Russia's military potential and its ability to wage substantial military operations in response to NATO's eastward expansion, and its military campaign against Yugoslavia. The overall assessment of Russian conventional military capabilities and the combat performance of Russian forces in Chechnya leads to the conclusion that the Russian Armed Forces are currently capable of staging one theatre-level defensive, or one army-level offensive operation.

Vladimir Putin: a New Hope for the Russian Military?

After Vladimir Putin was appointed Russia's Prime Minister in early August 1999, he made crystal clear his intention to provide the Russian military with real, not declarative, support. Born into the family of a Soviet naval officer, and being a professional security officer himself, Putin makes no secret of the fact that he has a special attitude to men in uniform. When Chechen guerrillas invaded Dagestan in late August 1999, Putin showed that he put more trust in the might of the Russian military machine, rather than the power of negotiations. The military were given the green light to wage full-scale military operations against the rebels; their actions were backed politically and financially. Also, the new Putin-led government began paying off debts to the officer corps. As the army newspaper *Krasnaya zvezda* reported in January 2000, for the first time since 1996 Russian military personnel actually received their December 1999 wages without any delay.[33]

Moreover, more funding was promised to resolve the housing dilemma, which continues to remain one of the most painful difficulties faced by the military. At the beginning of 2000, around 40,000 personnel of the Russian Armed Forces required accommodation; every fifth officer family had to share accommodation. The Air Force had approximately 28,000 personnel with no accommodation. Even officers of the elite Airborne Troops experience some severe problems with housing. According to Colonel-General Georgiy Shpak, in 1999, nearly 40% of all of the Airborne Troops' officers did not have their own accommodation.[34]

While trying to finally resolve social problems of the military Putin has also concentrated the efforts of his government upon modernisation of the armed forces. The urge for the restoration of military might has been driven both by domestic and external circumstances. From a Russian perspective the shifting strategic balance in favour of NATO poses a threat to its security. NATO's new borders with the Russian Federation have significantly added to the former's ability to deliver either conventional or nuclear strikes deep into Russia's core territory, notably the Moscow region. There is concern in Russia that NATO could use this new strategic advantage for political blackmail in times of crisis. The Secretary of Russia's Security Council, Sergei Ivanov, stated in May 2000 that Russia strongly objects any further eastward expansion of NATO and is prepared to undertake adequate measures to counter the alliance.[35]

Apart from the shifting strategic balance in Europe, resentment at US-dominated NATO operations in the Balkans, ongoing tension over US ABM initiatives, war in Chechnya and the possibility of the emergence of similar conflicts along the periphery of the former USSR, have all combined to persuade Moscow that this is a good time both to flex nuclear muscles and to boost conventional capabilities. One of the reasons behind Russia's decision to finally ratify the START-2 was a pragmatic assessment of the nation's defence needs. While it was acknowledged that the country did not have the capacity to maintain strategic deterrent forces at the level of START-1, the Russian military-political leadership also noted that in the current geo-political situation it is more efficient for the country's national security to re-allocate state funds for the modernisation of conventional armaments and the restoration of the combat potential of the Navy and the Air Force.[36] Putin's Government has already increased procurement in its 2000 Defence Budget by 50%, to 62 billion roubles (US$2.1 billion). The total defence budget for 2000 has been set at 143 billion roubles or 2.64% of GDP (Novichkov, 2000). Later, the military received nearly an additional 27 billion roubles, thus increasing the share of defence in the state budget for 2000 to 29.2%. In 2001, Russia's military spending will be at a level of 2.68% of national GDP.[37]

As new Supreme Commander-in-Chief, Putin apparently has his own vision of military reform and construction. While making a commitment to continue to preserve substantial strategic deterrent capabilities, Putin indicated that special attention has to be paid to general-purpose forces. The ongoing conflict in the North Caucasus has shown the necessity of strengthening GF in particular. The conventional forces are being promised new equipment. At the end of 1999, Russia's Ministry of Defence received an additional 4 billion roubles for conventional arms procurement and modernisation, mainly to re-equip GF (Novichkov, 1999). In 1999, GF acquired and received 30 T-90 MBTs, 100 BTR-80A APCs and 24 self-propelled howitzers (probably *Msta-S*). The 2000 state defence order includes the acquisition of another 30 T-90 MBTs and 100 BTR-80A APCs.[38]

The Navy has also been targeted for particular support from the new Federal Government, its share of the state defence order will be significantly increased, from 9.3% in 1999 to 20% in 2000 (Sokut, 2000b). Before 2010 the Navy plans to commission warships of different types, ranging from minesweepers to guided-missile destroyers.[39] The construction of the new-generation SSBN *Yuri Dolgorukiy* and the new SSN series also continues in Severodvinsk. New attention is being given to modernisation of the SSBN fleet as well. In September 1999 the government decided to resume series production of the improved RSM-54 *Sineva* (SS-N-23) SLBM in Krasnoyarsk (Aleksin, 1999). Efforts have been made to refit *Typhoon* class SSBNs. The operational life of the 6 Pacific Fleet *Delta III* class SSBNs will be prolonged until 2005; while the submarines will be modernised (IISS, 1999, p.107).

The Air Force will focus its efforts on modernising its most modern aircraft, such as the Su-25, Su-27, Su-30 and MiG-29, upgrading their capabilities to the level of 4+-generation combat aircraft. The Russian helicopter fleet of Mi-8s and Mi-24s will also undergo significant modernisation, even if it means fewer acquisitions of the advanced Ka-50 *Black Shark* assault helicopter.[40] Design work on new combat aircraft is already underway. In particular, the Air Force expects to receive its fifth-generation fighter in 2008-10 (Sokut, 2000a). The MTA will receive the first batch of the An-70 transport aircraft in 2000. A new-generation air defence complex S-400 *Triumph* will be fielded by the end of 2000 (Butowski, 2000a and 2000c). However, the Air Force Command warns that without allocation of additional funds, the overall combat potential of the service will be significantly reduced by 2005; and the number of operational combat aircraft will fall by 3-4 times.[41]

Table 10.1   Evolution of Russian society's trust in its armed forces, 1992-2000

Year	Percentage of Trust
1992	55-60
1994	38
1996	27
1998	24
2000	44

Source: Nezavisimoe voennoe obozrenie, no.13, 1999, p.4; *Nezavisimaya gazeta*, 21 April, 2000, p.3.

While making efforts to keep the military machine effective, Putin and the new government continue to strengthen Russia's military-political positions in the expanse of the former Soviet Union. The creation of the political union between Russia and Belarus has only accelerated further integration of military establishments of two allied nations. In April 2000 the formation of the 300,000-strong Joint Group of Forces it was declared (Georgiev, 2000). Efforts have been made for the creation of a Russia-Belarus joint regional air defence system, responsible for the air defence of the western zone.[42] Russia was also successful in expanding the so-called Integrated Air Defence System of the Commonwealth of Independent States (CIS). In March 2000, two more Central Asian states, Tajikistan and

Uzbekistan joined Russia, Armenia, Belarus, Kazakhstan and Kyrgyzstan (Drobyshevsky, 2000). A new CIS Anti-Terrorist Centre with the support and under the patronage of the FSB has also been established. On 2 April 2000, Armenia, Belarus, Kazakhstan, Kyrgyzstan, Russia and Tajikistan renewed the 1992 Tashkent Collective Security Treaty. Russia promised to offer military support, assistance and protection to the members of the Treaty, thus further strengthening its military-political influence within the CIS.[43]

Putin's ambition to restore Russia's military has strong public support. NATO's military campaign against Russia's traditional ally Serbia, followed by the invasion of the Chechen militants into Dagestan, have led to a re-assessment of the pacifist views that dominated Russian society in the early-mid 1990s. In July 1999, some 55% of the Russians supported an increase in military expenditure, while only 8% had an opposite view. Some of the country's prominent sociologists noticed an increase in respect for the military by society. According to some opinion polls, by 2000 more than 44% of the population looked positively on the Russian military establishment compared to only 29% a couple of years ago.[44]

Table 10.2   Changes to 'Great Power' sentiments in Russian society *

	1999	2000
Yes	31	53
No	65	43
Uncertain	4	4

* Percentage of respondents' answers to the question 'Is Russia a Great Power Today?'

Source: Nezavisimaya gazeta, 22 April, 2000, p.3.

Society also strongly favours Putin's desire to reclaim Russia's superpower status. After the end of the Cold War many Russians were left with a feeling of shame at the bloodless defeat the West perceives as a triumph. Opinion polls show a significant increase of 'great power' sentiments among Russians over just one year (table 16.2). It is likely this shift was caused by strong support for Putin's tough crackdown on rebellious Chechnya.

Prospects for the Development of Russian Military Power in the 21st Century

When, in 1998, Yeltsin approved the detailed concept paper he had commissioned in late 1996, 'The Fundamental (Concept) of State Policy in Defence Building Until 2005', it foreshadowed a transition over seven years to three fighting services in the armed forces. These would correspond to the three spheres of warfare: land, aerospace and sea. Accordingly, it can be anticipated that there will be further integration of existing fighting services. Ultimately, after 2005 the Russian Armed Forces will comprise the Integrated Air Force (air force and air defence, SMF, MSF and MSD), the Navy and GF. The number of UCCRs will continue to grow, especially in Russia's western and south-western MDs. Strategic nuclear forces will remain the backbone of Russian deterrence in the 21st Century; they are intended to prevent either a nuclear or large-scale conventional war against Russia. At the same time, tactical nuclear weapons, particularly air-launched ones, will also play a crucial role in deterring potential attack. Before 2006, the Russian Armed Forces do not expect to start rearmament *en masse*. Instead, the emphasis will be made upon radical upgrades and the modernisation of existing equipment and weapons systems, upgrading them to the standards of 4/4+-generation weapons systems. The improvement of control and management structures and information and reconnaissance systems also has high priority.[45] However, in 2006 the Russian military-political leadership anticipates the start of mass acquisitions of advanced armaments and equipment for the armed forces.[46]

Conclusion

The next decade may become crucial for Russia and its Armed Forces. A preliminary assessment of the actions of Vladimir Putin and his team leads to the conclusion that the new Russian President has so far been acting more like a military strongman. After years of decline under Yeltsin, his successor is flexing Russia's military might. Putin has made quite clear his ambition to see Russia's reincarnation as a world superpower because he knows that his goal resonates with the desires of millions of ordinary

Russians after the Yeltsin years. Ironically, it is US world domination that has eased Putin's rise and the adoption of this new strategy.

Apart from plans to reclaim the country's superpower status, Russia's new President has a clear desire to restore his country's influence across that great swathe of territory that once followed Moscow's line without question. In order to achieve these goals Putin plans to rebuild Russian military power out of the wreckage of the old Soviet war machine. However, it should still be kept in mind that the army has been underfunded for several years, and that this has entailed negative consequences for the nation's defence potential. While Moscow cannot currently devise credible responses to large-scale conventional contingencies on its frontiers, *Zapad-99* and the second Chechen war have shown that Russia still has the capability to counter local and regional conflicts. However, with no significant increase in defence spending in the very near future, strong doubts may be raised about the possibility of Russia having a modern professional army equipped with state-of-the-art weaponry in the 21st Century. Russia would be unable usefully to deploy conventional forces except possibly in local or regional police actions. However, if the new Russian government and the new President continue to provide firm support to the military, the world will witness the restoration of Russia's military might. The Russian Federation will then be able to retain its status as a military power and a nuclear superpower in the 21st Century.

Notes

1   *Krasnaya zvezda*, 4 September, 1999, p.1.
2   Own estimates.
3   *Krasnaya zvezda*, 4 September, 1999, p.1.
4   The operational life of RS-20 ICBMs will expire in 2006-2007.
5   *Krasnaya zvezda*, 20 March, 1999, p.3.
6   *Nezavisimaya gazeta*, 5 May, 2000, p.2.
7   *Krasnaya zvezda*, 15 July, 1999, p.2.
8   *Jane's Defence Weekly*, 13 May, 1995, p.5.
9   According to the Chief of the Main Directorate of the Ground Forces, Colonel-General Yuri Bukreev, this problem will be apparently resolved by 2001 (*Krasnaya zvezda*, 5 March, 1999, p.1).
10   Note that most of the stored equipment is obsolete.
11   *Nezavisimaya gazeta*, 5 March, 1999, p.2.

12   *Nezavisimoe voennoe obozrenie*, no.10, 1999, p.1; *Krasnaya zvezda*, 31 July, 1999, p.1.
13   *Nezavisimoe voennoe obozrenie*, no.10, 1999, p.1.
14   For example, the 201st Division is manned only with contract personnel.
15   *Jane's Defence Weekly*, 17 May, 2000, p.6; *Nezavisimoe voennoe obozrenie*, no.45, 1999, p.8.
16   See General Anatoly Kornukov, 'Nebo otchizny pod nadezhnoi zashchitoi', *Krasnaya zvezda*, 8 April, 2000, p.1.
17   *Krasnaya zvezda*, 27 May, 1999, p. 1; Dobrovol'sky, 1999; author's estimates.
18   The fleet of Russian strategic bombers (Tu-160 *Blackjack* and Tu-95MS *Bear*) is capable of delivering a total load of approximately 800 airborne cruise missiles (ALCMs).
19   See the interview with the MTA Commander, Major-General Viktor Denisov, in *Nezavisimoe voennoe obozrenie*, no.3, 2000, p.1.
20   The average number of daily combat sorties, carried out by the Russian AF in Chechnya is about 50. During the most intensive periods of fighting, the AF conducted more than 100 combat sorties a day.
21   Quoted from an article by the Commander-in-Chief of the Russian Navy (Kuroyedov, 1998, pp.8-9).
22   Naval infantry units from all Russian fleets are taking part in operations in Chechnya. As in the first Chechen war, the combat performance of the Russian marines was quite high.
23   See interview with the Head of Combat Training of the Russian Navy Vice-Admiral Nikolai Mikheev in Aleksin, 2000.
24   *Krasnaya zvezda*, 21 July, 1999, p.1. Note that some of the above-mentioned warships were under construction and trials for several years due to the lack of funding.
25   *Nezavisimoe voennoe obozrenie*, no.18, 2000, p.1.
26   *Jane's Defence Weekly*, 18 February, 1998, p.5; *Nezavisimoe voennoe obozrenie*, no.10, 2000, p.6.
27   The full name of the Commission in Russian is *Gosudarstvennaya Komissiya Pravitel'stva Rossiiskoi Federatsii po voprosam VPK*.
28   *Nezavisimoe voennoe obozrenie*, no.30, 1999, p.1.
29   *Nezavisimaya gazeta*, 25 May 2000, p.2. There was an obvious misprint in the article regarding currency.
30   *Nezavisimoe voennoe obozrenie*, no.14, 2000, p.6.
31   Information is based on a variety of reports published by the Russian press.
32   *Nezavisimaya gazeta*, 7 April, 1999, p.2.
33   *Krasnaya zvezda*, 15 January, 2000, p.1.
34   *Krasnaya zvezda*, 8 April, 2000, p.2, 26 January, 2000, p.2 and 31 July, 1999, p.1.
35   *Krasnaya zvezda*, 31 May, 2000, p.1.
36   See Putin's remarks in *Nezavisimoe voennoe obozrenie*, no.14, 2000, p.1.
37   *Krasnaya zvezda*, 7 June, 2000, p.1.
38   *Nezavisimoe voennoe obozrenie*, no.16, 2000, p.6.
39   See remarks of Admiral Kravchenko in *Morskoi sbornik*, no.2, 2000, p.12.
40   *Nezavisimoe voennoe obozrenie*, no.16, 2000, p.6.
41   *Nezavisimoe voennoe obozrenie*, no.16, 2000, p.1.
42   *Krasnaya zvezda*, 30 May, 2000, p.1.

220   *Russia After Yeltsin*

43   *Nezavisimaya gazeta*, 23 May, 2000, p.1.
44   *Nezavisimoe voennoe obozrenie*, no.28, 1999, p.1; *Nezavisimaya gazeta*, 21 April, 2000, p.3.
45   *Krasnaya zvezda*, 30 May, 2000, p.1.
46   *Nezavisimoe voennoe obozrenie*, no.14, 2000, p.6.

References

Aleksin, V. (1999), 'Vozrozhdenie morskogo raketostroeniya', *Nezavisimoe voennoe obozrenie*, no.50, p.3.
Aleksin, V. (2000), 'Voennye moryaki idut v Sredizemnoe more', *Nezavisimoe voennoe obozrenie*, no.14, p.1.
Baichurin, I. (1999), 'Itogi goda', *Nezavisimoe voennoe obozrenie*, no.45, p.1.
Butowski, P. (2000a), 'Russia's First S-400 Squad to be Deployed by Next Year', *Jane's Defence Weekly*, 26 January, p.13.
Butowski, P. (2000b), 'Russian Air Force Gets Another Tu-160', *Jane's Defence Weekly*, 24 May, p.12.
Butowski, P. (2000c), 'Ukraine Becomes Second An-70 Customer', *Jane's Defence Weekly*, 26 January, p.5.
Chernorechensky, A. and Sokut, S. (2000), 'Vykhod iz shtopora otkladyvaetsya', *Nezavisimoe voennoe obozrenie*, no.2, p.3.
Dick, C.J. (2000), 'Russia's New Doctrine Takes Dark World View', *Jane's Intelligence Review*, vol.12, no.1, January, p.15.
Dobrovol'sky, A. (1999), 'VVS budut spasat' svoyu tekhniku', *Nezavisimoe voennoe obozrenie*, no.18, p.6.
Drobyshevsky, A. (2000), 'PVO rasshiryaetsya', *Nezavisimoe voennoe obozrenie*, no.9, p.1.
Georgiev, V. (1999), 'Yubilei rossiiskoi armii', *Nezavisimoe voennoe obozrenie*, no.17, p.1.
Georgiev, V. (2000), 'Sozdaetsya sovmestnaya gruppirovka', *Nezavisimoe voennoe obozrenie*, no.14, p.1.
Grigoriev, S. (2000), 'Put' k ustoichivomu razvitiyu', *Nezavisimoe voennoe obozrenie*, no.8, p.6.
IISS (1999), *The Military Balance 1999-2000*, International Institute for Strategic Studies, London.
Kedrov, I. (1999), 'Rossiya igraet strategicheskimi muskulami', *Nezavisimoe voennoe obozrenie*, no.39, p.1.
Kedrov, I. (2000), 'Vesennee popolnenie v dal'nei aviatsii', *Nezavisimoe voennoe obozrenie*, no.8, p.8.
Korbut, A. (1999), 'Na poroge uchebnogo goda', *Nezavisimoe voennoe obozrenie*, no.46, p.3.
Korbut, A. (2000), 'Moskva ustupila Tbilisi', *Nezavisimoe voennoe obozrenie*, no.15, p.1.
Kuroyedov, V. (1998), 'O morskoi strategii Rossii', *Voenny parad*, no.2 (26), pp.8-9.
Litovkin, D. (2000), '*Sineva* podnimetsya nad morem', *Nezavisimoe voennoe obozrenie*, no.16, p.1.
Novichkov, N. (1999), 'Russian Funds for Procurement Reallocated', *Jane's Defence Weekly*, 20 October, p.4.

Novichkov, N. (2000), 'Russia Doubles Defence Procurement', *Jane's Defence Weekly*, 2 February, p.3.

Pimenov, V. (1999), 'Organizatsionnye bluzhdaniya oboronnogo kompleksa', *Nezavisimoe voennoe obozrenie*, no.33, p.4.

Polkovnikov, P. (1999), 'Ot Kaliningrada do granitsy s Kitaem', *Nezavisimoe voennoe obozrenie*, no.25, p.5.

Russian Government (1997), 'O pervoocherednykh merakh po reformirovaniyu Vooruzhennykh Sil Rossiiskoi Federatsii i sovershenstvovanii ikh struktury', *Rossiiskaia Gazeta*, 19 July, p.5.

Russian Government (2000a), 'Kontseptsiya natsional'noi bezopasnosti', *Nezavisimoe voennoe obozrenie*, no.1, pp.6-7.

Russian Government (2000b), 'Osnovy politki Rossiiskoi Federatsii v oblasti voenno-morskoi deyatel'nosti na period do 2010 goda', *Morskoi sbornik*, no.4, pp.6-9.

Russian Government (2000c), 'Voennaya doktrina Rossiiskoi Federatsii', *Nezavisimoe voennoe obozrenie*, no.15, pp.4-5.

Sokut, S. (1999a), 'Gosudarstvo vspomnilo pro oboronku', *Nezavisimoe voennoe obozrenie*, no.21, p.1.

Sokut, S. (1999b), 'Krug pocheta nad Islandiei', *Nezavisimoe voennoe obozrenie*, no.25, p.5.

Sokut, S. (1999c), 'Novaya tekhnika RVSN', *Nezavisimoe voennoe obozrenie*, no.30, p.1.

Sokut, S. (2000a), 'Istrebitel pyatogo pokoleniya postupit v voiska cherez 8-10 let', *Nezavisimoe voennoe obozrenie*, no.9, p.6.

Sokut, S. (2000b), 'Novaya vlast' imeet shans vyvesti voennuyu reformu iz krizisa', *Nezavisimoe voennoe obozrenie*, no.1, p.2.

Sokut, S. (2000c), 'Siloviki ukreplyayut svoi pozitsii', *Nezavisimoe voennoe obozrenie*, no.18, p.1.

Sokut, S. (2000d), 'Zabytaya oboronka', *Nezavisimoe voennoe obozrenie*, no.10, p.3.

Soloviev, V. (1999), 'Federal'nye voiska uspeshno zavershayut operatsiyu v Dagestane', *Nezavisimoe voennoe obozrenie*, no.33, p.1.

Zolotarev, V. (1998), *Voennaya bezopasnost' Otechestva*, Kanon Press Kuchkovo Pole, Moskva.

11 Personality, Politics and Power: Foreign Policy under Putin

PETER SHEARMAN

Introduction: Leadership Succession and Policy Initiative

Succession of political leadership provides an occasion for reflection on and analysis of the past, and for a tentative assessment of the future. It has been demonstrated in a large number of academic studies in comparative politics that leadership succession brings in its wake significant changes in public policy. This has been shown to be the case not only in countries where leadership succession is determined by free and open competitive elections, but also in authoritarian states (Bunce, 1981). Although perhaps counterintuitive, it was found that in Soviet-type communist ('totalitarian') states new leaders had less ability to implement new policies than did their counterparts in liberal democracies, despite their seemingly 'total' power. This was due to the different methods of succession between political systems. In liberal democracies new leaders, gaining power through the ballot box, are able to—indeed, *expected* to—choose a new government and to institute new policy initiatives. New policy initiatives, especially any radical reforms, usually take place in the early period of a new leader's tenure in office—referred to in popular discourse as the 'honeymoon period'. In the former Soviet Union, new leaders were chosen by the existing ruling elite, not on the basis of regular elections, but rather upon the death of the previous incumbent leader.[1] New policy initiatives would only come about slowly, once the new leader had managed over time to successfully accumulate power through personnel renewal, bringing into the top echelon of the party/state apparatus people that he could trust (Breslauer, 1982).[2] At least this was the case after Stalin's death in 1953 through to the 1980s when Gorbachev came to power. The system became rigid, and was resistant to radical change due in part to the constraints on personnel turnover, leading to what became known as the 'stability of cadres' or what Gorbachev termed the 'period of stagnation' in Russian politics.[3]

Most of these studies highlighted a linkage between the *process* of succession and changes in public policy; however, other works, mostly in the area of psychology, have stressed the role of *individuals* themselves (Jervis, 1976). It is widely accepted that certain individuals have made a significant impact on the course of political history: for example, Napoleon, Hitler, Churchill, Gandhi, Mao, Castro, Saddam Hussein, Milosevic are individuals that have made their mark on history, for better or ill. The personality of a leader will determine what type of leader one has. Each person has unique life experiences, likes and dislikes, lovers and enemies, levels of education, cognitive and analytical skills, and other properties and characteristics, which together influence the decisions reached. Indeed, in liberal democracies 'character' is seen by many as a crucial issue when calculating which party or leader to vote for in elections for political office.

Russia is now an electoral democracy, if not a fully-fledged one. The last decade of the twentieth century in Russia is commonly referred to as the 'Yeltsin era', indicative of the importance attached to Boris Yeltsin in political developments during this period. The first years of the twenty-first century, depending upon what takes place and assuming he retains the presidency could go down as the Putin era in Russian politics. The fact that it was the ballot box which brought him to power—marking the first ever democratic leadership transition in Russian history—has provided Putin with similar opportunities to form a new government and initiate new policies that other democratically elected leaders have enjoyed in western countries. Thus we could expect the immediate post-election honeymoon period to be marked by new policy initiatives, as Putin puts his stamp on the presidency.

Individuals are important, but (as Karl Marx noted) they do not make history as they please for they are inevitably confronted with and restricted by the objective circumstances pertaining at any specific time. Thus, for any comprehensive evaluation of a state's foreign policy, in addition to the individual, we need to take account of the domestic arrangement of government and the systemic, structural properties of the international system. In other words we need to consider *personality, politics*, and *power*.[4] As other chapters in this volume have demonstrated, Yeltsin made a difference to the course of Russian politics in the 1990s, but his policies were conditioned by both domestic politics and the international configuration of power. Similarly, Putin's ability to affect the conduct of Russian foreign policy will be in part determined by forces at these different levels of analysis. In this chapter I will provide an assessment of

Russian foreign policy under Putin, with a consideration of these three separate but linked influences.

(1) Personality

Who is Putin?

Little was known about Putin when he was suddenly catapulted to power following Yeltsin's surprise resignation on the night of 31 December, 1999.[5] Before his rapid rise to power during the last two years of Yeltsin's presidency, Putin spent almost his entire professional career in the KGB. It was popularly assumed on the basis of this limited biographical background that Putin would usher in a new authoritarianism in Russian politics, resulting in increasing anti-Westernism. Ariel Cohen (2000) argued that due to his links to the KBG Putin's presidency does '...not bode well for Russian democracy'.[6] As Amy Knight (2000) put it, if we judge Putin by his past then '...it does not bode well for the future of Russian democracy or for Russia's relations with the West' (p.33). However, such an assessment is extremely simplistic. It ignores not only the roles of personality, politics, and power: it also misrepresents the influences of bureaucratic and institutional processes.

In the late Soviet period the KGB was the one institution that recognised the huge technological gap between East and West, and the importance for the future of the Soviet system in overcoming this gap. This was especially the case among lower level operatives engaged in direct industrial espionage. Putin, operating in this area in East Germany, experienced this first hand.[7] Whilst serving in the KGB Putin (2000) recalls that '...we were allowed to think differently. And we could say things that few normal citizens could permit themselves to say' (p.68). Putin made this comment in the series of frank interviews he gave to three Russian journalists, providing us with the most detailed source yet available for assessing Putin the man. During these conversations a picture emerges of a person who is patriotic but not nationalistic; hard-working, but not driven by a lust for power; sober, but likes an occasional drink; intelligent, but not overly intellectual. Putin emerges as a conservative, but one who is willing to listen to other arguments and points of view.[8] He is also someone who is able to adapt and learn from experience, rather than being wedded to any particular ideology.[9] He has a commitment to family, and on a wider level he is an advocate of a strong Russian state. Putin comes across as confident in his own abilities, but not cocky; strong, mentally and physically, but not a gambler or someone to take undue risks. In most of these character traits we can contrast Putin with his predecessor. For Yeltsin was an unpredictable risk taker, often physically weak, unhealthy, and inebriated. Yeltsin was also prone to fall into depression, at several times verging on suicide. The picture painted of Yeltsin by Lilia Shevtsova is one of '…a man who lost contact with reality' and who learned about events in the real world not through the media or his government officials, but through his family. Shevtsova said that Yeltsin would sit for hours looking at a blank piece of paper: 'He knew he was in Russia but nothing else. Nothing interested him. He went to Sweden, but thought he was in Finland'.[10] Yeltsin also lacked higher education and had an inability to grapple with complex issues or gain control over the details of policy. In contrast Putin, a law graduate from Leningrad University, speaks fluent German, and has shown an impressive ability to master the detail of policy. As he demonstrated on numerous occasions with his sudden replacement of prime ministers, Yeltsin held little loyalty to his staff, whereas for Putin trust and loyalty appear to be important ingredients in his personal make-up.

Putin's background and contacts in the KGB could have given him an opportunity when the Soviet Union disintegrated to take advantage of state and party collapse to enrich himself during the initial 'transition' period, when state assets were being divided up among the apparatchiks. However, he chose to work in regional politics in St.Petersburg, alongside one of the then democratic reformers, Mayor Anatoly Sobchak, whom Putin referred to as a 'friend and mentor' (Putin, 2000, p.119). The choice Putin made was to engage directly in the new democratic process. During the attempted coup in August 1991, carried out by members of the KGB and other members of the military industrial complex, Putin sided openly and actively with the 'democrats', holed up in the city council buildings where he assisted Sobchak in countering the plotters. It was at this moment that Putin the patriot decided finally to officially resign his office in the KGB (Putin, 2000, p.93). Similarly, during the standoff between parliament and president in Moscow in 1993, Putin instigated measures to counter any potential plot against the democratically elected mayor in St.Petersburg.

Putin might have been selected by Yeltsin as his chosen successor, but the Russian people did not then vote for him to continue with Yeltsin's legacy. On the contrary, most people recognised the contrast in character, style, and personality between the two leaders, and opinion polls suggested that the Russian people also recognised what Putin stood for politically. Nearly 70 percent of Russians believed Yeltsin did more harm than good for Russia during his presidency.[11] Putin received most votes in fully 84 of Russia's 89 regions; receiving equally strong support in the cities and rural areas; among blue-collar workers and farmers; among the poor, the middle class, and the wealthy; among the young and the old.[12] The Russian people seemed to recognise that Putin was a person who was strong, principled, and dynamic. But what type of policies were people voting for?

What does Putin stand for?

Madeleine Albright and other members of the U.S. Administration were quick to make the point that Putin should be judged by his deeds, rather than what he says. Indeed; but we should not ignore completely what he says, for it is possible to gain some insight into Putin the man by analysing carefully his speeches and writings, whilst being sensitive to their context and the audience to which they are addressed. Although Putin did not have a printed election manifesto setting out in detail his policy priorities, the vast majority of Russian voters had a clear idea of what he stood for – principally for order and stability (the 'dictatorship of laws'). In fact he did publish some important indicators of what he stood for on the very day that Yeltsin resigned, entitled 'Russia at the Turn of the Millennium'.[13] In this document Putin sounds rather like a conservative republican in the U.S., stressing the sanctity of the individual; the importance of the capitalist market; the need to strengthen family values; and the dangers posed by drugs, alcohol, and crime. Although Putin (2000) states that Russia cannot simply apply foreign models or mechanically copy other nations' experiences, he does stress clearly that there is 'no alternative to democracy and the market' (p.212).

On the basis of his public statements, Putin's basic foreign policy orientation reflects what one might term a 'robust nationalism'. This involves highest loyalty and devotion to country, patriotism, an assertion of Russian culture and values in the international arena, and integration into global institutions to further Russian state interests (rather than fostering these institutions for their own sake, as advocated by 'liberals').[14] Patriotism for Putin is not to be equated or confused with 'nationalism' or 'imperialism': it is rather 'pride in one's country'. Putin (2000, p.214) stresses the importance of what one might term the psychological dimension of power: '[i]f we lose patriotism and the national pride and dignity that are connected with it, we will no longer be a nation capable of great achievements'. Putin is aware of the dangers of hyper-nationalism or all-encompassing ideologies. It is perhaps revealing that one of his most admired political leaders is Ludwig Erhard, who was the architect of the German 'miracle' of economic recovery following defeat in war in 1945. But for Putin the most important quality that Erhard displayed was that '...his entire conception for the reconstruction of the country began with the creation of new moral values for society', which was critical after the danger inflicted by Nazi ideology (Putin, 2000, p.194). This is further indication that Putin's personal experiences and knowledge of Germany have helped to shape his politics, and in particular his desire to develop a new sense of pride and hope in Russia whilst avoiding simple ideological solutions and nationalist extremism.

During his first few months in power Putin's Cold War was waged not against the West but closer to home, against those engaged in tax evasion, asset-stripping, and illegal capital flight. Putin's initial priorities clearly lay in the economic realm, both in domestic and foreign policy, whilst recognising that the two are clearly linked. It has not been so much that ordinary people have feared the secret police knocking on the door in the middle of the night, but rather the oligarchs fearing a visit from the tax police at their company headquarters. Putin's clear message has been that he wishes to strengthen the Russian state not in order to be able to rule as a dictator, or to return to Soviet methods, but for the overriding priority of economic development and stability in Russian society. Putin sees the key to Russia's recovery, the development of democracy and a strong economy with Russia integrated into the global economy as being determined by the re-establishment of state power. He stresses, however, that '[a] strong state power in Russia is a democratic, law-based, workable federal state' (Putin, 2000, p.215). It is worth pointing out that when he was head of the FSB under Yeltsin he spoke out in support of those calling for charges to be laid against Albert Makashov for making anti-Semitic comments in the Duma, calling for the removal of his parliamentary immunity from prosecution.[15] Putin was more outspoken in his criticism of Makashov than many other so-called 'democrats' at that time, and it reflects his fear that extremism could threaten the security of the state. Again, perhaps his knowledge and experience of German politics and history provide the background for understanding Putin's stance.

What does Putin see as the major threats to Russian security? The answer to this question can be gleaned quite clearly from his statements and policy prescriptions. Putin has explicitly stated, and consistently so, that the main threats to Russia come not from external sources, but from internal problems relating principally to continuing economic stagnation. These economic problems are responsible for increasing crime, and for undermining the infrastructure of education, health, and welfare provision. Putin sees this as being responsible ultimately for a demographic and spiritual crisis, with a shrinking population and increasing societal breakdown.

If the main threat is economic decay, then the rational response is to follow a policy that would result in economic growth. The logical consequence of this in the foreign policy realm would be to stimulate increasing direct foreign investment, foreign aid and trade. Indeed, judging by the substance of Putin's policy statements and his foreign travels and diplomacy, the Russian president is doing all in his power to stimulate a commitment from Western states and entrepreneurs to invest in Russia. In his 'millennium' article Putin (2000, p.217) wrote: '[f]rankly speaking, without foreign capital, our country's road back to recovery will be long and hard...[w]e must do our best to attract foreign capital to the country'. Soon after coming to power Putin promised, in the context of attracting foreign investors, to institute laws on tax, profit repatriation, bankruptcy, and business regulation. On a visit to the United Kingdom soon after he became acting president Putin told an audience of British businessmen and women that '[o]ur main goal is to make the Russian economy attractive for Russian and foreign investment'. Whilst in London Putin also made a promise that Russia would cut back on red tape and bureaucratic hurdles and impose strict regulations for the operating of business procedures, including '...a truly effective and independent judiciary'.[16] The same message was sent via Putin's foreign minister, Igor Ivanov, when he met the U.S.-Russia Business Council in Washington, D.C., in April 2000. Ivanov stated: '[n]ow about foreign policy. President Putin has set Russian diplomacy a precise task – to ensure favourable external conditions for continuing internal transformations in Russia'.[17]

Much has been made of the war unleashed in Chechnya whilst Putin was Prime Minister in 1999, with many seeing this as indicative of both Putin's hard-line stance, and also his unprincipled manipulation of violence to serve his own political ends. Yet there is no evidence that Putin orchestrated events leading up to the war in order to garner public support for his election bid. Indeed, evidence suggests that plans for the Russian military actions in Chechnya were underway well before Putin became Prime Minister. Nevertheless, it is true that Putin has articulated strong support for the military campaign, arguing that '[n]o government can stand idly by when terrorism strikes'.[18] It is also worth recalling that the first war unleashed in Chechnya, in 1994, led not to an increase in Yeltsin's popularity, but, on the contrary, to an undermining of his popular support. It was not at all obvious at the time that unleashing a second war in Chechnya would have any different result for the incumbent political leadership in Moscow. It has also been suggested that the timing and the nature of the war unleashed in Chechnya owe much to NATO's earlier war in Kosovo.[19] If NATO could use air warfare against the Serbs, then why should not the Russians use the same methods against 'terrorists' in Chechnya?

Recognising that we need ultimately to judge Putin by his actions, and not simply his statements, it is noteworthy nevertheless that his political discourse is one that reflects a commitment to keeping Russia on the road towards the market and democracy. In his address to the UN millennium summit of world leaders in September 2000, Putin stressed the virtues of the United Nations for ensuring international peace and security, stressing in particular the Declaration of Human Rights as the '...most important international regime of the modern world'.[20] It is perhaps not surprising that Russia should turn attention to the UN, as the Security Council is the one forum in which it retains its status as a great power. Yet, it is at least reassuring that a Russian leader accords such saliency in his political rhetoric to the discourse of human rights. Gorbachev it will be recalled also used the UN as a platform for articulating new Soviet initiatives in arms control, whilst stressing the importance of the UN as a vehicle for managing international security.[21] At the millennium summit Putin, somewhat reminiscent of Gorbachev's tendency to unveil arms control initiatives in the UN, proposed that Russia should host a new international conference in 2001 on preventing the militarisation of space. Also as with Gorbachev, and perhaps even more forcefully than Yeltsin did, Putin sees ·

Russia's place as a part of the West, and in particular part of a wider Europe. He has made the comment many times that due to Russia's history, geography, and culture, it is, in his estimation, a component part of Europe, and hence Russia's relations with Europe are a top priority.[22] When assessing at this early stage of his presidency what he stands for, one can perhaps identify a close resemblance to Gorbachev in the late 1980s. This is not to imply that he wishes to restore the USSR (on the contrary, he has made it clear that is not his desire or goal);[23] but rather to state that the evidence points to a man who wishes to see Russia as a great power, as a strong democratic state, and one which is integrated into the world economy as part of what Gorbachev used to refer to as the 'common European home'. Much of course will depend on the forces of domestic politics.

(2) Politics

When the Soviet Union suddenly collapsed the demarcation of power and authority between the partially reformed and partially democratic institutions of the new Russian Federation were uncertain. The USSR collapsed despite Gorbachev's attempts to hold it together, due to the dynamics of domestic politics beyond his control. The first years of the new Russian state were marked by acute tensions between the presidency and the parliament, and between the regions and the centre. This was made all the more acute by deep divisions within society about the very future of the Russian state. Yeltsin, despite his seemingly dictatorial tendencies, was nevertheless inclined to support democratisation and market reform, linked to a pro-western foreign policy. However, Yeltsin was inhibited in pursuing his favoured policies due to a recalcitrant legislature, constantly challenging the president's policies and authority. At one point Yeltsin was forced to postpone a visit to Japan due to opposition from the Supreme Soviet at the very last minute, much to the chagrin of the government in Tokyo (Miller, 1995). These domestic political constraints should not be seen as anything other than natural, especially in states undergoing a process of democratisation.

As Kenneth Waltz (1968) pointed out in a comparative study of foreign policy, increased levels of democracy raise the competencies of parliaments, and in the past this has caused anguish to eminent diplomats such as Bismarck and Lord Salisbury (p.11).[24] In Yeltsin's case the conflict between president and legislature came to a head with the storming of the parliament in 1993. Nevertheless, the new Duma that was elected under the new constitution in December that year turned out to be equally as uncooperative to Yeltsin as the one it replaced, keeping Yeltsin under constant pressure in the conduct of Russian foreign policy. It is generally considered that the parliament was instrumental in turning policy more intently toward the former republics of the Soviet Union, whilst simultaneously influencing a more pragmatic, less romantic, approach to the West (Shearman, 1997). Apart from opposition in the parliament, Yeltsin was also restricted in pursuing his own policies by the power of the so-called 'oligarchs'. Especially in the second term of his presidency Yeltsin appeared to be strongly under the influence of a small group of advisers and oligarchs who basically sought to maintain the status quo, for this was considered to be in their own financial interests. It was Yeltsin and this small group of oligarchs who were responsible for selecting Putin as the presidential successor.

Thus Richard Rose (2000) wrote that 'Putin owes nothing to parties or Duma members; the only obligation he has is to the people who promoted him from obscurity' (p.59). With a more cooperative parliament (following the success of Putin's new party of power, Unity, in the Duma elections in December 1999) those like Rose have argued that Putin would be effectively a puppet manipulated by those responsible for bringing him to power (i.e., Yeltsin's family and the oligarchs).[25] However, the new Duma has been more compliant since Putin came to power (finally ratifying the START-2 Treaty; signing off on the Comprehensive Nuclear Test Ban Treaty; and generally supporting foreign policy initiatives), and Putin's freedom has not been hampered by the oligarchs. Indeed, Putin was fairly quick to preside over a number of clear attempts by the authorities to 'reign in the oligarchs' by instituting procedures against some of them to ensure they pay their fair share of taxes. That Putin had unsettled the oligarchs is evidenced by the resignation of Boris Berezovsky from the Duma, his hostile and open comments about Putin's leadership, indications of an unusual coalition of forces among previously competing oligarchs in solidarity against Putin, and Putin's own stated intentions of ensuring that what he terms 'clans' will not become a 'class' that threatens the state.[26] Hence, the domestic political constraints on Putin's foreign policy are less than those faced earlier by Yeltsin.

Putin has also taken measures to reduce the powers of the regions, some of which in recent years have been governed by individuals who have sought to conduct their own foreign policies, separate from the Federal centre in Moscow. For a number of years officials in Moscow have referred to the possible breakdown of central authority leading to instability and even threatening the very survival of the state. For example Ivan Rybkin, then Secretary of the Security Council, stated in 1997 that the main threats to Russia came from the economic, social, ecological, informational, and constitutional realms (Rybkin, 1997, p.132). But it has only been since Putin came to power that practical steps have been undertaken to deal with these security threats. Putin has issued an informational security doctrine; established presidential representatives to manage seven new regions (roughly corresponding with the existing Russian military districts); reduced the power of elected regional leaders; and signed new military, defence, and foreign policy doctrines and concepts that have as their central focus economic and social problems.[27] Perhaps the most important factor in these new documents is not the stated linkage between Russia's economic situation and its foreign policy goals (for this was always recognised in the Yeltsin era), but the linkage between these domestic developmental tasks and the acknowledgement of the limited resources Russia can employ to fulfil them. Shortly after Putin approved the new Foreign Policy Concept, Foreign Minister Igor Ivanov stated explicitly that Russian foreign policy will hitherto be based upon solid realism, '...taking into account the country's real possibilities and resources'.[28] There is now a domestic consensus in Russia that foreign policy should be solidly based upon a pragmatic assessment of interests and resources, rather than seeking to maintain the pretence of a great military power.

In order to ensure control over decision-making in the foreign policy realm Putin has appointed close associates whom he can trust, many of them from the security services, to leading positions in relevant institutions. It is worth pointing out that the Russian people too have more trust in the military and the FSB than they do in any other institutions, including the Orthodox Church.[29] The most important of these was the appointment of Sergei Ivanov as Secretary of the Security Council. This institution has been seen by some observers as the main vehicle under Putin for devising and coordinating foreign and security policies. When asked whom he trusted from among his political appointees Putin unhesitatingly came up with one name, that of Sergei Ivanov (Putin, 2000, p.200).[30] Yet Putin has clearly been offered conflicting policy advice from senior members of government and the armed forces. Indeed during the first few months of his presidency he was confronted with the unprecedented public argument between the Russian defence minister, Igor Sergeyev and the chief of the general staff, Anatoly Kvashnin. Sergeyev supported increased funds for the strategic nuclear forces, whereas Kvashnin wanted a larger slice of the defence budget to go to improving the quality of conventional forces. Sergeyev's argument was that Russia's nuclear forces were both a deterrent against attack and a symbol of super power status. Kvashnin argued that nuclear weapons do not make for an effective force for maintaining security in contemporary conflicts or for containing threats. Recent proposals for reforming the military implies that Putin's priority is to develop a more sophisticated, technologically advanced conventional force, whilst maintaining the minimum nuclear forces deemed necessary for stable deterrence. Overall, Putin appeared to have built up his authority in the foreign policy arena, with an overall domestic consensus on aims, with little in the way of powerful political forces at the domestic level acting as a restraint. We should turn now to assess the more systemic factors pertaining to material power resources, and their impact on Putin's foreign policy.

(3) Power

The global structure of power and relative power capabilities provide both opportunities and constraints for member states of the international system. Russian foreign policy under Putin will continue to be determined, as it was in the Yeltsin period, in large part by the relative capabilities Russia enjoys compared to other states in the system. Although many processes of international economics take place on a global level, often taking little account of state territorial boundaries, politics, as noted above, generally still takes place at the domestic level. I have tried in the previous section to show how these domestic processes and issues impact on foreign policy. Here I will assess the extent to which the structure of power at the international level determines Russian foreign policy.

Defining power

There are many ways of defining relative power capabilities, but most definitions would include some or all of the following: economic capacity; size, health, education levels, and technical skills of the population; military capabilities, including the ability to project power globally; natural resources and mineral wealth. It is also important not only to have the empirical referents of power: to be effective a state needs also to be able to marshal that power, and to convincingly demonstrate to potential adversaries a willingness and ability to employ it. I do not wish here to get involved in a detailed discussion of the various uses of power, nor distinctions between using power, authority, and influence. Suffice it to say that relative power capabilities, based on those listed above, clearly affect the extent to which states are able to operate in the international arena. If we think back, for example, to the second half of the twentieth century it is evident that any explanation of the conflict between East and West must consider relative power capabilities. Indeed, the Cold War conflict that ensued was waged between what were commonly referred to as two 'superpowers' the term itself indicative of the importance of power in understanding the conflict. Also, the common reference to the conflict as being bipolar is indicative of the role of structural systemic power configurations as determining the Cold War confrontation. The Soviet Union and the United States were super in the sense that they could wipe each other out with nuclear weapons, both had massive conventional military forces, enjoyed high levels of economic growth after 1945, and were large countries, with sizeable populations. Furthermore, both the United States and Soviet Russia had high levels of education and health, and were largely self-sufficient in natural and other critical resources. Perhaps irrespective of their opposing social and economic systems the two sides were destined to be in conflict due to the structure of the international system. Alliance systems that did develop, with often strange alliance partners (in ideological terms) are here understood on the basis of relativities in power (i.e. the 'balance of power'). With the demise of bipolarity with the end of the Cold War and the collapse of the Soviet Union, one would expect that different opportunities and constraints on Russian foreign and security policy would manifest themselves.

Assessing Russia's power and its place in the international system

As already indicated throughout this chapter Russian power has declined precipitately. On any indicator of power listed above, including even the actual size of the country and its population, Russia has suffered a radical and sudden decline in power. The world has not only ceased to be bipolar, Russia really no longer figures as a major global power. Russia's economy, as detailed in earlier chapters in this volume, has suffered constant crises during the past ten years. Without a strong economy it is not possible to develop a competitive edge with other states in the global trading network; it is also not possible to maintain a strong and effective military force with international power projection capabilities. With a weak economy in perpetual crisis it is not possible to ensure security from poverty for large sections of the population, or even to maintain the infrastructure of a modern economy. Russia has in many ways been suffering a demodernisation process as the economy has been unable to stimulate growth, and hence provide the resources necessary for the provision of state collective goods such as education, health, and welfare. The UN World Health Organisation issued a report in June 2000 in which countries were ranked according to their level of health care - and Russia was ranked a lowly 130th out of 191 countries. Russia came just above Honduras, but far behind eleven of the other fourteen former republics of the Soviet Union, with Kazakhstan ranked 64th, way ahead of Russia (WHO, 2000). Also in 2000 the UN's *Human Development Report*, an annual assessment of progress of member states, employing a number of economic and social indicators, found that Russia ranked in the bottom half of all countries listed (UN, 2000). In terms of national disparities between rich and poor the gulf in Russia was found to be widening dramatically.

The bombing in Pushkin Square, the sinking of the *Kursk* submarine, and the fire in the Ostankino Television Tower all within a few weeks in August 2000, together symbolised how Russian power has declined in three key areas. These are the ability to maintain security and law and order; the deterioration of the once might military machine; and declining infrastructure. As Pavel Felgenhauer put it after the sinking of the *Kursk*: '[w]e may claim to be great power, but the truth is we can barely afford to change the light bulbs in these ships, much less keep them running properly'.[31] Russia's armed forces have declined from 4 million in 1992 to 1.2 million in 1999, and those forces that remain are poorly trained, ill-

236 Russia After Yeltsin

equipped, and lacking in morale.[32] Only 13 percent of the draft intake to the Russian military in 2000 had turned up for service, and of those that do show up 1,000 each year commit suicide.[33] In September 2000 the Security Council announced plans to cut the armed forces further, to 850,000 personnel. Former Secretary of the Security Council, Andrei Kokoshin, stated in an interview that it had been recognised since 1995 that clinging to a massive army was a strategy that would actually serve to weaken it.[34] It is only under Putin that effective measures are finally being implemented to improve the technical competencies and skills of the military, reflecting a new sense of realism in relation to power capabilities.

In terms of both 'hard', material factors of power, and 'soft' factors of power relating to national morale and societal well-being, Russia has suffered a massive decline in the relative balance of power. In 1999 Russia's budget revenues for the entire year ($25 billion) were less than the private wealth of Bill Gates ($30 billion). Capital flight exceeded foreign direct investment; and IMF loans were used to pay off debts accumulated in the previous year.[35] In his 'millennium' essay Putin states that 'Russia was and is a great power'. But he goes on to say that '[in] today's world, a country's power is manifested more in its ability to develop and use advanced technologies, ensuring a high level of general well-being, protecting its security, and upholding its national interests in the international arena, than in its military strength'. Putin is frank in portraying the reality of Russia's condition, acknowledging that simply to catch up with the levels of Portugal and Spain, calculated at an eight percent annual growth in GDP, would take Russia approximately 15 years (Putin, 2000, p.213). Given the relative power capabilities of contemporary states it is only logical that Russia has been pursuing a multipolar diplomacy.

Multipolarism

The term 'multipolarism' has been used by Russia's foreign policy community for the past few years. Indeed, one can trace its usage back to the immediate post-Soviet period when Andrei Kozyrev was foreign minister.[36] However, multipolarism is a term most often associated with the more recent foreign and security policy discourse in Russia, particularly since the tenure of Primakov as foreign and then prime minister. In the West the term has come to symbolise a more hardline stance in Russian foreign policy, indicative of a move away from a western-oriented approach. This is perhaps only partially true. Although the term itself, utilising the vocabulary of realist theory, would imply a policy based upon the 'balance of power', this should not be equated with a militaristic or aggressive approach to foreign policy. On the contrary, it reflects more recognition of Russia's weak position in the overall global distribution of power.

In a round-table discussion on multipolarity in the Russian journal *International Affairs* it was pointed out recently that international politics today is no longer carried out for control over territories, but rather for influence over multilateral financial, informational, and intellectual flows. In this forum N.Nikonov suggested that '[e]xpansion is becoming less and less military and more and more economic and cultural', noting that smaller countries with well-developed science and technology play a greater role in international relations than bigger states like Russia. Nikonov offers the notion that 'real-politik' is being superseded not by 'ideal-politik', but by 'real-economics'.[37] Although this reflects thinking among foreign policy elites in Moscow that can be traced back a number of years, it is really only under Putin that such ideas are becoming central to actual policy in a systematic way, reflected in recent concepts and doctrines and in practical diplomacy. Although the new Military Doctrine of the Russian Federation, and the National Security Concept, only came into operation in 2000, this should not be read to imply that they do not reflect Putin's thinking. These documents were drawn up before he came to power, but it should be noted that Putin was Secretary of the Security Council in March 1999, and it was principally the Security Council which had responsibility for coordinating work on these documents. The documents are striking for attaching highest priority to economics in the formulation of foreign and security policy goals.

In its relations with the Asia Pacific Region, and with China in particular, Russia has for a number of years articulated opposition to a 'unipolar world' (for which read U.S. hegemony). Putin has continued with this approach, evidenced during his trip to China in July 2000 when he signed a bilateral statement in opposition to U.S. plans for a National Missile Defence (NMD).[38] Putin also at this time became the first Russian leader to pay an official visit to North Korea, where he gained a commitment from the government in Pyongyang, in return for assistance in developing satellites for communications and space exploration, that it would refrain from developing an independent nuclear capability. Again, this should be seen in terms of the global balance of power, and an effective demonstration of multipolar diplomacy, in an attempt to give Russia some influence and leverage in issue areas that it considers important for its own national interests. It is worth noting that former foreign minister Kozyrev stated in an interview with the BBC at the time that Putin's visit to North Korea was a very good diplomatic move.[39] Putin's multipolar diplomacy is designed in this instance to help prevent the U.S. going ahead with the development of the NMD, something which is clearly viewed in Moscow as undermining the central components of mutual nuclear deterrence, in particular the ABM Treaty of 1972, and hence ultimately Russian security. If the United States undertakes an anti-missile programme, then Russia would either be forced to respond with its own programme, which it can ill afford, or else make other costly countermeasures. Either way it is in Russia's own perceived interests to counter NMD.

Putin came to power at a time when Russia's relations with NATO were tense, following the war in Kosovo. Russia had been forced to sit on the sidelines as the UN Security Council, the one arena in which Russia still has an equal vote with the United States and other major powers, was deliberately bypassed. NATO initiated a war against Serbia, one of Russia's fellow Slavic nations, without the sanction of the UN, marking a radical new departure in the conduct of international relations. This first military action undertaken by NATO took place soon after the alliance had expanded to include three former Warsaw Pact states (Poland, Hungary, and the Czech Republic). Russia had been opposed to the process of expanding NATO; but given the realities of power could do nothing to prevent it happening. Russia had reluctantly accepted an institutional relationship with the alliance that gave it only a 'voice', but not a 'veto', over its decisions.

Despite this backdrop, Putin moved fairly quickly to normalise relations with NATO, hosting a meeting with George Robertson, NATO Secretary General in Moscow, and involving Russia again fully in the Russia-NATO Permanent Joint Council. In justifying this more positive attitude towards NATO Putin stated that 'Russia should be and will be an integral part of the civilised world and in this context we will cooperate with NATO'.[40]

In a BBC television interview and again in his interview in *First Person* Putin has even stated that he sees no reason eventually why Russia itself should not belong to the alliance as a full member. However, this is more an indication of Putin's desire for Russia to be viewed as part of Europe than any immediate intentions or hopes of being invited to join the alliance. Putin, as noted, recognises only too well Russia's weakened position in international affairs.

Graham Allison has referred to Russian foreign policy under Putin as 'extreme realism', noting that since he came to power Russia is acting more in line with its relative power capabilities, rather than trying to maintain a global role. Allison provides some figures that demonstrate clearly the impossibility for Russia to try and compete with the United States - for example, whereas Russia's defence budget projections were less than $5 billion, the US annual defence budget is close to $300 billion! Allison also notes that Russia's GNP provides a per capita purchasing power equivalent to that of Guatemala, and to half that of Mexico.[41] Putin, in his 'Millennium' article noted himself that Russia's GDP halved in the 1990s and was now five times smaller than China's, and that following the crisis of 1998 Russia's GDP dropped to roughly five times smaller than the average for the G7 states. Putin went on here to highlight the poor state of Russia's manufacturing industry, its poor productivity, its low levels of Research and Development, and the lack of capital investments.

In the overall balance of power the most important arena for Russia is the former republics of the Soviet Union, perhaps especially in terms of potential threats those in the South and in Central Asia. Policy and strategic documents relating to defence, security, and foreign policy since Putin came to power all highlight the threats Russia faces from national and religious extremism, economic decay, illegal immigration, and the trafficking of drugs. The one area where all of these threats come together is in Central Asia; and it is here that Russian foreign policy has been very active. In the first few weeks as president Putin undertook intense shuttle diplomacy in the region, signing a number of bilateral relations with the Central Asian states. At a meeting of the Shanghai Forum in Dushanbe, Putin promised to increase Russian military forces in Tajikistan, and assist in deterring the spread of Islamic fundamentalism throughout the region.[42] The members of the forum have produced confidence building measures and declarations to combat terrorism, extremism, illegal immigration, and the spread of weapons of mass destruction. In these areas China and Russia face similar threats, and during his July visit to Beijing Putin reiterated

Russia's support for a bilateral strategic partnership between the two countries.

Conclusion

It is clear that in his honeymoon period Putin has sought to stamp his authority on Russian foreign policy. It is also clear that his personality - who he actually is - has had an impact, if not in the substance of policy, then certainly on its style and in regard to the perceptions that Russians have of their leader. This in itself could have an important psychological impact on the collective identity of Russia, helping to restore a more positive attitude conducive to social cohesion. It is, at the time of writing, far too early to state confidently what ultimate direction he will take in domestic political developments. Early indications have been contradictory: for example whilst taking measures to undermine the influence of the oligarchs, Putin has demonstrated an impatience with the media, with signs of increasing state control. Whilst restricting the ability of regional leaders to undermine the federal authorities, central controls have increased which could be used by Putin to further develop his own powers. Through his public statements, important policy and strategic documents, and his own intensive international diplomacy, there can be little doubt of Putin's own foreign policy priorities: to assist the economic development of the Russian Federation. This key strategic goal involves a continuing focus on the major – western – powers as the most promising source of direct foreign investment. With a cooperative parliament and few domestic political groups in opposition to his basic goals, Putin has much more freedom than had his predecessor in formulating and implementing foreign policy.

What has not changed since Putin took office is the structure of power in the international system. This structure provides similar constraints on the conduct of foreign policy to those faced by the Yeltsin administration. Putin's multipolar diplomacy is far more assertive, dynamic, and active than that of the previous administration, but in essentials it remains very much the same, due to the distribution of power capabilities in the international system. Whilst pushing a multipolar diplomacy (which has taken him to Europe, Asia, North America, and the Subcontinent), during which anti-unipolarism and opposition to U.S. plans for NMD have been paramount, Putin has been careful not to antagonise the administration in

Washington. Indeed, the Russian president has been careful to foster more cooperative relations with the United States, including through Russian participation in the NATO-Russia Permanent Joint Council. Although during his visit to Beijing the Russian and Chinese leaders expressed a desire to continue developing a 'strategic partnership', this does not indicate moves towards an anti-U.S. military alliance. Russia and China do both face threats, but they are not in reality direct threats of likely military aggression from the U.S. As noted above, real threats to Russia and China are closer to home, within their borders or on their borders.

There are different kinds of threats that face states in the international system, what one might term objective, subjective, and creative threats. Objective threats are real threats that can be readily defined and calculated. Subjective threats are those that are perceived, and not as materially existing in themselves; whereas creative threats are those that are created - deliberately constructed - for individual political gain. Even with the expansion of NATO and the war in Kosovo, few in Russia would argue that the US and the West countenance a direct and immediate military threat. Subjective threats can of course be used as a basis of policy, and hence perceptions of threat to all intents and purposes are real threats. One could argue that there are many in the Russian Federation who perceive the US as a real potential military threat; but these are not dominant in the current political leadership, hence have little influence on policy. There are of course groups in Russia who seek to create a U.S. threat in order to further their own political ambitions.

The important point to note is that in so far as there is a consensus in Russia on the U.S. as a threat, it is as an economic threat in that the U.S. has decisive influence in global financial institutions and in the international trading system. Given Russia's goals of market development and integration into the world capitalist system, the U.S. is courted as a partner rather than played off as an enemy. However, the development of NMD is an area that is perceived as threatening to Russia, hence if this were to go ahead under Clinton's successor as U.S. president then this could lead to increasing antagonism between the two states. Also, if NATO were to expand further to incorporate the former Baltic Republics of the Soviet Union this would also increase perceptions of an American threat to Russia itself; it would also fuel ammunition for those who want to foment this threat in order to undermine Putin's position. Such external policies could also ultimately create the domestic political situation that forces Putin himself to undertake an anti-Western aggressive foreign policy turn.

In conclusion then it can be argued that external factors relating to material factors of power have been the most important determinants of Russian foreign policy since the break up of the Soviet Union, and are likely to continue to be so under Putin's leadership. However, in his first six months in power Putin has made a difference in style and tactics in the conduct of Russian foreign policy. But the basic strategic objectives remain the same as they were under Yeltsin.

Notes

1   The exception to this rule was the overthrow of Khrushchev in 1964. Gorbachev's leadership position was made redundant in December 1991 with the dissolution of the Soviet Union.
2   Interestingly Brezhnev utilised a shift in foreign policy in building up his authority as leader by employing a policy of détente (Brown, 1982). Also see Archie Brown's and Richard Sakwa's assessments of Gorbachev's role in transforming international relations leading to an end to the Cold War (Brown, 1996; Sakwa, 1990).
3   Gorbachev stated that 'The atmosphere of complacency and the ...process of leadership change gave rise to stagnation and retardation in the country' (Gorbachev, 1987, p.44).
4   This relates to the so-called 'level of analysis' problem in political science, a discussion about which can be found in almost any introductory text on international relations. For an overview see Buzan (1995).
5   For a positive appraisal of the Yeltsin era and its legacy see Leon Aron (1999).
6   The simple fact that a small number of ex KGB officials were promoted to senior Kremlin positions under Putin is indicative for Cohen of a return to a non-democratic path of development, whereas this in itself really says nothing more than perhaps Putin is promoting people he knows and trusts. Cohen decries the replacement of 'the reformers who came to power with Yeltsin'! One wonders precisely who Cohen has in mind, given the prominence of the unelected oligarchs in Yeltsin's inner circle (Cohen, 2000).
7   Putin served in the KGB in Dresden from 1985 to the fall of the Berlin Wall in 1990. He began his service in the KGB in 1975, and finally resigned in 1991, before the collapse of the Soviet Union.
8   This is a point made in *Obshchaya gazeta*, 1 June, 2000, where it is pointed out that unlike Yeltsin, Putin has been careful to sound out opinion among various branches of the military and security community on defence issues when making security policy. Thus, when he held the summit in Moscow with US President Bill Clinton, Putin was very well briefed on issues relating to arms control and US plans for a National Missile Defence. Putin has impressed western leaders with his knowledge of the various issues that have formed the subject of negotiations. Putin is also not afraid to utilise the skills

of people who had previously opposed his election bid. For example on his official visit to Spain Yevgeny Primakov, former foreign minister, prime minister, and one-time possible contender for the presidency was part of his delegation. And during his visit to Italy Moscow Mayor Yuri Luzhkov was included in the delegation.

9   Putin's initial response to the tragic sinking of the *Kursk* nuclear submarine, deciding not to interrupt his vacation on the Black Sea, was viewed in the West as indicative of a Soviet-type personality. Zbigniew Brzezinski argued that it showed Putin for what he really is: '...an old Soviet-type apparatchik and not a democrat', noting that there was not a single member of his government that was previously a 'democratic dissident' (*Wall Street Journal*, 29 August, 2000). Yet perhaps the significant point to make is how quickly Putin learned from his initial mistake. Following media criticism he joined the relatives of the deceased, making public expressions of sadness, and even guilt. And it is difficult to understand why the absence of 'dissidents' in his government would necessarily imply, as Brzezinski puts it here, that Putin is '...the last gasp of the Soviet past'! After all Chubais, Gaidar, and Kozyrev, to take just a handful of examples, were hardly 'democratic dissidents' in the Soviet era. One conservative dissident of that era, the writer Alexander Solzhenitsyn, was invited to the Kremlin to meet with Putin in September 2000. In a later interview Solzhenitsyn said that he had been very impressed with Putin as a man with a quick mind who nevertheless showed '...extreme caution and prudence' when making decisions, showing '...absolutely no thirst for personal power' (*Trud*, 23 September, 2000, from *Johnson Russia List (JRL)*, no.4537, 25 September, 2000).

10 Lilia Shevtsova, in an interview on the U.S. Frontline Television documentary, 'Return of the Tsar: Yeltsin's Legacy', shown on PBS Television 22 June, 2000.

11 From a VTsIOM nationwide survey, 8-10 January, 2000.

12 However, here it should be noted that according to an investigation by *The Moscow Times* Putin only managed to gain election through ballot rigging and falsification of election results (*The Moscow Times*, 9 September, 2000). The report can also be found at www.themoscowtimes.com/stories/2000/09/ 09/119.html. But it should be noted that opinion polls all had Putin out in front leading up to the election. Even in August 2000 when many media commentators were suggesting that Putin's approval rating had sunk along with the *Kursk* nuclear submarine opinion surveys saw only a drop of 6%, leaving him with still a very high approval rating above 70%. See *Argumenty i fakty*, no.35, 4 September, 2000, p.2. For details of opinion surveys and the election results themselves see www.russiavotes.org. The *Moscow Times* itself (10 August, 2000) cited Putin's approval rating at 73%.

13 This was first published on the Russian government's website www.gov.ru/ ministry/isp-vlast47.html. It is also available in English at www.pravitelstvo.gov.ru/ english/statVP_engl.1.tml, and can be found at the Public Affairs website at www.publicaffairsbooks.com. It is also published as an appendix in Putin, 2000, pp.209-19. References to the Millennium piece below will be from Putin (2000).

14 The term 'robust nationalism' comes from the article by Samuel P. Huntington (2000) in which he prescribes such a foreign policy orientation for the United States. Given his conservative approach to politics it is not surprising that Putin would find support from the likes of Solzhenitsyn (see note 9 above).

15 As reported by *Reuters*, 13 November, 1998.

16 *Weekly Telegraph*, no.456, April 2000.

17 *Interfax*, 11 April, 2000.

18 Putin made this point in a piece he wrote in the *New York Times*, 14 November, 1999. In this article Putin compared the situation in Chechnya to one in which armed terrorists in Montana and Idaho, assisted by foreigners with their own agenda, launched violent raids against a neighbouring US state whilst blowing up apartment blocks in New York and Washington.

19 *Daily Telegraph*, 6 June, 2000.

20 *JRL*, no.4496, 6 September, 2000.

21 Gorbachev was in attendance at Putin's official inauguration as Russian president, and later had an audience with him in the Kremlin. Following this meeting, which lasted for two hours, Gorbachev made some very positive comments about the new Russian leader, referring to him as '...in essence, a social democrat'. Gorbachev also said '...Putin is being guided by Russia's national interests, not by the interests of a clan' (*Kommersant*, 11 August, 2000, and *Interfax*, 10 August, 2000).

22 For example, Putin made this claim in discussions with the President of the European Union in Moscow (*The Financial Times*, 30 May, 2000). He makes a similar point in *First Person*, at one point regretting the 'major mistakes' of Soviet military interventions into Eastern Europe in 1953, 1956, and 1968. When discussing Russia's recent difficult relations with NATO Putin noted that 'Russia is a country of European culture--not NATO culture' (Putin, 2000, p.178).

23 As with Yeltsin before him, Putin has stated that any Russian who has a heart will regret the dissolution of the USSR; but that anyone who wants to put it back together again doesn't have a head! (*Reuters*, 31 May, 2000).

24 Kenneth Waltz here cites de Tocqueville's opinion that a popularly elected parliament would undermine an active and effective foreign policy (Waltz, 1968, p.11). It is interesting to note that Waltz is of course more noted for his structural theory of the international system, rather than any focus on the domestic determinants of foreign policy (Waltz, 1979).

25 Jerry Hough has argued that Yeltsin resigned from office when he did as a long term plan to regain institutional power using a similar path to Milosevic in Yugoslavia – by putting his name forward as president of a new union between Russia and Belarus. Yeltsin was prevented by the constitution for running for a third term as president of Russia. In the interim Putin is merely a puppet, serving the interests of Yeltsin and his closest aides. Asked what Putin would do when gaining office, Hough stated it wasn't clear because 'Putin probably doesn't know because Yeltsin probably hasn't told him yet'. For Hough's 'Yeltsin still rules' thesis see his postings on the *JRL* list over the past few months (e.g., *JRL*, no.4225, 4 April, 2000).

26 Putin made a promise before his election that he would not tolerate such a class, and to defend the market from illegitimate interference from the clans. See Putin's 'open letter' to the voters at www.putin.2000.ru. *Newsweek* (2 October, 2000) notes that Vladimir Gusinsky and Berezovsky, two of the most influential of the oligarchs in the 1990s, previously in direct conflict with each other, were now united in their strong opposition to Putin.

27 See for example the Military Doctrine of the Russian Federation. The text was published in *Nezavisimaya gazeta*, 22 April, 2000.

28 *Itar-TASS*, 1 July, 2000.

29   In a poll taken in March 2000 it was found that fully 77% of respondents, when asked
     which state, public and other institution they trusted the most, nominated the army and
     the FSB (*Itar-TASS*, 18 March, 2000). Given the massive resurgence in religious belief
     that occurred in the initial transition period it is surprising that the church did not
     receive a higher rating for trust. On the radical increase in religious belief during this
     period see Filatov and Furman (1992).
30   Ivanov is also a veteran of the KGB. Some observers in the summer of 2000 were
     predicting that Ivanov would eventually replace Kasyanov, thought to be too close to
     the oligarchs, as Prime Minister.
31   Cited in the *Christian Science Monitor*, 15 August, 2000.
32   *Sevodnya*, 19 May, 1999.
33   *JRL*, no.4315, 21 May, 2000.
34   *Vremya novostei*, 25 September, 2000, in the *JRL*, no.4537, 25 September, 2000.
35   Russia's economy has declined by almost a half since the collapse of the Soviet Union
     in 1991. See UNICP (1999) and CIA (1999).
36   The term was actually used in Soviet discourse before the collapse of the USSR. See,
     for example, Lukin (1983) and Lukin and Nagorny (1988). As Kozyrev has noted the
     'stage of wooing the West' (i.e. the stage of Russian foreign policy associated with his
     name) was 'based upon a nationwide consensus' (Kozyrev, 1996, p.24).
37   'A Multipolar World Already Exists', round-table in *International Affairs* (Moscow),
     vol.42, no.3, 1996, pp.25-42.
38   Putin and Chairman Jiang Zemin stated in this document that the ABM Treaty is the
     'cornerstone of global strategic stability and international security'. The full text is in
     Krasnaya zvezda, 19 July, 2000. It should be noted also that many of America's allies
     are also opposed to or deeply concerned about the potential negative consequences for
     global security of a US missile defence system.
39   U.S. plans for NMD are designed to counter what are termed 'rogue states', such as
     North Korea. It should be noted here that the term 'rogue state' has absolutely no
     scientific or objective definition, but is simply an ideological term devised by the
     United States to describe certain states that Washington opposes. That it has gained
     common currency is a further reflection of the power of the United States in global
     politics after the Cold War.
40   Cited in Antonenko, 2000, p.137.
41   *Boston Globe*, August 23, 2000.
42   Initially referred to as the Shanghai 5 (made up of China, Russia, Kazakhstan,
     Kyrgyzstan, and Tajikistan following a meeting in Shanghai in April 1996) the
     organisation was renamed the Shanghai Forum at the Dushanbe meeting following the
     inclusion of Uzbekistan.

References

Antonenko, O. (2000), 'Russia, NATO and European Security After Kosovo', *Survival*,
     vol.41, no.4, Winter, pp.124-44.
Aron, L. (1999), *Yeltsin: A Revolutionary Life*, St. Martin's Press, New York.
Breslauer, G.W. (1982), *Khrushchev and Brezhnev as Leaders: Building Authority in Soviet
     Politics*, Allen & Unwin, London.

Brown, A. (1982), 'Leadership Succession and Policy Innovation', in A.Brown and M.Kaser (eds), *Soviet Policy for the 1980s*, Macmillan, London, pp.223-53.

Brown, A. (1996), *The Gorbachev Factor*, Oxford University Press, Oxford.

Bunce, V. (1981), *Do New Leaders Make a Difference? Executive Succession and Public Policy Under Capitalism and Socialism*, Princeton University Press, Princeton, New Jersey.

Buzan, B. (1995), 'The Level of Analysis Problem in International Relations Reconsidered', in K.Booth and S.Smith (eds), *International Relations Theory Today*, Polity, Cambridge, pp.198-216.

CIA (1999), *World Fact Book 1999*, U.S. Central Intelligence Agency, www.odci.gov/publications/factbook.html.

Cohen, A. (2000), 'The Rise of Putin: What it Means for the Future of Russia', *Backgrounder*, March 28, 2000, The Heritage Foundation, http://www.heritage.org/library/backgrounder/ bg1353.html.

Filatov, S.B. and Furman, B.E. (1992), 'Religiya: politika v massovom soznanii', *Sotsiologicheskie issledovaniya*, no. 7, pp.3-12.

Gorbachev, M. (1987), *Perestroika: New Thinking for Our Country and the World*, Collins, London.

Huntington, S.P. (2000), 'Robust Nationalism', *The National Interest*, No. 58, Winter, pp.31-40.

Jervis, R. (1976), *Perception and Misperception in International Politics*, Princeton University Press, Princeton.

Knight, A. (2000), 'The Two Worlds of Vladimir Putin: 1 the KGB', *The Washington Quarterly*, Spring, pp.32-7.

Kozyrev, A.V. (1996), 'Consensus on Russia's Foreign Policy?', *International Affairs* (Moscow), vol.42, no.1, January-February, pp.21-4.

Lukin, V. (1983), *Tsentry sily: kontseptsii i realnosti*, Moscow.

Lukin, V.P. and Nagorny, A.A. (1988), 'Kontseptiya treugolnika SSSR-SShA-KNR: novye real'nosti mirovoi politiki', *SShA: ekonomika, politika, ideologiiia*, no. 6.

Miller, R.F. (1995), 'Russian Policy Toward Japan', in P.Shearman (ed.), *Russian Foreign Policy Since 1990*, Westview, Boulder, pp.135-58.

Putin, V. (2000), *First Person*, Hutchinson, London.

Rose, R. (2000), 'A Supply-Side View of 'Russia's Elections', *East European Constitutional Review*, vol.9, nos, 1/2, Winter/Spring, pp.53-9.

Rybkin, I. (1997), 'Domestic Challenges to Russia's Security', *International Affairs* (Moscow), no. 4, pp.132-43.

Sakwa, R. (1990), *Gorbachev and his Reforms, 1985-1990*, Philip Allen, Hemel Hempstead.

Shearman, P. (1997), 'Defining the National Interest: Russian Foreign Policy and Domestic Politics', in R.Kanet and A.V.Kozhemiakin (eds), *The Foreign Policy of the Russian Federation*, Basingstoke, Houndmills, pp.1-27.

UN (2000), *United Nations Human Development Report 2000*, United Nations, New York.

UNICP (1999), *United Nations International Comparison Program (UNICP)*, United Nations, New York.

Waltz, K.N. (1968), *Foreign Policy and Democratic Politics: The American and British Experience*, Longman, London.

Waltz, K.N. (1979), *Theory of International Politics*, Random House, New York.
WHO (2000), *United Nations World Health Organisation Report*, United Nations, Geneva, July.

Bibliography

Aleksin, V. (1999), 'Vozrozhdenie morskogo raketostroeniya', *Nezavisimoe voennoe obozrenie*, no.50, p.3.

Aleksin, V. (2000), 'Voennye moryaki idut v Sredizemnoe more', *Nezavisimoe voennoe obozrenie*, no.14, p.1.

Antonenko, O. (2000), 'Russia, NATO and European Security After Kosovo', *Survival*, vol.41, no.4, Winter, pp.124-44.

Arkhangel'skaya, N. (2000), 'Vertikal'naia Rossiya', *Ekspert*, no.19, 22 May, 2000, pp.53-6.

Aron, L. (1999), *Yeltsin: A Revolutionary Life*, St. Martin's Press, New York.

Auer, S. (2000), 'Nationalism in Central Europe - A Chance or a Threat for the Emerging Liberal Democratic Order?', *East European Politics and Societies*, vol.14, no.2, pp.1-33.

Aukutsionek, S., Kapelushnikov, R., Filatotchev, I. and Zhukov, V. (1998), 'Dominant Shareholders, Restructuring and Performance of Privatized Companies in Russia: An Analysis and Some Policy Implications', *Communist Economies and Economic Transformation*, vol.10, no.4, pp.495-517.

Babasyan, N. (2000), 'Semiya otpravila Yeltsina v otsatvku', *Deadline.ru* (http://archive.deadline.ru/babas/bab991231.asp).

Baichurin, I. (1999), 'Itogi goda', *Nezavisimoe voennoe obozrenie*, no.45, p.1.

Belotserkovsky, V. (2000), 'Na kogo pokhozh Stalin?', *Nezavisimaya gazeta*, 29 January.

Berezovsky, V. (1994), 'Dva politicheskikh lagerya federal'noi elity Rossii', *Svobodnaia mysl'*, no.9, June, pp.82-3.

Black, B., Kraakman, R. and Tarassova, A. (1999), *Russian Privatization and Corporate Governance: what went wrong?* John M. Olin Program in Law and Economics, Working paper No.178, Stanford Law School, Stanford.

Blasi, J.R., Kroumova, M. and Kruse, D. (1997), *Kremlin Capitalism. Privatizing the Russian Economy*, Cornell University Press, Ithaca and London.

Blommestein, E.T. (1998), 'The Development of Securities Markets in Transition Economics - Policy Issues and Country Experiences', in *Capital Market Developments in Transition Economies. Country experience and policies for the future*, OECD, Paris.

Bovt, G. (2000), 'Va-bank', *Izvestia*, 20 September.

Bovt, G. and Kolesnikov, A. (2000), 'Tainaya demokratiya', *Izvestia*, 9 February.

Bowser, D. (1999), 'Corruption in Post Soviet States: A Question of Cultural Identity?', unpublished paper given at the Fourth Annual ASN Conference, New York.

Boycko, M., Andrei S. and Vishny, R. (1995), *Privatizing Russia*. The MIT Press, Cambridge MA.

Breslauer, G., Brada, J., Gaddy, C., Ericson, R., Saivetz, C. and Winston, V. (2000), 'Russia at the End of Yel'tsin's Presidency', *Post-Soviet Affairs*, vol.16, no.1, pp.1-32.

Breslauer, G.W. (1982), *Khrushchev and Brezhnev as Leaders: Building Authority in Soviet Politics*, Allen & Unwin, London.

Brown, A. (1982), 'Leadership Succession and Policy Innovation', in A.Brown and M.Kaser (eds), *Soviet Policy for the 1980s*, Macmillan, London, pp.223-53.

Brown, A. (1996), *The Gorbachev Factor*, Oxford University Press, Oxford.

Brown, J.D. and Earle, J.S. (2000), *Privatization and Restructuring in Russia: New Evidence from Panel Data on Industrial Enterprises*, Working paper series No.1, Russian-European Centre for Economic Policy, Moscow.

Bruszt, L. (2000), 'The Russian Lesson: A Market Economy Needs an Effective State', *Transition Newsletter*, vol.11, nos.3-4, May-July, pp.21-2.

Bunce, V. (1981), *Do New Leaders Make a Difference? Executive Succession and Public Policy Under Capitalism and Socialism*, Princeton University Press, Princeton, New Jersey.

Butowski, P. (2000a), 'Russia's First S-400 Squad to be Deployed by Next Year', *Jane's Defence Weekly*, 26 January, p.13.

Butowski, P. (2000b), 'Russian Air Force Gets Another Tu-160', *Jane's Defence Weekly*, 24 May, p.12.

Butowski, P. (2000c), 'Ukraine Becomes Second An-70 Customer', *Jane's Defence Weekly*, 26 January, p.5.

Buzan, B. (1995), 'The Level of Analysis Problem in International Relations Reconsidered', in K.Booth and S.Smith (eds), *International Relations Theory Today*, Polity, Cambridge, pp.198-216.

Buzgalin, A. (1998), 'Russia: "Capitalism's Jurassic Park"', *Prism*, vol.4, no.15, part 4, July.

'"Can't Pay, Don't Need to Pay": How Russians view Taxation' (1998). *www.strath.ac.uk/Departments/CSPP/nrb7pr.html* (accessed 26 April 2000).

Chernorechensky, A. and Sokut, S. (2000), 'Vykhod iz shtopora otkladyvaetsya', *Nezavisimoe voennoe obozrenie*, no.2, p.3.

Chubais, A. (1995), 'The Results of Privatisation in Russia and the Tasks of the New Stage', *Problems of Economic Transition*, vol.38, no.1, May.

CIA (1996), *Handbook of International Economic Statistics. 1996*, U.S. Central Intelligence Agency, Directorate of Intelligence, Washington, D.C.

CIA (1997), *Handbook of International Economic Statistics. 1997*, U.S. Central Intelligence Agency, Directorate of Intelligence, Washington, D.C.

CIA (1999a), *Handbook of International Economic Statistics. 1999*, U.S. Central Intelligence Agency, Directorate of Intelligence, Washington, D.C.

CIA (1999b), *World Fact Book 1999*, U.S. Central Intelligence Agency, www.odci.gov/publications/factbook.html.

Cohen, A. (2000), 'The Rise of Putin: What it Means for the Future of Russia', *Backgrounder*, March 28, 2000, The Heritage Foundation, www.heritage.org/library/backgrounder/bg1353.html.

Considine, T.J. and Larson, D.F. (1996), *Uncertainty and the Price for Crude Oil Reserves*, Policy Research Working Paper 1655, The World Bank, Washington, D.C., September.

Coulloudon, V. (1997), 'Crime and Corruption after Communism: The Criminalization of Russia's Political Elite', *Eastern European Constitutional Review*, vol.6, no.4.

Custine, de, M. (1991), *Letters from Russia*, Penguin, Harmondsworth, 1991.

Davydova, M. and Manvelov, N. (2000), 'Yukos idet na vostok', *Segodnya*, 25 September.

Desai, M. and Estrin, S. (1992), *Some Simple Dynamics of Transition: From Command to Market Economy*, Discussion Paper No.85, Centre for Economic Performance, London School of Economics, London, July.

Desai, P. (2000), 'A Russian Optimist: an interview with Yegor Gaidar', *Challenge*, May-June, pp.15-16.

Diamond, L., Plattner, M.F., Chu, Yu. and Tien, H. (eds) (1997), *Consolidating The Third Wave Democracies: Themes and Perspectives*, Johns Hopkins University Press, Baltimore.

Dick, C.J. (2000), 'Russia's New Doctrine Takes Dark World View', *Jane's Intelligence Review*, vol.12, no.1, January, p.15.

Dikun, Ye. (1997), 'A Profile of Boris Nemtsov', *Prism*, vol.3, no.5, part 2, April.

Dikun, Ye. (1999), 'Vsya kremlevskaya rodnya', *Obschaya gazeta*, no.29, 22 July.

Dittus, P. and Prowse, S. (1996), 'Corporate Control in Central Europe and Russia. Should Banks Own Shares?', in R.Frydman, C.W.Gray and A.Rapaczynski (eds), *Corporate Governance in Central Europe and Russia*, vol.1, *Banks, Funds, and Foreign Investors*, Central European University Press, Budapest.

Dixon, R. (2000), 'Pushing the Boundaries of a Free Press', *Los Angeles Times*, 1 June.

Djankov, S. (1999), 'Enterprise Restructuring in Russia', in H.G.Broadman (ed.), *Russian Enterprise Reform. Policies to Further the Transition*, World Bank Discussion Paper No.400, World Bank, Washington D.C.

Dobrovol'sky, A. (1999), 'VVS budut spasat' svoyu tekhniku', *Nezavisimoe voennoe obozrenie*, no.18, p.6.

Drobyshevsky, A. (2000), 'PVO rasshiryaetsya', *Nezavisimoe voennoe obozrenie*, no.9, p.1.

Duparc, A. (2000), 'New light thrown on Vladimir Putin's past', *The Guardian Weekly*, 1-7 June, 2000.

Dyker, D.A. (2000), 'The Structural Origins of the Russian Economic Crisis', *Post-Communist Economies*, vol.12, no.1, March, pp.5-24.

Earle, J. and Estrin, S. (1996), *Privatization Versus Competition: Changing Enterprise Behavior in Russia*, Discussion Paper No. 316, Centre for Economic Performance, London School of Economics.

EIA (2000), *Short-Term Energy Outlook, September 2000*, Energy Information Administration, Washington, D.C., 6 September.

Elster, J., Offe, O., Preuss, U.K. (1998), *Institutional Design in Postcommunist Societies: Rebuilding the Ship at Sea*, Cambridge University Press, Cambridge.

Filatov, S.B. and Furman, B.E. (1992), 'Religiya: politika v massovom soznanii', *Sotsiologicheskie issledovaniya*, no. 7, pp.3-12.

Finansovo-promyshlennye gruppy i konglomeraty v ekonomike i politike sovremennoi Rossii, Tsentr politicheskikh tekhnologii, Moscow, 1997.

Fischer, S. (1998), *The Russian Economy at the Start of 1998*. Speech at the 1998 U.S.-Russian Investment Symposium, at Harvard University, on January 9 1998. IMF, Washington, D.C. http://www.imf.org/external/np/speeches/1998/010998.htm.

Fortescue, S. (1992), 'The Privatisation of Soviet Large-Scale Industry', in H.Hendrischke (ed.), *Market Reform in the Changing Socialist World*, Macquarie Studies in Chinese Political Economy, No.4, Macquarie University, Sydney.

Fortescue, S. (1997), *Policy Making for Russian Industry*, Macmillan, London and Basingstoke.

Fortescue, S. (1998a), 'Ownership and Corporate Strategy in the Russian Mining and Metals Sector', *Soviet and Post-Soviet Review*, vol.25, no.2, pp.163-80.

Fortescue, S. (1998b), 'Privatisation, Corporate Governance and Enterprise Performance in Russia', *Russian and Euro-Asian Bulletin*, vol.7, no.5, pp.1-9.

Fortescue, S. (2000), 'Enterprise Adaptation in the Russian Mining and Metals Sector', Paper presented to the 6th ICCEES World Congress, Tampere, July-August.

Gaddy, C.G. and Ickes, B.W. (1998), 'Russia's Virtual Economy', *Foreign Affairs*, vol.77, no.5, September-October.

Gaidar, E. (1999), *Days of Defeat and Victory*, University of Washington Press, Seattle WA, 1999.

Galbraith, J.K. (1994), *The World Economy Since the Wars: a Personal View*, Sinclair-Stevenson, London.

Galeotti, M. (1996), *Mafiya: Organized Crime in Russia*. Jane's Intelligence Review, special report No 10. Jane's Information Group, Coulsdon.

Galeotti, M. (1997), *Policing Russia: Problems and Prospects in Turbulent Times*. Jane's Intelligence Review, special report No 15. Jane's Information Group, Coulsdon.

Georgiev, V. (1999), 'Yubilei rossiiskoi armii', *Nezavisimoe voennoe obozrenie*, no.17, p.1.

Georgiev, V. (2000), 'Sozdaetsya sovmestnaya gruppirovka', *Nezavisimoe voennoe obozrenie*, no.14, p.1.

Gill, G. (2000), 'The Russian Duma Elections of 1999: The Main Game?', *Russian and Euro-Asian Bulletin*, vol.9, no.1, pp.1-9.

Gill, G. and Markwick, R. (2000), *Russia's Stillborn Democracy? From Gorbachev to Yeltsin*, Oxford University Press, Oxford.

Glinski, D. and Reddaway, P. (1999), 'The Ravages of Market Bolshevism', *Journal of Democracy*, vol.10, no.2, April.

Gobbin, N. and Merlevede, B. (2000), 'The Russian Crisis: a Debt Perspective', *Post-Communist Economies*, vol.12, no.2, 2000, pp.141-63.

Goldman, M. (2000), 'Reprivatizing Russia', *Challenge*, vol.43, no.3, May-June.

Golovkov, A. (2000), 'Vtoroi president Rossii', *Nezavisimaya gazeta*, 28 March.

Golts, A. (2000), 'The Arming of Russia's Economy', *The Russia Journal*, 7-13 February.

Gorbachev, M. (1987), *Perestroika: New Thinking for Our Country and the World*, Collins, London.

Gorbachev, M. (2000), 'Lyudi bez printsipov', *Nezavisimaya gazeta*, 15 January.

Goskomstat (1992), *Narodnoe khozyaistvo Rossiiskoi Federatsii. 1992*, Goskomstat Rossii, Moscow.

Goskomstat (1993), *Sotsial'no-ekonomicheskoe polozhenie Rossii, yanvar'-noyabr' 1993 g.*, Goskomstat Rossii, Moscow.

Goskomstat (1994), *Rossiiskii statisticheskii ezhegodnik. 1994*, Goskomstat Rossii, Moscow.

Goskomstat (1995), *Rossiiskii statisticheskii ezhegodnik. 1995*, Goskomstat Rossii, Moscow.

Goskomstat (1996), *Promyshlennost' Rossii. 1996*, Goskomstat Rossii, Moscow.

Goskomstat (1998), *Promyshlennost' Rossii. 1998*, Goskomstat Rossii, Moscow.

Goskomstat (1999a), *Regiony Rossii 1998, Volume 2*, Goskomstat Rossii, Moscow.

Goskomstat (1999b), *Rossiiskii statisticheskii ezhegodnik. 1999*, Goskomstat Rossii, Moscow.

Goskomstat (1999c), *Rossiya v tsifrakh. 1999*, Goskomstat Rossii, Moscow.

Goskomstat (2000a), *Regiony Rossii 1999, Volume 2*, Goskomstat Rossii, Moscow.

Goskomstat (2000b), *Rossiya v tsifrakh. 2000*, Goskomstat Rossii, Moscow.

Goskomstat (2000c), *Sotsial'no-ekonomicheskoe polozhenie Rossii. 1999 god*, Goskomstat Rossii, Moscow.

Goskomstat (2000d), *Sotsial'no-ekonomicheskoe polozhenie Rossii, yanvar' 2000 goda*, Goskomstat Rossii, Moscow.

Goskomstat (2000e), *Sotsial'no-ekonomicheskoe polozhenie Rossii, yanvar'-iyun' 2000 goda*, Goskomstat Rossii, Moscow.

Goskomstat (2000f), *Sotsial'no-ekonomicheskoe polozhenie Rossii. yanvar'-mai 2000 goda*, Goskomstat Rossii, Moscow.

Gregory, R.S. (1990), *Soviet Economic Structure and Performance*, Forth Edition, Harper and Row, New York.

Grigoriev, S. (2000), 'Put' k ustoichivomu razvitiyu', *Nezavisimoe voennoe obozrenie*, no.8, p.6.

Hanson, P. (1999), 'The Russian Economic Crisis and the Future of Russian Economic Reform', *Europe-Asia Studies*, vol.51, no.7, November, pp.1141-66.

Held, D. (1980), *Introduction to Critical Theory*, University of California Press, Berkeley.

Hoffman, D. (1997), 'The Man who Rebuilt Moscow: Capitalist Style Could Propel Mayor to National Power', *Washington Post*, 27 February.

Hoffman, D. (2000), 'Putin's Actions Seem to Belie Promise on Tycoons', *Washington Post Foreign Service*, 7 May, 2000.

Holmes, L. (1993), *The End of Communist Power: Anti-Corruption Campaigns and Legitimation Crisis*, Melbourne University Press, Melbourne.

Holmes, S. (1993-4), 'A Forum on Presidential Power', *East European Constitutional Review*, vo.2, no.4, Fall 1993, and vol.3, no.1, Winter 1994, pp.36-9.

Huntington, S.P. (1991), *The Third Wave. Democratization in the late Twentieth Century*, University of Oklahoma Press, Norman.

Huntington, S.P. (2000), 'Robust Nationalism', *The National Interest*, No. 58, Winter, pp.31-40.

Huskey, E. (1995), 'The State-Legal Administration and the Politics of Redundancy', *Post-Soviet Affairs*, vol.11, no.2, pp.115-43.

IISS (1999), *The Military Balance 1999-2000*, International Institute for Strategic Studies, London.

Illarionov, A. (2000), 'Mify i uroki avgustovskogo krizisa', *Polit.ru*, 13 and 19 April (http://www.polit.ru).

IMF (1999), *World Economic Outlook. October 1999*, IMF, Washington, D.C.

Jack, A. (2000), 'Russian Reform Plan Strikes Liberals as Too Good to Last', *The Financial Times*, 4 July.

Jervis, R. (1976), *Perception and Misperception in International Politics*, Princeton University Press, Princeton.

Kabalina, V. (1996), 'Privatisation and Restructuring of Enterprises under "Insider" or "Outsider" Control', in S.Clarke (ed.), *Conflict and Change in the Russian Industrial Enterprise*, Elgar, Cheltenham.

Kagarlitsky, B. (2000), 'Pereraspredeleniye mechty: pochemy oligarkhi budut zashishat' ne demokratiyu, a tol'ko sobstvennost'', *Obschaya gazeta*, 24 February.

Kamenka, E. (1975), 'Political Nationalism—The Evolution of the Idea', in E.Kamenka (ed.), *Nationalism: The Nature and Evolution of an Idea*. Australian National University Press, Canberra, pp. 2–20.

Kazakevitch, G. (1994 and 1995), 'Macroeconomic Issues of Privatisation in Russia and Eastern Europe', *Ekonomika i matematicheskie metody*, Moscow, no.3, 1994. Translation into English in *MATECON*, Spring 1995, vol.32 (3).

Kedrov, I. (1999), 'Rossiya igraet strategicheskimi muskulami', *Nezavisimoe voennoe obozrenie*, no.39, p.1.

Kedrov, I. (2000), 'Vesennee popolneniye v dal'nei aviatsii', *Nezavisimoe voennoe obozrenie*, no.8, p.8.

Kelley, D.R. (1994), 'Yel'tsin and Russo-Gaullism', *The Soviet and Post-Soviet Review*, vol.21, no.11, pp.44-55.

Knight, A. (2000), 'The Two Worlds of Vladimir Putin: 1 the KGB', *The Washington Quarterly*, Spring, pp.32-7.

Korbut, A. (1999), 'Na poroge uchebnogo goda', *Nezavisimoe voennoe obozrenie*, no.46, p.3.

Korbut, A. (2000), 'Moskva ustupila Tbilisi', *Nezavisimoe voennoe obozrenie*, no.15, p.1.

Kornai, J. (1980), *Economics of Shortage*, vols. A and B, North-Holland, Amsterdam.

Kornai, J. (1982), *Growth, Shortage and Efficiency*, Basil Blackwell, Oxford.

Kornai, J. and Martos, B. (eds) (1981), *Non-Price Control*, North-Holland, Amsterdam.

Kovalev, S. (2000), 'Putin's War', *The New York Review of Books*, 10 February, 2000, pp.4-8.

Kozyrev, A.V. (1996), 'Consensus on Russia's Foreign Policy?', *International Affairs* (Moscow), vol.42, no.1, January-February, pp.21-4.

Krygier, M. (1996), 'The Sources of Civil Society', Second Richard Krygier Memorial Lecture, 29 August 1996, *http://abc.net.au/rn/talks/bbing/stories/510754.htm*.

Kubicek, P. (1994), 'Delegative Democracy in Russia and Ukraine', *Communist and Post-Communist Studies*, vol.27, no.4, pp.423-41.

Kuroyedov, V. (1998), 'O morskoi strategii Rossii', *Voenny parad*, no.2 (26), pp.8-9.

Linz, J.J. and Stepan, A. (1996), *Problems of Democratic Transition and Consolidation: Southern Europe, South America and Post-Communist Europe*, Johns Hopkins University Press, Baltimore.

Litovkin, D. (2000), '*Sineva* podnimetsya nad morem', *Nezavisimoe voennoe obozrenie*, no.16, p.1.

Lloyd, J. (1999), 'The Russian Devolution', *The New York Times Magazine*, August 15, p.34.

Lukin, V. (1983), *Tsentry sily: kontseptsii i realnosti*, Moscow.

Lukin, V.P. and Nagorny, A.A. (1988), 'Kontseptiya treugolnika SSSR-SShA-KNR: novye real'nosti mirovoi politiki', *SShA: ekonomika, politika, ideologiiia*, no. 6.

Maley, W. (1991), 'Ethnonationalism and Civil Society in the USSR', in C.Kukathas, D.W.Lovell and W.Maley (eds), *The Transition from Socialism: State and Civil Society in the USSR*, Longman Cheshire, Melbourne, pp.177–97.

Malle, S. (1999), 'Foreword', in V.Tikhomirov (ed.), *Anatomy of the 1998 Russian Crisis*, CERC, Melbourne, pp.1-8.

Malleret, T., Orlova, N. and Romanov, V. (1999), 'What Loaded and Triggered the Russian Crisis?', *Post-Soviet Affairs*, vol.15, no.2, April-June, pp.107-29.

Marsh, C. (2000), 'Social Capital and Democracy in Russia', *Communist and Post-Communist Studies*, vol.33, no.2, pp.183-99.

Matlack, C. (1998), 'What Disasters Lie Ahead in Moscow?', *Business Week*, 19 October.

Matloff, J. (2000), 'Putin Who? Russia's Presidential Enigma', *Christian Science Monitor*, 28 January.

McFaul, M. (1995), 'State Power, Institutional Change, and the Politics of Privatization in Russia', *World Politics*, vol.47, no.2, pp.210-43.

McFaul, M. (2000), 'Russia's 2000 Presidential Elections: Implications for Russian Democracy and US-Russian Relations', *Testimony before the Committee on Foreign Relations*, US Senate, 12 April, 2000.

Medvedev, R. (2000), 'Byla li u Putina maska?', *Rossiiskaya gazeta*, 5 April.

Miller, R.F. (1995), 'Russian Policy Toward Japan', in P.Shearman (ed.), *Russian Foreign Policy Since 1990*, Westview, Boulder, pp.135-58.

Nellis, J. (1999), *Time to rethink privatization in transition economies?* International Finance Corporation Discussion Paper No.38, The World Bank, Washington, D.C.

Nelson, L.D. and Kuzes, I.Y. (1995), *Radical Reform in Yeltsin's Russia. Political, Economic, and Social Dimensions*, Sharpe, Armonk N.Y.

Nikitinsky, L. and Shpakov, Yu. (2000), 'Putin v razvedke: "zavklubom" ili "superagent"', *Moskovskie novosti*, 25 January.

Novichkov, N. (1999), 'Russian Funds for Procurement Reallocated', *Jane's Defence Weekly*, 20 October, p.4.

Novichkov, N. (2000), 'Russia Doubles Defence Procurement', *Jane's Defence Weekly*, 2 February, p.3.

Novoprudsky, S. (2000a), 'U nas vsyakii mozhet stat' Abramovichem', *Izvestia*, 27 April.

Novoprudsky, S. (2000b), 'Unizhayushiisya kapitalizm', *Izvestia*, 22 March.

Nunberg, B. (1999), *The State After Communism: Administrative Transitions in Central and Eastern Europe*, World Bank, Washington D.C.

Obolonsky, A.V. (1995), 'Russian Politics in the Time of Troubles: Some Basic Antinomies', in A.Saikal and W.Maley (eds), *Russia in Search of its Future*, Cambridge University Press, Cambridge, pp.12–27.

OECD (1997), *OECD Economic Surveys 1997: Russian Federation*, OECD, Paris.

OECD (2000), *OECD Economic Surveys 1999-2000: Russian Federation*, OECD, Paris.

Oilnergy (2000), *OilEnergy Website* (www.oilnergy.com, accessed on 16 October, 2000).

Okolicsanyi, K. (1991), 'Hungary: the Nonexistent Long-term Economic Plan', *Radio Liberty Research Report*, 18 December.

Panfilov, O. (2000), 'Glasnost under Siege: Putin and the Media - No Love Lost', *East European Constitutional Review*, vol.9, no.1-2, online at http://www.law.nyu.edu/eecr/ vol9num_onehalf/feature/lovelost.html.

Payer, C. (1989), 'Causes of the Debt Crisis', in B.Onimode (ed.), *The IMF, The World Bank and African Debt: The Social and Political Impact*, Zed Books, London.

Peach, G. and Bivens, M. (1998), 'Primakov's Six weeks Magically Confused', *The Moscow Times*, 24 October.

Peregudov, S.P. (1998), 'Novyi Rossiiskii korporativizm: ot byurokraticheskogo k oligarkhicheskomu?', *Polis*, no.4.

Perekhod k rynku, Moscow, 1990.

Phillips, A. (1999), 'Changing Characterisations of the Roots of Russia's Problems: A Look at the Virtual Economy Thesis', *Russian and Euro-Asian Bulletin*, vol.8, no.3, March.

Piirainen, T. (1994), 'Introduction', in T.Piirainen (ed.), *Change and Continuity in Eastern Europe*, Dartmouth, Aldershot, pp.1-9.

Pimenov, V. (1999), 'Organizatsionnye bluzhdaniya oboronnogo kompleksa', *Nezavisimoe voennoe obozrenie*, no.33, p.4.

Piñera, J. (2000), 'A Chilean Model for Russia', *Foreign Affairs*, vol.79, no.5, pp.62-73.

Pipes, R. (1964), *The Formation of the Soviet Union: Communism and Nationalism, 1917–1923*, (revised edition), Harvard University Press, Cambridge MA.

Plasser, F., Ulram, P.A. and Waldrauch, H. (1998), *Democratic Consolidation in East-Central Europe*, Macmillan, London.

Politkovskaya, A. (1999), 'Esli vraga nel'zya kupit', ego unichtozhayut', *Novaya gazeta*, 26 July.

Polkovnikov, P. (1999), 'Ot Kaliningrada do granitsy s Kitaem', *Nezavisimoe voennoe obozrenie*, no.25, p.5.

Polonsky, G. and Aivazian, Z. (2000), 'Restructuring Russian Industry: Can It Really Be Done?', *Post-Communist Economies*, vol.12, no.2, June, pp.229-40.

Porfiriev, A. (2000), 'Pravilo silnoy ruki', *Segodnya*, 25 July.

Pravosudov, S. and Mason, H. (2000), ' My ponimayem, chto biznes i vlast' v vashei strane tesno svyazany', *Nezavisimaya gazeta*, 20 June.

Proskurnina, O. (2000), 'Missing Points from Strategic Development Plan', *Gazeta.Ru*, 14 June.

Putin, V. (2000), *First Person*, Hutchinson, London.

Putnam, R. D. (1993), *Making Democracy Work: Civic Traditions in Modern Italy*, (with R.Leonardi and R.Y.Nanetti), Princeton University Press, Princeton.

Remington, T. (2000), 'Putin's Third Way; Russia and the "Strong State" Ideal', *East European Constitutional Review*, vol.9, no.1-2, online at http://www.law.nyu.edu/ eecr/vol9num_onehalf/feature/strongstate.html.

Roitman, L. (2000), 'Izbiratel' kak grazhdanin', *Radio svoboda*, 21 March (http://www.svoboda.org/programs/RT/2000/RT.032100.shtml).

Rose, R. (2000), 'A Supply-Side View of Russia's Elections', *East European Constitutional Review*, vol.9, nos.1/2, Winter/Spring, pp.53-9.

Russian Central Bank (1998), *Godovoi otchyot Tsentral'nogo banka Rossiiskoi Federatsii, 1997,* Tsentral'nyi bank Rossii, Moscow.

Russian Central Bank (1999), *Godovoi otchyot Tsentral'nogo banka Rossiiskoi Federatsii, 1998,* Tsentral'nyi bank Rossii, Moscow.

Russian Government (1997), 'O pervoocherednykh merakh po reformirovaniyu Vooruzhennykh Sil Rossiiskoi Federatsii i sovershenstvovanii ikh struktury', *Rossiiskaia Gazeta*, 19 July, p.5.

Russian Government (1999), 'Russia at the turn of the Millennium', *www.pravitelstvo.gov.ru/english/statVP_engl_1.html* (accessed 26 April 2000).

Russian Government (2000a), 'Kontseptsiya natsional'noi bezopasnosti', *Nezavisimoe voennoe obozrenie*, no.1, pp.6-7.

Russian Government (2000b), 'Osnovy politki Rossiiskoi Federatsii v oblasti voenno-morskoi deyatel'nosti na period do 2010 goda', *Morskoi sbornik*, no.4, pp.6-9.

Russian Government (2000c), 'Voennaya doktrina Rossiiskoi Federatsii', *Nezavisimoe voennoe obozrenie*, no.15, pp.4-5.

Ryabov, A. (1999), 'Politicheskaya stabil'nost', institut prezidenta i raskol vlastnykh elit: est' li u Rossii shansy izbezhat' politicheskogo khaosa?', *Brifing moskovskogo tsentra Karnegi*, vol.1, no.4, April, pp.1-2.

Rybkin, I. (1997), 'Domestic Challenges to Russia's Security', *International Affairs* (Moscow), no. 4, pp.132-43.

Sakwa, R. (1990), *Gorbachev and his Reforms, 1985-1990*, Philip Allen, Hemel Hempstead.

Schleifer, A. and Treisman, D. (1998), *The Economics and Politics of Transition to an Open Market Economy. Russia*, Development Centre Studies, OECD, Paris.

Schmidt, H. (1999), *Auf der Suche nach einer öffentlichen Moral*, Gütersloh, Rheda-Wiedensbrück.

Schroeder, G. (1998), 'Dimensions of Russia's Industrial Transformation, 1992 to 1998: An Overview', *Post-Soviet Geography and Economics*, vol.39, no.5, May, pp.243-70.

Sharyi, A. (2000), 'Mozhno li provesti parallel' mezhdu Putinym i Leninym?', *Radio svoboda*, 26 March (http://www.svoboda.org/archive/elections2000/0300/ ll.032600-22.shtml).

Shearman, P. (1997), 'Defining the National Interest: Russian Foreign Policy and Domestic Politics', in R.Kanet and A.V.Kozhemiakin (eds), *The Foreign Policy of the Russian Federation*, Basingstoke, Houndmills, pp.1-27.

Shelley, L. (2000), 'Why a Corrupt State can't be a Strong State: Corruption in the Post-Yeltsin Era', *East European Constitutional Review*, vol.9, no.1-2, online at http://www.law.nyu.edu/eecr/vol9num_onehalf/feature/corruption.html.

Shukshin, A. (2000), 'Russia Sets Out to Tackle "2003 Problem"', *Reuters*, 13 September.

Sikri, A. (2000), 'Debt Deal Prompts Fresh Investor Interest in Russia', *Reuters*, 11 February.

Slay, B. (1999), 'An Interpretation of the Russian Financial Crisis', *Post-Soviet Geography and Economics*, vol.46, no.1, pp.24-33.

Smith, J. (1999), *The Bolsheviks and the National Question, 1917–23*, Macmillan, London.

Sokut, S. (1999a), 'Gosudarstvo vspomnilo pro oboronku', *Nezavisimoe voennoe obozrenie*, no.21, p.1.

Sokut, S. (1999b), 'Krug pocheta nad Islandiei', *Nezavisimoe voennoe obozrenie*, no.25, p.5.

Sokut, S. (1999c), 'Novaya tekhnika RVSN', *Nezavisimoe voennoe obozrenie*, no.30, p.1.

Sokut, S. (2000a), 'Istrebitel pyatogo pokoleniya postupit v voiska cherez 8-10 let', *Nezavisimoe voennoe obozrenie*, no.9, p.6.

Sokut, S. (2000b), 'Novaya vlast' imeet shans vyvesti voennuyu reformu iz krizisa', *Nezavisimoe voennoe obozrenie*, no.1, p.2.

Sokut, S. (2000c), 'Siloviki ukreplyayut svoi pozitsii', *Nezavisimoe voennoe obozrenie*, no.18, p.1.

Sokut, S. (2000d), 'Zabytaya oboronka', *Nezavisimoe voennoe obozrenie*, no.10, p.3.

Soloviev, V. (1999), 'Federal'nye voiska uspeshno zavershayut operatsiyu v Dagestane', *Nezavisimoe voennoe obozrenie*, no.33, p.1.

Soros, G. (2000), 'Who Lost Russia', *New York Review of Books*, April 13.

Statkom (1996), *Finansy i tseny stran Sodruzhestva Nezavisimykh Gosudarstv v 1991-1995 gg. i pervom polugodii 1996 g.*, Statkom SNG, Moscow.

Statkom (1997), *Finansy i tseny stran Sodruzhestva Nezavisimykh Gosudarstv v 1995-1996 gg. i pervom polugodii 1997 g.*, Statkom SNG, Moscow.

Statkom (1999), *SNG i strany mira*, Statkom SNG, Moscow.

Statkom (2000), *Sodruzhestvo Nezavisimykh Gosudarstv v 1999 godu*, Statkom SNG, Moscow.

Statkom (2000), *Sodruzhestvo Nezavisimykh Gosudarstv v 1999 godu*, Statkom SNG, Moscow.

Stiglitz, J. (2000), 'What I Learned at the World Economic Crisis', *The New Republic*, 17 April.

Stuart, R.C. and Panayotopolous, C.M. (1999), 'Decline and Recovery in Transition Economies: the Impact of Initial Conditions', *Post-Soviet Geography and Economics*, vol.40, no.4, pp.267-80.

Szporluk, R. (1991), *Communism and Nationalism: Karl Marx versus Friedrich List*, Oxford University Press, New York.

Taras, R. (1997), 'Separating Power: Keeping Presidents in Check', in R.Taras (ed.), *Postcommunist Presidents*, Cambridge University Press, Cambridge, pp.15–37.

Tennenbaum, J. (2000), '"National Liberals" Try to Kidnap Russia's Economic Policy', *Executive Intelligence Review*, vol.27, no.15, 7 April.

Thornhill, J. (1999), 'Vladimir Putin: The Family's Sinister Son', *Financial Times*, 14 August, 1999.

Tikhomirov, V. (1997), 'Capital Flight from Post-Soviet Russia', *Europe-Asia Studies*, vol.49, no.4, June, p.591-615.

Tikhomirov, V. (1998), 'Investment Crisis in Post-Soviet Russia' in H.Shibata and T.Ihori (eds), *Welfare State, Public Investment and Growth*, Springer-Verlag, Tokyo, p.221-55.

Tikhomirov, V. (1999a), 'State Finances and the Effectiveness of the Russian Reform' in V.Tikhomirov (ed.), *Anatomy of the 1998 Russian Crisis*, CERC, Melbourne, pp.164-203.

Tikhomirov, V. (1999b) (ed.), *Anatomy of the 1998 Russian Crisis.* CERC, Melbourne.

Tikhomirov, V. (2000a), 'The Second Collapse of the Soviet Economy: Myths and Realities of the Russian Reform', *Europe-Asia Studies*, vol.52, no.2, pp.207-36.

Tikhomirov, V. (2000b), *The Political Economy of Post-Soviet Russia*, Macmillan Press, London, St.Martin's Press, New York.

Timakova, N. (1998), 'Yeltsin vs. Yeltsin', *Intellectual Capital*, vol.2, no.46, 9-16 December.

Tolz, V. (1998), 'Forging the Nation: National Identity and Nation-Building in Post-Communist Russia', *Europe-Asia Studies*, vol.50, no.6, pp.993-1022.

Tompson, W. (2000), 'Putin's Power Plays', *World Today*, vol.56, no.7, pp.14-16.

Treisman, D. (1998), 'Fighting Inflation in a Transitional Regime. Russia's Anomalous Stabilization', *World Politics*, vol.50, January, pp.235-65.

Tretyakov, V. (1999), 'Stalin - eto nashe vsyo', *Nezavisimaya gazeta*, 22 December.

Tsipko, A. (1993), 'Democratic Russia as a Bolshevik as well as a National Party', *Nezavisimaya gazeta*, 9 April, p.5.

TsSU (1984), USSR Central Statistical Department, *Narodnoe khozyaistvo SSSR v 1983 g.*, Finansy i statistika, Moscow.

TsSU (1985), USSR Central Statistical Department, *Narodnoe khozyaistvo SSSR v 1984 g.*, Finansy i statistika, Moscow.

Tsuladze, A. (2000), 'Ot demokratii ostanetsya tol'ko forma', *Nezavisimaya gazeta*, 1 June.

Tsyganov, Yu. (1999), 'Political Background of the Economic Crisis in Russia', in V.Tikhomirov (ed.), *Anatomy of the 1998 Russian Crisis*, CERC, Melbourne, pp.259-94.

UN (2000), *United Nations Human Development Report 2000*, United Nations, New York.

UNICP (1999), *United Nations International Comparison Program (UNICP)*, United Nations, New York.

USSR Goskomstat (1987), *Narodnoe khozyaistvo SSSR za 70 let*, Finansy i statistika, Moscow.

USSR Goskomstat (1988), *Kapital'noe stroitel'stvo SSSR. Statisticheskii sbornik*, Finansy i statistika, Moscow.

USSR Goskomstat (1989), *Narodnoe khozyaistvo SSSR v 1988 g.*, Finansy i statistika, Moscow.

USSR Goskomstat (1990a), *Narodnoe khozyaistvo SSSR v 1989 g.*, Finansy i statistika, Moscow.

USSR Goskomstat (1990b), *The USSR in Figures for 1989*, Finansy i statistika, Moscow.

USSR Goskomstat (1991), *Narodnoe khozyaistvo SSSR v 1990 g.*, Finansy i statistika, Moscow.

Voschanov, P. (2000), 'Yesli b Lubyanka mogla...', *Delovoi vtornik*, 21 September.

Walicki, A. (1980), *A History of Russian Thought from the Enlightenment to Marxism*, Oxford University Press, Oxford.

Waltz, K.N. (1968), *Foreign Policy and Democratic Politics: The American and British Experience*, Longman, London.

Waltz, K.N. (1979), *Theory of International Politics*, Random House, New York.

Ward, B. (1958), 'The Firm In Illyria: Market Syndicalism', *American Economic Review,* vol.48 (4), pp.566-89.

Weber, M. (1978), *Economy and Society. An Outline of Interpretive Sociology*, University of California Press, Berkeley, (eds G.Roth and C.Wittich).

Wedel, J.R. (2000), 'Tainted Transactions: Harvard, the Chubais Clan and Russia's Ruin', *The National Interest*, no.59, Spring.

White, S. (1997), 'Russia: Presidential Leadership under Yeltsin', in R.Taras (ed.), *Postcommunist Presidents* Cambridge University Press, Cambridge, pp.38-66.

White, S. (2000), *Russia's New Politics*, Cambridge University Press, Cambridge.

WHO (2000), *United Nations World Health Organisation Report*, United Nations, Geneva, July.

Willerton, J.P. (1998), 'Post-Soviet Clientelist Norms at the Russian Federal Level', in G.Gill (ed.), *Elites and Leadership in Russian Politics*, Macmillan, Basingstoke 1998, pp.52-80.

World Bank (1998), *Knowledge for Development. World Bank Annual Report 1998*, World Bank, Washington D.C.

World Bank (1999), *Entering the Twenty-First Century. World Development Report 1999-2000*, Oxford University Press for World Bank, New York.

World Bank (2000), *Attacking Poverty. World Development Report 2000-2001*, Oxford University Press for the World Bank, New York.

Yanovskiy, R.G. (ed.) (1999), *Armiya Rossii: sostoyaniye i perspektivy*, ISPI RAN, Moscow.

Yavlinsky, G. (1992), 'Spring '92 Reforms in Russia' (Report from the Centre for Economic and Political Research), *Moscow News*, nos.21-22.

Zolotarev, V. (1998), *Voennaya bezopasnost' Otechestva*, Kanon Press Kuchkovo Pole, Moskva.

Zotov, V.B. (1998), *Kak mer Luzhkov upravliaet Moskvoi (materialy lektsii)*, IM-INFORM, Lyubertsy.

Zyuganov, G.A. (ed.) (1998), *Voyennaya reforma. Vooruzhennyye sily Rossiyskoi Federatsii*, AO RAU-Universitet, Moscow.

Index

Khodorkovsky, M. 93, 95
Khrushchev, N. 242n, 245n
Kirienko, S. 19, 32n, 83, 87, 89, 120
Kiselev, O. 95
Kizner 202
KKR investment group (USA) 117n
Klebanov, I. 209-10
Knight, A. 224
Kokh, A. 92, 93, 95
Kokoshin, A. 236
Kola Peninsula 206
Korea, North 186, 237, 245n
Korea, South 109, 185, 189
Kornai, J. 146, 159-60
Kornukov, A. 219n
Korzhakov, A. 97
Kosovo 8, 187, 194, 197, 204, 206, 229, 238, 241, 245n
Kostunica, V. 14n
Kovalev, N. 82
Kovalev, S. 31n, 32n
Kozyrev, A. 236, 238, 243n, 245n
Kraakman, R. 110-1, 113-5
Krasnoyarsk 93, 214
Kravchenko, V. 208, 219n
Kryuchkov, V. 99n
Kudrin, A. 139n
Kulikov, A. 76n
Kuril Islands 184
Kursk 195
Kuwait 186
Kvashnin, A. 186-7, 233
Kyrgyzstan 196, 216, 245n

Latin America 14n, 168, 177, 179
Latyshev, P. 32n
Lebed, A. 83-4
Lebedinsk Ore Enrichment Combine 117n
Leningrad 23, 32n, 195, 200, 211
Leningrad State University 23, 225
Leonidovka 202
Lesin, M. 92
Liberal Democratic Party of Russia 49, 87
Lisin, V. 95
'Lomo' enterprise 209
Lomonosov Porcelain Factory 117n
London 228
London Club 127, 141n

Lukashenka, A. 4, 11, 14n
Lukoil company 7, 94, 98
Luxembourg 188
Luzhkov, Yu. 20-1, 27, 48, 64, 83, 87, 91, 100n, 242n

Mabetex company 3, 20, 22, 31n
Main Intelligence Directorate of the Russian Armed Forces 210
Makashov, A. 227
Malaysia 171, 189
Maley, W. 44, 50
Malle, S. 99n
Mamut, A. 98
Mao, Z. 3, 223
Maradykovsky 202
Marx, K. 223
Maschitsky, V. 95
Maslyukov, Yu. 76n
MDM-Bank 98
Media Most 6, 9, 91-2, 100n, 139n
Medved see Unity party
Menatep bank 93
Mexico 184, 239
Mikheev, N. 219n
MIKOM investment bank 117n
Milosevic, S. 14n, 223, 244n
Moldova 204
Mongol Empire 52
Mongolia 195-6
Montana 243n
Moody's Investor Services 140n
Mordashev, A. 95
Mordashov, A. 111
Morev, V. 6
Morgan Stanley 75n
Mormons 46
Moscow 4, 5, 17, 20-1, 23, 24, 27, 29-30, 44, 47-8, 62, 64, 81-3, 86-7, 91, 117n, 184, 192n, 195, 200-1, 204, 211, 213, 225, 229, 232, 237-8, 242n, 244n
Moscow region 205
Moscow State University 98
Most-Bank 32n, 91

Napoleon 223
NATO see North Atlantic Treaty Organisation

264

Tyumen Oil Company 7

UES *see* Unified Energy Systems
Ukraine 180, 182, 185, 187, 190
Ukrainka 205
Uneximbank 92-3
Uneximbank-Interros Financial Group
     93, 114
Unified State Register of Enterprises and
     Organisations 191
Union of Rightist Forces 27, 32n, 87
United Energy Systems 7
United Kingdom 42, 47, 167-8, 171,
     174, 177-8, 180-5, 188-9, 192n,
     228
United Nations 197, 229, 235, 238
United Nations Security Council 229,
     238
United States of America 5, 11, 29, 33,
     47, 53, 75n, 76n, 166-8, 171, 174-
     5, 177-82, 184, 186, 188-9, 192n,
     195, 197, 202, 210, 212-3, 218,
     226, 228, 234, 237-9, 240-1, 242n,
     243n, 245n
Unity party 1, 2, 24-5, 27, 80-1, 85-7,
     100n, 87, 231
Urals Machinery Plant 95
Urals region 32n, 194, 196, 200, 211
Uruguay 185
USA *see* United States of America
USSR 10, 14n, 37, 40, 44-5, 47, 40, 53,
     55-7, 61, 63, 68-9, 74, 89, 125,
     129, 166, 168, 174, 182, 184, 187,
     190, 192-4, 204-5, 213, 215, 222,
     225, 230-1, 234-5, 239, 241-2,
     244n, 245n
USSR State Planning Committee 55
Uzbekistan 187, 190, 216, 245n

'Vakhrushi' leather goods plant 111
Vaknin, S. 79
Vaziani 204
Vekselberg, V. 95
Victoria (Australian State) 178
Vietnam 204
Vinogradov, V. 90
Vladivostok 200

Vneshekonombank 91
Volga region 32n
Volgodonsk 24
Voloshin, A. 29, 96
Vyakhirev, R. 92, 94-5
Vympelcom Company 95
Vyugin, O. 141n

Waltz, K. 230, 244n
Warsaw Pact 182, 187, 195, 238
Washington (D.C.) 57, 60, 75n, 117-9,
     140n, 142-3, 228, 241, 244n, 245n
Weber, M. 12
World Bank 57, 59, 68, 72, 75n, 77n,
     98, 125, 138, 140n, 141n, 142n,
     166-8, 171-3
World Health Organisation 235
World Trade Organisation 10

Yabloko party 27, 59, 87
Yakovlev Aircraft Construction Bureau
     209
Yakovlev, V. 201
Yavlinsky, G. 56, 59, 71, 74n, 76n, 106
Yekaterinburg 204
Yeltsin, B. 1-3, 6, 9-10, 13-20, 22-3, 25-
     6, 28-31, 35, 48, 52, 54-7, 61-2,
     64, 67-8, 71-2, 75n, 81-5, 88-91,
     94, 96-7, 99n, 166, 186-7, 191,
     198-9, 202, 217, 223-33, 240, 242,
     243n, 244n, 245n
Yeltsina, N. 96
Yevtushenkov, V. 95
Yew, L.K. 11
Yugoslavia 37, 157-8, 197, 204, 212,
     244n
Yukos 93, 101n
Yumashev, V. 82, 96, 98
Yuriev, D. 89
Yurubcheno-Takhomsky 93

Zemin, J. 245n
Zhirinovsky, V. 49
Zhukovskiy 205
Zimin, L. 95, 100n
Zyuganov, G. 2, 20, 25, 27, 60, 75n

University of Plymouth Library
Subject to status this item may be renewed
via your Voyager account
http://voyager.plymouth.ac.uk
Tel: (01752) 232323